NEPALI GRAMMAR & VOCABULARY

NEPALI GRAMMAR & VOCABULARY

REV. A. TURNBULL

THIRD EDITION

Edited by the

REV. R. KILGOUR, D.D.

GYAN

Published by

Gyan Publishing House
5, Ansari Road
Daryaganj, New Delhi-110002
Phone: 011-47034999, 9811692060
E-mail: books@gyanbooks.com

Distribution Network
gyanbooks.com
India, USA, Canada, UK, Australia, France

ISBN : 9788121244718 (PB)
First Published, 1923 (Third Edition)

2nd Impression 2020

Printed at: Gyan Press, Delhi.

Nepali Grammar & Vocabulary
Author: Rev. A. turnbull

PREFACE TO THE SECOND EDITION.

THIS "second edition" of my 1887 attempt to reduce to standard rule the Nepali tongue, as spoken at cosmopolitan Darjeeling, is really an entirely new work.

In preparing it I have had the advantage of elaborate critical notes on the first edition by the most exalted authority in Kathmandu; in passing it through the press, the invaluable assistance of the Rev. G. P. Pradhan, the highest authority in Darjeeling; and in meeting the expense, the practical patronage of the Government of Bengal, the advance purchaser of an adequate number of the copies.

In perusing it the student will perhaps allow some of its shortcomings—to be excused by my distance from the printer, and himself to be persuaded to learn the *native* alphabet at the outset—the language is much easier in its own character than in the ill-fitting Roman—and to procure in due course *The Acts of the Apostles* in Nepali (Bible House, 23, Chowringhi, Calcutta) and in English (R.V.), as complemental textbooks.

The Vocabulary is not so full as in the first edition, but may prove of working utility pending its purposed extension and publication in a separate volume.

A. TURNBULL.

LINLITHGOW, SCOTLAND,
JANUARY, 1904.

PREFACE TO THE THIRD EDITION.

BY request, this edition is practically a page for page reproduction of the earlier work with the correction of obvious mistakes.

It may assist the scholar to know that the whole Bible is now available in Nepali. Before his death, Mr. Turnbull, with the help of his and my fellow-worker, the Rev. Ganga Prashad Pradhan, had completed the translation of the New Testament.

A Nepali Dictionary begun on the lines laid down by Mr. Turnbull is now in the press.

R. KILGOUR.

THE BIBLE HOUSE, LONDON,
MAY, 1923.

INDEX.

NEPALI GRAMMAR.

NEPALI

by which name we call the Court language and *lingua franca* of Nepal * (*ne-pāl*), is no longer Newārī, the language of the Newars (*ne-wār*), but Gorkhālī,† or as the natives themselves call it, Parbate, or Parbatiyā, the language of the Gorkhās, who have ruled the country since 1768.

It is really a dialect of Hindī, akin to those of Rajputana, very like Kumāonī and Gaṛhwālī, and spoken "from the Gogarī to the Sankhassī River."

It varies more or less with locality, as all dialects do, but the scope of the present attempt to reduce it to a common standard, or "High Nepālī" form, only admits of reference to its Kāṭhmāṇḍū variations, as being the most important. ‡

---

* Length, 500 miles; breadth, 150; population, over 5,600,000, now mostly Hindus; Capital, Kāṭhmāṇḍū (commonly pronounced *Kāṭhmāṇṛu*). The name "Nepal," applied in political geography to the whole country, and so used in the present work, is restricted by the natives themselves to the Kāṭhmāṇḍū valley; the rest of the country they distinguish as "Pahāṛ" ("the hills"). "Parbate," their term for the "Nepālī" of the present work, means "hill,"—the "hill" dialect of the Gorkhās. They also frequently refer to the language as "Pahāṛī," or "Pahāṛiyā," though, strictly speaking, it is only one of the many forms of Pahāṛī. (The figures are quoted from *The Statesman's Year Book*, 1922.)

† Also called "Khas Kurā" from "Khas" the name of the real Gorkhā caste, and "Kurā" meaning "word." "Gorkhālī" (or "Gorkhe") is the adjective of "Gorkhā."

‡ Sir G. A. Grierson's *Linguistic Survey of India*, Vol. IX, Part IV, pp. 1–99, has an interesting survey of the language, which he prefers to spell Naipālī.

THE ALPHABET

is practically that of Sanskrit and Hindī, the "Devanāgarī," or "Nāgarī."

In the following table the first column gives the "Devanāgarī" letters in their alphabetic order; the second, their "Roman" equivalents; and the third, by the italics, their approximate "English" pronunciation.

The second form of vowel in the first column is the medial, used except at the beginning of a word or syllable.

Blanks in the third column mean that the pronunciation has no example in English.

Vowels.

1.	अ	*a*	*u*ndone
2.	आ ा	*ā*	*a*rm f*a*r
3.	इ ि	*i*	*e*ternal s*ee*n
4.	ई ी	*ī*	*e*dict s*ei*ze
5.	उ ु	*u*	*u*lema w*oo*d
6.	ऊ ू	*ū*	*oo*ze w*oo*ed
7.	ऋ ृ	*ṛi*	*re*ply t*re*at *
8.	ए े	*e*	*ai*d m*ai*n
9.	ऐ ै	*ai*	*ai*sle m*i*ne
10.	ओ ो	*o*	*oa*k n*o*
11.	औ ौ	*au*	*ow*l n*ow*

* But the *ṛ* has really no English equivalent.

GUTTURALS.

12.	क	*ka*	*kick*
13.	ख	*kha*	kic*k* *h*im
14.	ग	*ga*	*gag*
15.	घ	*gha*	ga*g* *h*im
16.	ङ	*ña*	ki*ng*

PALATALS.

17.	च	*cha*	*church*
18.	छ	*chhạ*	chur*ch* *h*im
19.	ज	*ja*	*judge*
	ज़	*za*	size
20.	झ (or झ or ऊ)	*jha*	jud*ge* *h*im
21.	ञ	*ṅa*	li*n*ch

CEREBRALS.

22.	ट	*ṭa*	*to treat*
23.	ठ	*ṭha*	trea*t* *h*im
24.	ड	*ḍa*	*do dread*
	ड़	*ṛa*	
25.	ढ	*ḍha*	drea*d* *h*im
	ढ़	*ṛha*	
26.	ण	*ṇa*	re*n*d

Dentals.

27.	त	*ta*	
28.	थ	*tha*	
29.	द	*da*	
30.	ध	*dha*	
31.	न	*na*	

Labials.

32.	प	*pa*	*pop*
33.	फ	*pha*	pop *h*im
	फ़	*fa*	*ph*ase
34.	ब	*ba*	*b*ri*b*e
35.	भ	*bha*	bri*b*e *h*im
36.	म	*ma*	*mem*ber

Semi-vowels.

37.	य	*ya*	*y*ou be*y*ond
38.	र	*ra*	*r*a*r*e
39.	ल	*la*	*l*oya*l*
40.	व	*wa*	*w*e be*w*ail
	व़	*va*	*v*al*v*e

Sibilants.

41.	श	*sha*	*sh*un ocean

42. ष *sha* *sh*ut u*sh*er

43. स *sa* *s*en*s*e

ASPIRATES.

44. ह *ha* *h*a*h*

45. ः *ḥ* hu*h*

ANUSVĀR.*

46. ं *ṉ* mo*n* (French)

VIRĀM.

As seen above, each consonant is vocalised by inherent *a*. For instance, क is not merely *k*, but *ka*. To make क *k*, the virām is written below it thus, क्. So तर *tara*, तर् *tar*; कांड़ *kāṉṛa*, कांड़् *kāṉṛ*. But Nepālī writing frequently omits the virām when it ought to appear.

CONJUNCTS.

When, in the same word, two or even three consonants come together without vowel intervention, written or inherent, they are usually conjoined in one compound of the two or three. प् च coming together, with, as the virām shews, no vowel between, make the conjunct प्च; प् च् य, the conjunct प्च्य or प्च्य.

The following is a list of the commonest :—

क्क	क्ख	क्त	क्म	क्य	क्र	क्ल	क्व	क्ष क्ष	ख्य	ख्व
kka	*kkha*	*kta*	*kma*	*kya*	*kra*	*kla*	*kwa*	*ksha*	*khya*	*khwa*

ग्ग	ग्घ	ग्ध	ग्द	ग्न	ग्म	ग्य	ग्र	ग्व	ग्ल	घ्य	घ्न	घ्र
gga	*ggha*	*gdha*	*gda*	*gna*	*gma*	*gya*	*gra*	*gwa*	*gla*	*ghya*	*ghna*	*ghra*

ङ्क	ङ्ख	ङ्ग	ङ्घ	च्च	च्छ	च्य	छ्य	छ्र
ñka	*ñkha*	*ñga*	*ñgha*	*chcha*	*chchha*	*chya*	*chhya*	*chhra*

---

* ANUNĀSIK is frequently used for nasalization weaker than anusvār; and is often written with two dots ·· instead of the ·. See p. 9.

ज्ज	ज्झ	ज्ञ*	ज्म	ज्य	ज्र	ज्व	झ्य	ञ्च
jja	jjha	jña	jma	jya	jra	jwa	jhya	ñcha

ञ्छ	ञ्ज	ञ्झ	ट्ट	ट्ठ	ड्ग	ड्ड	ड्र	ण्ण
ñchha	ñja	ñjha	ṭṭa	ṭṭha	ḍga	ḍḍa	ḍra	ṇṇa

ण्य	ण्ट	ण्ठ	ण्ड	ण्ढ	त्क	त्त	त्थ	त्प	त्न
ṇya	ṇṭa	ṇṭha	ṇḍa	ṇḍha	tka	tta	ttha	tpa	tna

त्म	त्य	त्र	त्व	त्स	थ्य	द्ग	द्द	द्ध
tma	tya	tra	twa	tsa	thya	dga	dda	ddha

द्भ	द्न	द्म	द्य	द्व	ध्य	ध्र	ध्व	न्न	न्त
dbha	dna	dma	dya	dwa	dhya	dhra	dhwa	nna	nta

न्थ	न्द	न्ध	न्म	न्य	न्र	न्ह	न्छ	प्प	प्फ
ntha	nda	ndha	nma	nya	nra	nha	nchha	ppa	ppha

प्त	प्न	प्म	प्य	प्र	प्ल	प्स	ब्ब	ब्भ
pta	pna	pma	pya	pra	pla	psa	bba	bbha

ब्ज	ब्द	ब्ध	ब्य	ब्र	भ्य	भ्र	म्म	म्न
bja	bda	bdha	bya	bra	bhya	bhra	mma	mna

म्य	म्र	म्ल	म्ह	य्य	र्र	र्ण	र्म	र्य	र्व
mya	mra	mla	mha	yya	rra	rṇa	rma	rya	rwa

र्श	र्ष	र्ह	र्क	र्ख	र्ग	र्घ	र्च	र्छ	र्ज	र्झ
rsha	rs̲h̲a	rha	rka	rkha	rga	rgha	rcha	rchha	rja	rjha

र्ट	र्ठ	र्ड	र्ढ	र्त	र्त्त	र्द	र्ध	र्न	र्प	र्फ	र्ब
rṭa	rṭha	rḍa	rḍha	rta	rtta	rda	rdha	rna	rpa	rpha	rba

र्भ	र्का	र्कि	र्की	र्कु	र्कू	र्के	र्कै	र्को	र्कौ
rbha	rkā	rki	rkī	rku	rkū	rke	rkai	rko	rkau

र्कं	र्कौं	रु	रू	ल्ल	ल्म	ल्य	ल्ह	ल्द	ल्प
rkan̲	rkaun̲	ru	rū	lla	lma	lya	lha	lda	lpa

ल्व	व्व	व्य	व्र	श्न	श्र	श्ल	श्च
lba	wwa	wya	wra	shna	shra	shla	shcha

श्व	श्य	ष्म	ष्य	ष्व	ष्क	ष्ट	ष्ठ	ष्प
shwa	shya	s̲h̲ma	s̲h̲ya	shwa	s̲h̲ka	s̲h̲ṭa	s̲h̲ṭha	s̲h̲pa

* Pronounced *gyā* (one syllable): ज्ञान *g-yān*; आज्ञा *āg-yā*.

स्स	स्न	स्म	स्य	स्ल	स्र	स्व	स्क	स्त	स्त्र	स्थ
ssa	*sna*	*sma*	*sya*	*sla*	*sra*	*swa*	*ska*	*sta*	*stra*	*stha*

स्प	स्फ	ह्म	ह्य	ह्ल	ह्व	हु हु	हू हू
spa	*spha*	*hma*	*hya*	*hla*	*hwa*	*hu*	*hū*

REMARKS ON THE ALPHABET.

The letters are named by adding *kār* to each: अकार् *akār*, 'the letter *a*'; ककार् *kakār*, 'the letter *ka*.'

1–11. The first form of each of the 11 vowels in the table is used only initially at the beginning of words and syllables: अक *aka*, अकअक *akaaka*, कइ *ka-i*. The second form is used in every other position, medially. अ *a*, being inherent in each consonant has no written medial form: क *ka*. The medial forms of the other 10 vowels, when used, are substituted for this inherent unwritten *a*: का *kā*, कि *ki*, की *kī*, कु *ku*, कू *kū*, कृ *kṛi*, के *ke*, कै *kai*, को *ko*, कौ *kau*. Notice that ि is written before the consonant it follows in pronunciation; ु, ू and ृ, under it; and े, over it.

It follows that after an immediately preceding vowel, inherent or written, in the same word, it is the first form that must be used: भई *bhaī*, भाई *bhāī*, पाईइ *pāīi*. Distinguish भै *bhai* (one syllable) from भइ *bha-i* (two syllables).

ु following र is written रु; following ह, हु or हु. ू following र is written रू; following ह, हू or हू.

12. How the consonants are pronounced is suggested by their classification as Gutturals, etc., and indicated by the examples furnished, but the only safe rule is to get a native *paṇḍit*, or teacher. The pronunciation of some of them cannot be learned otherwise.

13. ख *kha* is just क *ka* uttered with a forcible expiration. The same is the relation of *gha* to *ga*, *chha* to *cha*, etc.

In writing, Nepālis generally use ष *sha* for ख, which, however, of course, retains its own proper pronunciation: मुषिया (for मुखिया) *mukhiyā*, 'a chief.'

16. ञ ña can be conjoined, as the list of conjuncts has shewn, only with consonants of its own class—that is, with Gutturals, not with Palatals, etc. The same rule applies to the other nasals ङ ṅa and ण ṇa but not to न na, which occurring as it does in the stem of certain verbs, for instance, can be conjoined with छ chha, a Palatal: जान्छु jānchhu, 'I shall know.' For other न exceptions see the list of conjuncts.

20 Note the three ways of writing jha; झ, झ, ञ.

21. ङ ṅa is sometimes loosely used for य ya: ङाहाँ ṅāhān̲, for याहाँ yāhān̲ (more properly यहाँ yahān̲), 'here.'

24, 25. ड़ ṛa and ढ़ ṛha (which are just ड ḍa and ढ ḍha, with the diacritical point) have no corresponding sound in English. "Place the tongue in the same position as for ḍa and dha, on the roof of the mouth, that is, and then try to pronounce the English r."

27–31. The Dentals, त ta, etc., have no corresponding English sound. The English t, d, etc., correspond more nearly to the Nepālī Cerebrals ट ṭa, ड ḍa, etc.; though not exactly, for in pronouncing the latter the tongue has to strike, not the gums, as for the English t, d, etc., but the roof of the mouth. For the Dentals त ta, etc., place the tongue against the back of the teeth.

34. ब ba is often written व, which is properly the letter wa.

37. य ya is often written य़, and often pronounced ja: युग or युग् yug or jug, 'an age.' It is often written for ए e: यक yak, for एक् ek, 'one.'

38. र ra in combination with another consonant, as also with and ृ, must be carefully studied, as exhibited in the list of conjuncts.

When first in a conjunct, it is written as a semi-circle, called reph,' over the consonant following it: सर्ब sarba.

When a medial vowel follows the conjunct, the reph' is written over, or to the right of the vowel: सर्बा sarbā, सर्बी sarbī; when anusvār follows the 'reph' encloses it: सर्बं sarban̲. सर्बौं sarbaun̲.

When last in a conjunct, it is written in front of the foot of the consonant preceding it: स्रब sraba, क्रत krata. स्त्री strī.

Two exceptions to the 'reph' rule are important. Before य *ya* and ह *ha*, *ra*, in conjunction, is usually written, not as 'reph.' but as in the last preceding paragraph: गर्‍यो *garyo*, बार्‍है *bārhai*. In a word, र्‍य is not *yra*, but *rya*; र्‍ह is not *hra*, but *rha*.

40. व *wa*, since, as already seen, it often means ब *ba*, is itself often represented by व़; but it is desirable to reserve this latter form for *va*.

41, 42. Pronouncing ष *sha* the lingual contact is slightly further back than for श *sha*.

As already said, Nepālīs often write ष *sha* when they mean and say ख *kha*: षत् *shat*, for खत् *khat*. This has resulted in ष, in some words in which it is quite correctly written, being nevertheless pronounced as if it represented ख: विषय् *bishay*, 'a matter,' pronounced *bikhay*; इष् *ish*, 'zeal,' pronounced *ikh*.

43. स *sa*, before त *ta* and न *na*, at the beginning of a word, has often an incorrect *a* prefixed: अस्तुति *astuti*, for *stuti*, 'praise'; अस्नान *asnān*, for *snān*, 'bathing.' So before क *ka* it may have an incorrect *i*: इस्कुल् *iskul*, for *skul*

45. ः *h*, called '*visarg*,' is rare: अन्तःकरण् *antahkaran*, 'the heart' (in the moral sense).

46. *n*, called '*anusvār*,' denotes the nasalization of the preceding vowel, inherent or written. To nasalize an inherent vowel, or ु, ृ, or ू, it is written over the vocalised consonant: मं *man*, 'I'; मुं *mun*; मूं *mūn*; मृं *mrin*. To nasalize the other vowels, it is placed over, or to the right of them: मां *mān*, 'in'; मों *mon*; इं *in*; ईं *īn*; अंस *ansa*, 'an impression' (copy); अंश *ansha*, 'a part.' Its pronunciation is well indicated in the French 'mon.'

Besides its stricter use, it is often substituted for *ñ*, *ṅ*, *ṇ*, *n* and *m*, when these stand first in a conjunct: अंग *anga*, for अङ्ग *aṅga*; अंच *ancha*, for अञ्च *añcha*; अंड *anda*, for अण्ड *aṇḍa*; अंद *anda*, for अन्द *anda*; उंभो *ūmbho*, for उम्भो *ūmbho*, 'up.' In such cases its pronunciation is that of the nasal for which it is substituted.

It is gradually displacing ँ, 'anunāsik,' which is not uncommon in Nepālī works.

Conjuncts will not be found at all difficult, after the simple letters have been mastered.

Arithmetical Figures.

०	१	२	३	४	५	६	७	८	९	१०
0	1	2	3	4	5	6	7	8	9	10
sun	*ek*	*dui*	*tīn*	*chār*	*pāṉch*	*chha*	*sāt*	*āṭh*	*nau*	*das*

° is also used, like the English period, to mark abbreviation: ति° *ti.*, short for तिथि *tithi*, 'day of the month'; १°, '1st'; २°, '2nd.'

२ is also used to mark repetition: घर् २, for घर् घर् *ghar ghar*, 'houses.'

३ is used in the same way, after श्री *shrī*, 'illustrious,' for instance: श्री ३, for श्री श्री श्री *shrī shrī shrī*, 'thrice-illustrious.'

[See further, under Numeral Adjectives.]

Punctuation.

।, called '*chhewa*,' may be used at the end of sentences; ॥, '*ḍabal chhewa*,' at the end of paragraphs; ., '*nukta*,' for minor divisions within sentences: बुराई देखि न जीतौ . तर भलाईले बुराईलाइ जीत् । आमीन ॥

In verse, । is used at the end of the first line of a couplet, ॥ at that of the second.

In native works spaces are not left between words, and no attention is paid to syllabic division at the end of lines. The example given above would run, for instance, बुराईदेखिनजीतौतर भलाईलेबुराईलाइजीत् । आमीन् ॥

I. Exercise in Transliteration.

The student might cover over the one line when doing the other. The words are for the most part mere arbitrary collocations of letters for the purpose of the exercise. Some of the Roman could be transliterated in more ways than the one chosen in the exercise: *jasle* = जस्ले or जसले; *ārgghā* = आर्ग्‌घा or आर्ग्घा; and so on.

.. *taba jas jasle usko bachan khushī saña sunyera*

१° तब जस् जस्ले उस्को बचन् खुशी सङ सुन्येर

grahaṇ garye tiniharu baptismā bhaye. tyes din 3000

ग्रहण् गर्‍ये तिनिहरु बप्तिस्मा भये। त्येस् दिन् ३०००

janāko aṛkal shiksheharu saña misiye; hūnhūnhūnhūnza:

जनाको अड़कल् शिक्षेहरु सङ मिसीये. हूंहूंहूंऊंज़.

añkacnka.

अङ्कचंक ॥

2. *ārgghākāf dharmmī ichichhīījāañjhjhaḥkara.*

२। आर्ग्घाकाफ़् धर्म्मी इचिछ्ईईजाञ्झ्झःकर ॥

3. *ūnṭṭhūuḍaṛhuḍhūṭnuṇū jhījhījh ṛitrithṛidanadh.*

३। ऊंट्ठूउडढ़ुढूट्नुणू .झीझीज् ऋत्रिथृदनध् ॥

4. *kshamā makāmbhīnsambhītipphubon ṛiṇ.*

४। क्षमा मकांभींसम्भीतिप्फुबों ऋण् ॥

5. *eyenrainaileshaiv av bārhaun gardaunna.*

५। एयेंरैंऐलेशैवव़ बाऱ्हौं गर्दौंन ॥

6. *rurūnoshausohaaukshaujñakārchiṭutṛipaipāi.*

६। रुरूंओषौसोहओौक्षौज्ञकार्चिंटुटृपैपाइ ॥

7. *bār haun. ājñāruryonrhā; kārttīsiyan.*

७। बार् हौं। आज्ञारुर्‍योंऱ्हा. कार्त्तीसियन् ॥

8. *bārhābhratṛiya tyesmānutpanna janmye.*

८। बाऱ्हाभ्रातृय त्येस्मांउत्पन्न जन्म्ये ॥

9. *janmāūnjyāl samma khrīshṭa mānchhe.*

९। जन्माउंज्याल् सम्म ख्रीष्ट मान्छे ॥

10. *swapna swapna tyesle chichchyāyera.*

१०। स्वप्न २ त्येस्ले चिच्च्यायेर ॥

11. *lekhye bhakta ātmā mānyo mānryo.*

११। लेख्ये भक्त आत्मा मान्यो मांर्‍यो ॥

12. *buddhipashchāttāp īshwar strīorhlyepachchhyā.*

१२। बुद्धिपश्चात्ताप् ईश्वर् स्त्रीओऱ्ल्येपच्छ्या ॥

The exercise is a little up-hill, no doubt, but it is a short-cut to the top; and to love short-cuts, the steeper the better, is good Nepālī!

II. Exercise in Pronunciation of the Vowels.

[The third line gives the approximate pronunciation in English words.]

piṭāle	*ramāhaṭlāi*	*agambakṭā*	*āhan*
पिटाले	रमाहट्लाइ	अगम्बक्टा	आहन्
peat ah lay	rum ah hut lie	a gum buck't ah	ah Hun

āgo	*ago*	*aher*	*akāsh*	*bikul*	*boṭ*	*chīr*	*yeshū*
आगो	अगो	अहेर	अकाश्	बिकुल्	बोट्	चीर्	येशू
ah go	aga	a hare	a cash	be cool	boat	cheer	yea shoe

mail	*rog*	*ik*	*aul*	*bhoy*		*jīwan*	*apabe.*
मैल्	रोग्	इक्	औल्	भोय्		जीवन्	अपबे ॥
mile	rogue	eke	owl	'bhoy'	(Irish)	jee won	up a bay.

ARTICLE.

There is no **Article** in Nepālī : *chhoro* is 'son,' 'a son,' or 'the son,' according to the context. When the sense requires or admits of a word for the English article, एक् *ek*; or एक् जना *ek janā*, or येउटा *yeuṭā*, 'one' or कोई *koī*, 'some,' may be used for 'a'; यो *yo*, 'this,' त्यो *tyo*, 'that,' or चइं *chaiṇ*, 'the...one.' for 'the': *yeuṭā keṭo*, 'a boy'; *ti keṭāharu*, 'the boys.'

THE NOUN

has **two genders**: Masculine and Feminine; **two numbers**: Singular and Plural; **seven cases**: Nominative, Accusative, Dative, Agent, Genitive, Locative and Vocative.

All females, and females only, are **Feminine**.

For the **Plural**, हरु *haru* is, with the after-noted exceptions, added to the Singular. The pronunciation of this affix is peculiar, the *har* being almost like the English 'her.' Indeed, it is sometimes written हेरु *heru*.

[For a note on the formation of compound and abstract nouns, see Exercise VIII, 38.]

Declension.

Practically all possible changes are shewn in the following example :—

		Sing.	
N.	छोरो	*chhoro*	son..
Ac.	छोरोलाई	*chhorolāi*	..son
D.	छोरोलाइ	*chhorolāi*	to son
Ag.	छोरोले	*chhorole*	*by son
G.	छोरोको (की, का)	*chhoroko* (*kī*, *kā*)	of son
L.	छोरोमां	*chhoromā<u>n</u>*	†in son
V.	ए छोरा	*e chhorā*	O son
		Plu.	
N.	छोराहरु	*chhorāharu*	sons..
Ac.	छोराहरुलाइ	*chhorāharulāi*	..sons
D.	छोराहरुलाइ	*chhorāharulāi*	to sons
Ag.	छोराहरुले	*chhorāharule*	*by sons
G.	छोराहरुको (की, का)	*chhorāharuko* (*kī*, *kā*)	of sons
L.	छोराहरुमां	*chhorāharumā<u>n</u>*	†in sons
V.	ए छोराहरु हो	*e chhorāharu ho*	O sons

Remarks on Declension.

In the above example the final *o* of the noun is changed to *ā* for the V. sing., and throughout the plu., but it is practically only in nouns ending in *o* that such, or any changes occur.‡ All others, as a rule, remain **unmodified**; and even some nouns ending in *o*, e.g. :—

डालो *ḍālo*, 'a small basket'; *ḍālo*, 'a basket'; *e ḍālo*, 'O basket'; *ḍāloharuko*, 'of baskets'

ghoṛā, 'a horse'; *e ghoṛā*, 'O horse'; *ghoṛāharuko*, 'of horses'

chhoṛī, 'a daughter'; *e chhorī*, 'O daughter'; *chhorīharuko*, 'of daughters.'

phul, 'an egg'; *e phul*, 'O egg'; *phulharuko*, 'of eggs.

The **Feminine** of some masc. nouns is made, when they end in an unvocalised consonant, by adding *ī*; when they end in *ī*, by changing the *ī* to *inī*; when they end otherwise, by adding *nī*. This lengthening of the word may occasion the shortening of its stem vowel. Examples :—

* Or 'with,' etc., in the instrumental sense.

† Or 'into,' 'among,' 'on'; 'to,' 'at' (a place).

‡ It is not uncommon, however, to find this final *o* changed to *ā* in all the oblique forms, thus :—*chhorālai*, *chhorāle*, and *chhorāko*.

दास् *dās*	दासी *dāsī*	slave
पापी *pāpi*	पापिनी *pāpinī*	sinner
मित्र *mitra*	मित्रनी *mitranī*	friend
अगम्वक्ता *agambaktā*	अगम्वक्तानी *agambaktānī*	prophet
छिमेकि *kshimeki*	छिमेकिनी *kshīmekinī*	neighbour
शिक्षे *shikshe*	शिक्षेनी *shikshenī*	disciple
झांक्रि *jhānkri*	झंक्रेनी *jhankrenī*	diviner

It will be noticed that the last example is slightly irregular (probably due to the masc. also sometimes ending in *e*) but it exemplifies the shortening of the stem vowel *ā* to *a*.

The fem. final *ī*, and, indeed, final *ī* generally, is, as often as not, loosely written *i*.

For **emphasis**, as a rule, when a word ends in a consonant, *ai* is added; when a word ends in a vowel, the vowel is changed to *ai*, or *nai* or *i* is added: *dās*, *dāsai; chhoro*, *chhorai* (or *chhoronai*) *; pāpī*, *pāpīnai ; mitra*, *mitranai ; -lāi*, *-lāinai ; -le*, *-lei* (or *-lenai*) *; -ko* (or *-kī* or *-kā*), *-kai ; -man*, *-māni* (or *-mānnai*) *; -haru*, *-harui ; tyeso*, *tyesai*. But there are exceptions: *yo*, *yei ; tyahān*, *tihīn ;* etc. Emphasis may also, however, be secured for a word without changing its normal spelling, by merely changing its normal position in the sentence, or by the use of a following word, such as *tā*, 'indeed'; *po*, 'indeed'; *chain*, 'as for.'

The **Accusative**, especially of inanimate objects, is usually the same as the Nom. The affix, *-lāi*, is not used especially if there be also a Dative, expressed or understood, in the same clause: *chhorolāi kalam diyo*, he gave the son a pen.'

The **Dative** is used only in the strictly dative sense. 'To' a place is made by the Loc.: *kamānmān*, 'to the tea-garden.'

The Acc. and Dat. affix *-lāi* may be changed to *-kana* to indicate respect: राजाकन *rājākana*, instead of राजालाइ *rājālāi*, '..the king,' 'to the king.'

[The affix *-lāi* is to be distinguished from the word *lāi*, the conjunctive participle of *launnu*, 'to wear': जुत्तालाइ *juttālāī*, ..' boots'; जुत्ता लाइ *juttā lāi*, 'wearing boots.']

The **Agent** case is that of the instrument or cause, translated 'by,' 'with,' 'from,' 'through,' because of,' etc. It is accordingly used as the nominative to active transitive verbs: *chhoro* *āyo*, 'the boy came'; *chhorole garyo*, 'the boy did.' It is this important usage that gives it its name. See p. 98.

[The affix *-le* is to be distinguished from the word *le*, the regular 2nd sing. imperative of *li*n*nu*, 'to take,' and the irregular 2nd sing. imperative of *lyāu*n*nu*, 'to bring': *chhorole*, 'by the boy': *chhoro le*, 'take (or bring) the boy.']

The **Genitive** has three terminations: *-ko*, used before nouns masc. sing.; *-kī*, before nouns fem., sing. or plu.; *-kā*, before nouns masc. plu. It is the English Possessive:—

राजाको छोरोलाई	*rājāko chhorolāi*	to the king's son.
राजाकी छोरीलाई	*rājākī chhorīlāi*	,, ,, ,, daughter.
राजाकी छोरीहरु	*rājākī chhoriharu*	,, ,, ,, daughters.
राजाका छोराहरु	*rājākā chhorāharu*	,, ,, ,, sons.

[The affix *-ko* is to be distinguished from the word *ko*, the interrogative pronoun, 'who ?': *chhoroko ho*, 'it is the son's'; *chhoro ko ho*, 'who is the son ?': and from *ko* meaning 'at all' used in negative sentences *layak ko chhaina*, 'not at all worthy.' *-kō* and *-kā* are sometimes shortened to *o* and *ā*: जांचो *jā*n*cho*, for जांच्को *ja*n*chko*, 'of the examination'; अर्काआ *arkāā*, for अर्काका *arkākā*, 'of the others.']

[The form *-koni*, for *-ko*, is used **interrogatively**: छोरोकोनि *chhorokoni*, 'of the boy ?'. *-ni* may be added to any word in the same way, as an emphasis mark of interrogation: राज्दल्नि कहां छ *rājdalni kahā*n *chha*, 'where is Rajdal ?'; गर्योनि *garyoni*, 'did (he) do (it) ?' The affix *-koni* is to be distinguished from the word *koni*, 'who knows ?', to which, possibly, it owes its origin, or *vice versâ*.]

The G. of nouns is much used **adjectively**: *gā*n*uko keṭo*, 'the village boy'; *kāṭhko*, 'wooden'; *sunko*, 'golden.'

The **Locative** means 'in,' 'into,' 'among' (persons, places or things); 'on' (places or things); 'to,' 'at' (places). 'On' (persons) is *mā*n*thi*; 'to' (persons) is *thā*n*i*; 'at' (persons) is *-kā*n. See under Prepositions, p. 116.

The **Vocative**, in respectful address, substitutes *he* for *e*: हे ईश्वर् *he īshwar*, 'O God.' Final *o* is usually changed to *ā*: केटो *keṭo*, 'boy'; ए केटा *e keṭā*, 'O boy.' [The *ho* of the plu. is to be distinguished from the verb *ho*, 'is.']

The **Plural** affix *-haru* may be dropped, provided the plurality is clear from the context, and especially, therefore, when a numeral accompanies the noun: सात् केटा *sāt keṭā*, 'seven boys.' It is frequently omitted with words signifying inanimate objects.

Instead of the affix *-haru*, the word *log*, 'people,' may be used: केटा लोग् *keṭā log*, 'boys'; केटा लोगले *keṭā logale*, 'by boys'; or the sing. may simply be repeated: घर *ghar*, 'house'; घर् घर् *ghar ghar*, 'houses' (this is frequently used in distributive plural where each is thought of separately); or if the sing. have 'virām,' this, when there is an affix, may be removed: हात् *hāt*, 'hand,' हात् *hāt*, or हात्हरू *hātharu* (but not हात *hāta*) 'hands'; हातले *hātale*, 'by hands.' Nouns compounded of two nouns, both, or the first of which has 'virām,' may form their plu. by removing the 'virām' of the first: दुख्भोग् *dukhbhog*, 'suffering'; दुखभोग् *dukhabhog*, 'sufferings.'

Nouns ending in *u*, preceded by a vowel, generally change the *u* to *wa* in the oblique plu.; जीउ *jīu*, 'body,' जीवहरूको *jīwaharuko*, 'of bodies'; नांउ *nā̱nu*, 'name,' नांवहरूको *nā̱nwaharuko*, 'of names.' The *haru* may be dropped, of course.

III. Exercise in Translation.

As a rule, the order of words in a sentence is subject, predicate, copula: 'the king money gave.'

The indirect object precedes the direct: 'the king to his subjects money gave.'

Qualifying words—possessives, adjectives, adverbs—precede the words qualified; and prepositions (with one exception, *binā*) follow the words they govern: 'the adored king's many very wise ministers his famine-with afflicted many subjects-to the necessary money and clothes quite willingly gave.'

Supposing all the declension cases to occur in a sentence, the normal order would be, say: N., Ag., D., L., Ac., (mnemonically, 'Nagdlac'), with the G., as already said, always before its object, and the V., as a matter of course, always before everything: 'the king his subjects-to as follows loudly spoke, O my beloved people, I, my ministers-through, you-to, your own hands-into, the you-by needed money will give. But them-of one, that year-of high priest being, the king-to answering said, O king, they nothing need.'

But emphasis may have to be expressed, and a word is rendered emphatic in proportion as it is displaced, from its normal position. For instance, the verb, whose normal position is at the end, may be emphasized by being put at the beginning: '(he) *is* the house-in.'

In a word, seeing the connection can always be gathered from the inflexions, considerable freedom as to the collocation of words in a clause or sentence is permissible. The collocation must be that which best conveys the required meaning and emphasis.

In apposition, nouns usually reverse the English order: 'God our Father' is, in Nepālī, 'our Father God'; 'the word boy' is 'boy the word.' But the English order is not uncommon: 'his father Rāmlāl.' When the words in apposition are in an oblique case, only the last one receives the case affix: हांमिहरुको पिता ईश्वर्लाइ *hā̱nmiharuko pitā īsẖwarlāi*, 'to God our Father.' Of course in verb-apposition the order is as in English: *keṭo rāmlāl bhanī̱nda chha*, 'the boy is called Rāmlāl.'

The order of pronouns of different persons, following one another in the same construction, is the reverse of the English: not 'you and I,' as in English, but 'I and you.' A verb agreeing with 'I and you' would of course be in the 1st per. plu.

VOCABULARY (IN NEPĀLĪ ALPHABETIC ORDER).

āye	came (3d plu.)	*ḍālo*	basket
īshwar	God	*tarawār*	sword
kām	work	*tilaṉgā*	soldier
keṭī	girl	*dājyu*	elder brother
keṭo	boy	*dān*	gift
ganye	counted (3d plu.)	*didī*	elder sister
garye	did ,,	*diye*	gave (3d plu.)
gāṉu	village	*phūl*	flower
ghar	house	*bal*	force
chor	thief	*baiṉnī*	younger sister
chha	is	*bhāi*	,, brother
chhan	are ,,	*māṉrye*	killed (3d plu.)
chhorī	daughter	*mānchhe*	person
chhoro	son	*mālī*	gardener
juttā	shoes	*roṭī*	bread

lauro	stick	*sātai*	the seven
lāi	wearing	*sāp*	snake
le	take	*strī*	woman
sahar	city	*hāt*	hand
sāt	seven	*ho*	is.

mānchheko chhorokī bainnīharukā ḍālomā<u>n</u> sāp chha
मान्छेको छोरोकी बैंनीहरुका डालोमां साप् छ
There is a snake in the baskets of the person's son's y. sisters.

gā<u>n</u>ukā keṭāharu balle keṭīko gharmā<u>n</u> āye
गांउका केटाहरु बलले केटीको घर्मां आये
The village boys came by force into the girl's house.

tilan<u>g</u>āharule chorlāi tarawārale mā<u>n</u>rye
तिलंगाहरुले चोर्लाइ तरवारले मांर्ये
The soldiers killed the thief with swords.

mālīharule keṭīlāi ḍālomā<u>n</u> phūl diye
मालीहरुले केटीलाइ डालोमां फूल् दिये
The gardeners gave the girl flowers in the basket.

mānchheharu juttā lāi sahar saharmā<u>n</u> āye
मान्छेहरु जुत्ता लाइ सहर् २ मां आये
The persons came into the cities wearing shoes.

e didī roṭī le; he īshwar dān le
ए दिदी रोटी ले. हे ईश्वर दान् ले
O e. sister, take bread; O God, take the gift.

e chhorā chhorīharu ho dājyubhāīharuko kām ho
ए छोरा छोरीहरु हो दाज्युभाईहरुको काम् हो
O sons (and) daughters, (it) is the work of the brethren

sāt keṭā sātai gharmā<u>n</u> chhan
सात् केटा साते घर्मां छन्
Seven boys are in the seven houses.

tilan<u>g</u>ā logale hātale kām garye
तिलंगा लोगले हातले काम् गर्ये
The soldiers did the work with (their) hands.

sātai keṭāle strīko hātmā<u>n</u> lauro diye
साते केटाले स्त्रीको हात्मां लउरो दिये
The 7 boys gave the stick into the woman's hand.

chhạ gharmān̲. *pitā īshwarlāi.* *keṭo shabda.*

छ घर्मां। पिता ईश्वर्लाइ। केटो शब्द।

(He) *is* in the house. To God the Father. The word 'boy.'

mālīharule sātai tilan̲gālāi chor ganye.

मालीहरूले सातै तिलंगालाइ चोर् गन्ये।

The gardeners counted the seven soldiers thieves.

mānchhe ko ho. ghar chhani. koni.

मान्छे को हो। घर् छनि। कोनि॥

Who is the person ? Is there a house ? I am not sure.

THE PRONOUN.

* First Personal Pronoun.

Sing.

N.	मं	*man̲*	I
Ac.	मंलाइ	*man̲lāi*	me
D.	मंलाइ	*man̲lāi*	to me
Ag.	मैंले	*main̲le*	by me
G.	मेरो (ी, ा)	*mero* (*ī*, *ā*)	my
L.	मंमां	*man̲mān̲*	in me

Plu.

N.	हांमिहरू	*hān̲miharu*	we
Ac.	,, लाइ	*hān̲miharulāi*	us
D.	,, लाइ	*hān̲miharulāi*	to us
Ag.	,, ले	*hān̲miharule*	by us
G.	,, को (की, का)	*hān̲miharuko* (*kī*, *kā*)	our
L.	,, मां	*hān̲miharumān̲*	in us

Darjeeling colloquial for *man̲* is *mon̲*. In Kāṭhmāṇḍū it is simply *ma*.

Before nouns fem., sing. or plu., the G. sing. is *merī*; the G. plu., *hān̲miharukī*. Before nouns masc. plu., the G. is *merā*, *hān̲miharukā* : *mero*, *hān̲miharuko*. *chhoro*, 'my, our, son'; *merī*,

* '1st Person' is *uttam purus̲h̲*; '2nd,' *madhyam purus̲h̲*; '3d,' *anya purus̲h̲*.

hāṉmiharukī, chhorī, chhorīharu, **'my, our, daughter, daughters'; *merā, hāṉmiharukā, chhorāharu,* 'my, our, sons.'**

The plu. affix *haru* may be and generally is dropped, in which case the G. plu. is shortened to हांम्रो (ी, ा) *hāṉmro* (ī, ā)

Second Personal Pronoun.

Sing.

N.	तं	*taṉ*	thou
Ac.	तंलाई	*taṉlāi*	thee
D.	,,	,,	to thee
Ag.	तैंले	*taiṉle*	by thee
G.	तेरो (ी, ा)	*tero* (ī, ā)	thy
L.	तंमां	*taṉmāṉ*	in thee
V.	ए तं	*e taṉ*	O thou

Plu.

N.	तिमिहरु	*timiharu*	you..
Ac.	,, लाई	*timiharulāi*	..you

etc.

The plu. affix *haru* may be and generally is dropped, in which case the G. plu. is shortened to तिम्रो (ी, ा) *timro* (ī, ā), 'your.'

Third Personal Pronoun.

Sing.

N.	उ	*u*	he, she
Ac.	उसलाई	*uslāi*	him, her
D.	,,	,,	to him, her
Ag.	उसले	*usle*	by him, her
G.	उसको (ी, ा)	*usko* (ī, ā)	his, her
L.	उसमां	*usmāṉ*	in him, her

Plu.

N.	उनिहरु	*uniharu*	they
Ac.	,, लाई	*uniharulāi*	them

etc.

Instead of the above, the Demonstrative Pronoun त्यो *tyo* may, and for the English neuter, 'it,' must be used. *u* is more respectful than *tyo*. In our Nepālī translation of the Bible we have invariably used the former for the Divine Persons.

The plu. affix *haru* may be and generally is dropped, in which case, in the oblique cases, the *uni* may be changed to *un* or *una* : *unilāi*, or *unlāi*, or *unalāī*, 'them'; and so on.

HONORIFIC FORMS OF THE PERSONAL PRONOUNS

are used in token of eminence or respect, in the case of the First and Third persons singular, and of the Second person singular and plural. For the First and Third persons sing. the plu. is used, generally in its shortened form : *hāṉmī*, 'I' (or, as Royalty says in English, 'We') ; *uni*, 'he.' For the Second person the usage is as follows :—

Sing.

N.	*timi*	or	*āphu*	or	*tapāṉi*,	thou
Ac.	*timilāi*	,,	*āphulāi*	,,	*tapāṉilāi*,	thee.

etc.

Plu.

N.	*āphuharu*	or	*tapāṉiharu*,	you..
Ac.	*āphuharulāi*	,,	*tapāṉiharulāi*,	..you

hāṉmi, for 'I,' while correct at Kāṭhmāṇḍū, is not usual at Darjeeling, where they modestly say *māṉ*.

तपांइ *tapāṉi* is sometimes shortened to पांइ *pāṉi*, and sometimes written तपाञि *tapāñi*.

HOW THE HONORIFICS ARE USED WITH VERBS.

They take their verb in the plu. ; or, impersonally, in the Infinitive. For example, the ordinary indefinite perfect of the verb *āuṉnu*, 'to come,' being as follows :—

maṉ āyeṉ	I came	*hāṉmiharu āyūṉ*	we came
taṉ āis	thou camest	*timiharu āyau*	you ,,
u āyo	he came	*uniharu āye*	they ,,

—and *bhayo*, 'was,' being the 3rd sing. of the same tense of the verb *huṉnu*, 'to be,' the honorific usages of 'came' are :—

I came *hāṉmi āyūṉ*

thou camest	*timi āyau*			
	āphu / *tapāṉi*	*āyau*,	or *āuṉnu*	*bhayo*
he came	*uni āye*	,,	,,	,,
we ,,	*hāṉmiharu āyūṉ*	,,	,,	,,
you ,,	*timiharu*		,,	,,
	āphuharu		,,	,,
	tapāṉiharu		,,	,,
they ,,	*uniharu*		,,	,,

The respectful **Imperative** is of constant occurrence : ***timi*** (or *āphu*, or *tapāṉi*) or *timiharu* (or *āphuharu*, or *tapāṉiharu*) *āuṉnu hawas*, 'come.'

With Active Transitive verbs, of course, not the Nom., but the **Agent** case would be used : *āphule garnu bhayo*, 'thou didst' ; *āphule garnu hawas*, 'do.'

The student should master the Honorific idiom from the first. *taṉ*, 'thou,' addressed to other than inferiors or familiars, is disrespectful. *āphu* is more respectful than *timi*, and *tapāṉi* than either. In our Nepālī translation of the Bible, *tapāṉi* is reserved for the Divine Persons, and beings are made to address Jesus Christ as *taṉ*, *timi*, *āphu* or *tapāṉi*, according to their characteristic attitude towards Him.

The Kāṭhm. authorities give *uṉhāṉ*, for *uni*, and they translate, for instance, 'I am not' *hāṉmi hunnauṉ* ; 'thou art not' *tapāṉi huṉnu hunna* ; 'he is not' *uṉhāṉ huṉnu hunna* ; 'I shall not be' *hāṉmi huṉdainauṉ* ; 'thou wilt not be' *tapāṉi huṉnu hoina* ; 'he will not be' *uṉhāṉ huṉnu hoina*.

DEMONSTRATIVE PRONOUNS.

Sing.

	'this one'		'that one'	
N.	यो	*yo*	त्यो	*tyo*
Ac.	येस्लाइ	*yeslāi*	त्येस्लाइ	*tyeslāi*
D.	,,	,,	,,	,,
Ag.	येस्ले	*yesle*	त्येस्ले	*tyesle*
G.	येस्को (ी, ा)	*yesko* (ī, ā)	त्येस्को (ी, ा)	*tyesko* (ī, ā)
L.	येस्मां	*yesmāṉ*	त्येस्मां	*tyesmāṉ*

Plu.

	'these ones'		'those ones'	
N.	यिनिहरु	*yiniharu*	तिनिहरु	*tiniharu*
Ac.	,, लाई	*yiniharulāi*	,, लाई	*tiniharulāi*
		etc.		etc.

tes-, for ***tyes-***, is a common variant; and ***iniharu***, for ***yiniharu***, with the contractions, ***yi***, ***i***, ***yin***, ***in***, ***yina***, ***ina***, ***yini***, ***ini***; and ***ti***, ***tini***, ***tina***, ***tini***, for ***tiniharu***, especially for inanimate objects.

yo and *tyo* are also used as Demonstrative **Adjectives**, 'this,' 'that,' and for the **Definite Article**, 'the,' declined as above, except that the case affixes are dropped, and that the plu. is simply ***yi***, ***ti***: *yo thok*, 'this thing'; *yes thokko*, 'of this thing'; *yi thokamān*, 'in these things'; *tyes dailole*, 'by that door'; *ti dailāharu*, 'those doors.'

tyo is also used for *u*, the Third Personal Pronoun (page 20). *u* is used for *tyo*, both as pronoun and adjective: *u koṭhā*, 'that room'; *us koṭhāmān*, 'in that room'; *una koṭhāharumān*, 'in those rooms'; *usle*, 'by that one.'

'The same' is made by the emphatic of *tyo* or *u*: *tyei*, *ui*, 'the same one'; *tyesaile* (or *usaile*), 'by the same one'; *tyei* (or *ui*) *mālī*, 'the same gardener'; *tyesai* (or *usai*) *māliko*, 'of the same gardener'; *tinai* (or *unai*) *kūliharu*, 'the same coolies.' *tyei*, *ui* = literally 'that very.'

Relative or Conjunctive Pronouns.

'who,' 'which,' 'that.'

Sing.

N.	जो	*jo*	or	जुन्	*jun*
Ac.	जस्लाई	*jaslāi*		जुन्लाई	*junlāi*
D.	,,	,,		etc.	
Ag.	जस्ले	*jasle*			
G.	जस्को (ी, ा)	*jasko* (*ī*, *ā*)			
L.	जस्मां	*jasmān*			

Plu.

N.	जो जो	*jo jo*	or	जुन्हरु	*junharu*
Ac.	जस् जस्लाई	*jas jaslui*		जुन्हरुलाई	*junharulāi*

The plu. oblique cases of *jo* are sometimes made by doubling the *s* : *jasslāi*, 'to whom' (plu.)

The sing. is frequently used for the plu., especially as the subject of the verb, for then the verb shews the plurality : *jo āye*, 'who came' : '*jasle garye*,' 'who did.'

'that which,' 'what.'

	Sing.		Plu.	
N.	ज्ये	*jye*	ज्ये ज्ये	*jye jye*
Ac.	ज्येलाइ	*jyelāi*	ज्ये ज्येलाइ	*jye jyelāi*
	etc		etc.	

jye is often written *je*. As with *jo*, so with *jye*, the plu. may be the same as the sing.

'-ever' is *-sukai* : *josukai*, or *junsukai*, 'whoever' (Ac., *josukailāi*, or *junsukailāi* ; plu., *jo josukai*, or *junsukai*) ; *jyesukai*, 'whatever.' These compounds, with *pani*, 'even,' added, are much used in the sense of 'every' : *jyesukai kurāko bishaymān pani*, 'concerning every word.' Their noun is put in the plu.

Any of the above can be used adjectively, dropping their case affixes : *jun mānchhe*, 'the person who' (relatively) or, 'which person' (absolutely) ; *jas* (or *jun*) *mānchhelāi*, 'the person to whom,' or 'to which person' ; *jun mānchheharuko*, 'the persons whose,' or 'which persons' ' ; *jye kurole*, 'the word by which,' or 'by which word' ; *junsukai mānchhe*, 'whichever person' ; *jyesukai kuro*, 'whichever word' ; *prem garne junsukai pani*, 'whichever (= every) lover.'

Interrogative Pronouns.

'who ?'

Sing.

N.	को	*ko*	or	कुन्	*kun*
Ac.	कस्लाइ	*kaslāi*		कुन्लाइ	*kunlāi*
D.	,,	,,		etc.	
Ag	कस्ले	*kasle*			
G.	कस्को (ि, ा)	*kasko* (*i*, *ā*)			
L.	कस्मां	*kasmān*			

Plu.

N.	को को	*ko ko*	or	कुन्हरु	*kunharu*
Ac.	कस् कस्लाई	*kas kaslāi*		कुन्हरुलाई	*kunharulāi*
	etc.				

'what?'

	Sing.		Plu.	
N.	क्ये	*kye*	क्ये क्ये	*kye kye*
Ac.	क्येलाई	*kyelāi*	क्ये क्येलाई	*kye kyelāi*
	etc.		etc.	

The plu. oblique cases of *ko* may be made by doubling the *s* of the sing. : *kasslāi*, 'to whom?'

The sing. may be used for the plu., especially as the subject of a verb : *ko āye*, 'who came?'

kole, *kolāi*, etc., for *kasle kaslāi*, etc., are colloquial variants.

kun is more respectful than *ko*

ke is sometimes written for *kye*.

kyā, for *kye*, is used in verb-apposition : *tero nāṉu kyā ho*, 'what is thy name?'

kye is also used as a sign of interrogation : *kye u* (or *u kye*) *āyo*, 'did he come?' ; *kye tero nāṉu chha*, 'hast thou a name?'

kun is also used adjectively, dropping its affix : *kun mānchheharulāi*, 'to which persons?' ; *kun kārāṇle*, 'for what cause?' *ko* and *kye* also are so used, but not so frequently as *kun* : *kas mānchheko*, 'what person's?' ; *kye bhūlle*, 'by what mistake?' 'Which one?' is *kun chaiṉ* : *kun chaiṉ mānchheko* ; *kunchaiṉle*. [*kunai*, the emphatic of *kun*, means 'some or other,' 'any' ; *kunai rītle*, 'in some manner or other.']

Indefinite Pronouns.

'some one,' 'any one.' 'something,' 'anything.'

	Sing.		Sing.	
N.	कोई	*koī*	क्येइ	*kyei*
Ac.	कसैलाई	*kasailāi*	क्येइलाई	*kyeilāi*
D.	,,	,,	etc.	
Ag.	कसैले	*kasaile*		

G.	कसैको (ी, ा)	*kasaiko* (ī, ā)		
L.	कसैमां	*kasaimān̲*		
	Plu.		Plu.	
N.	कोई कोई	*koī koī*	क्येइ क्येइ	*kyei kyei*
Ac.	कसै कसैलाइ	*kasai kasailāi*	क्येइ क्येइलाइ	*kyei kyeilāi*
	etc.		etc.	

The plu. oblique cases of *koī* may by made by doubling the *s* of the sing. : *kassailāi*, 'to some ones.'

The sing. may be used for the plu., especially as the subject of a verb : *koī āye* 'some ones came'; *kasaile garye*, 'some ones did.'

koi and *kohi*, for *koī* ; and *kehi*, for *kyei*, are common variants.

koī and *kyei* may be used for 'a,' 'an'; *koī mānchhe*, 'a person'; *kyei kuro*, 'a word.'

The sense of '—soever' is imparted to *koī* and *kyei* by the word *pani*, 'even': *koī pani*, 'any one whatever'; *kyeilāi pani*, 'to anything whatever.'

'some.'

Sing.

N.	कति	*kati*
Ac.	कतिलाइ	*katilāi*

etc.

Plu.

N.	कति कति	or	कत्ति	*kati kati*	or	*katti*
Ac.	कति कतिलाइ	,,	कत्तिलाइ	*kati katilāi*	,,	*kattilāi*

etc.

'another,' 'the other.'

Sing

N.	अरु	or	अर्को (ी, ा)	*aru*	or	*arko* (ī, ā)
Ac.	अरुलाइ	,,	अर्कोलाइ	*arulāi*	,,	*arkolāi*

etc.

Plu.

N. अरु अरु or अरुहरु or अर्का (ी) *aru aru* or *aruharu* or *arkā* (ī)

etc.

The sing., *aru*, may also be used for the plu.

kati conveys the idea of quantity or number. It means, literally, 'how much?'

aru is properly indefinite, 'another'; *arko*, definite, 'the other'; but the distinction is not observed in practice. It may be the origin of the plu. affix *haru*, though a similar plural termination is found in Rajasthani and Kanauji.

arkā (ī) may take the plu. affix *haru*.

The Indef. Pronouns may be used adjectively, dropping their case affixes: *koī mānchhe* 'some, or any, person'; *kasai mānchhelāi* (Ac.); *kyei thok*, 'some, or any, thing'; *kati ḍar*, 'some fear'; *katti pāpīharu*, 'some sinners'; *aru ghar*, 'another house'; *aru aru rājāharu*, 'other kings'; *arkī bainnī*, 'the other y. sister'; *arkā dājyuharu*, 'the other e. brother.'

Used adjectively, *koī* may remain uninflected in the oblique cases: *koī na koī parile*, 'in some way or others.'

'None' [='not any,' 'not some'] is made by *koī* or *kyei* and the negative verb: *koī āyena*, 'none came'; *kyei chhaina* 'there is none.'

'Not one at all' [='not even some'] is made like 'none,' with *pani* added: *koī pani āyena*, 'not one came.'

'One another' is *ekā arkā*: *ekāle arkālāi pyāro gara*, 'love one another.' Loc., *āpastamāṉ*.

'One..another..' may be made by *arkai..arkai*: *keṭāharuko rīt arkai chha keṭīharuko rīt arkai chha*, 'boys have one custom; girls have another custom.' [And see Exercise VIII. 28, 30.]

Used adjectively *aru*, when it precedes its noun, means 'other' (different); when it follows it, 'more' (additional): *aru log āye*, 'other people came'; *log aru āye*, 'more people came.'

Reflexive Pronoun.

'-self,' '-selves.'

Sing.

N.	आफु	*āphu*
Ac.	आफुलाइ	*āphulāi*
D.	,,	,,
Ag.	आफुले	*āphule*

G. (आफ्नु) ी, ा — *āphnu* (*ī*, *a*)
आफुमां — *āphumān*

Plu.

N. आफु आफु — *āphu āphu*
Ac. ,, आफुलाइ — ,, *āphulāi*
D ,, ,, — ,, ,,
Ag. ,, आफुले — ,, *āphule*
G. आफ्नु (ी, ा) २ — *āphnu* (*ī*, *ā*) *āphnu* (*ī*, *ā*)
L. आफु आफुमां — *āphu āphuma̲n̲*

The plu. may also be the same as the sing.

The L. plu., when the meaning is 'among..selves,' is *āpastamān̲*.

'I myself' is *man̲ āphai;* Ac., *man̲ āphailāi;* G., *man̲ āphaiko,* or sometimes *mero āphnu;* Ag., *man̲ āphaile*, or *main̲le āphai*, according as the sense is 'I did it of myself' (without others), or 'I myself (as well as others) did it.'

Of course, when the 'self,' expressed or understood is a different person from the subject, not the Reflex., but the Pers. pron. is used: 'he put his own garment on him' is *usle uslāi āphnu* (Refl.)., or *usaiko* (Per.), *bastra lagāyo*, according as the garment is that of the subject, 'he,' or of the indirect object, 'him.' '(He) put his garment on him' may be *āphulāi āphn̲u*, or *āphulāi usko*, or *uslāi āphnu*, or *uslāi usko, bastra lagāyo*, according as 'he,' 'his,' 'him,' refer to one and the same person; or 'he,' 'him,' to one person, 'his,' to another; or 'he,' 'his' to one person, 'him,' to another: or 'he,' to one person, 'his,' 'him,' to another.

The **Honorific** *āphu* (p. 21) is declined like the Reflex., except that its G. is *āphuko* (*ī*, *ā*), and its plu. *āphuharu*. In other words, it is declined exactly like a noun.

Emphatic forms of the Pronouns

are much used. The following list contains typical examples :—

aru, arunai	for	*aru*
arkai		*arko* (*ī*, *ā*)
āphai, āphainai āphu aphai		*āphu* (Reflex.)
āphui, aphuinai		,, (Honor.)

āphnai, āphnu āphnai	*āphnu*
ui, uinai	*u*
usailāi	*uslāi*
katti, katinai	*kati*
kassailāi	*kasailāi*
kasslāi	*kaslāi*
jasaiko	*jasko*
jasailāi	*jaslāi*
junnai	*jun*
joi	*jo*
tan̲, tan̲nai	*tan̲*
tain̲lāi	*tan̲lāi*
tapān̲inai	*tapān̲i*
tinai	*ti*
tyei, tyeinai	*tyo*
tyesaiko	*tyesko*
main̲, man̲nai	*man̲*
main̲lāi	*man̲lāi*
main̲lei, main̲lenai	*main̲le*
merai, meroi	*mero*
yei, yeinai	*yo*
yesaiko	*yesko*
hān̲miharui, hān̲miharunai	*hān̲miharu*
hān̲miharuiko	*hān̲miharuko.*

Pronouns as Adjectives.

To the examples already given, this new one may be added that the Personal Pronouns themselves may be said to be used adjectively, though it is really a case of a noun in apposition to a pronoun: *man̲ rājā*, 'I, the king'; *man̲ rājālāi*, 'to me, the king'; *hān̲miterā chhorāharuko*, 'of us, thy sons'; *us mānchhelāi*, 'to him, the person,' 'to that person.'

So used, they drop their case and number affixes; but there is this exception, that qualifying *sabai*, 'all,' they themselves take the number affix: *hān̲miharu sabailāi* 'to us all.'

IV. Exercise.

Vocabulary.

man̲ chhu	I am

tan̲ chhas	thou art
u chha, or *ho*	he, she, is ; *chhaina, hoina*, 'is not'
hān̲miharu chhaun̲	we are
timiharu chhau	you ,,
uniharu chhan, or *hun*	they ,,
main̲le garyen̲, diyen̲	I did, gave
tain̲le garis, diis	thou didst, gavest
usle garyo, diyo	he did, gave
hān̲miharule garyūn̲. diyūn̲	we ,, ,,
timiharule garyau, diyau	you ,, ,,
uniharule garye, diye	they ,, ,,

āī	(she) came	*goṭhālā*	shepherd
āyena	(he) came not	*gohār*	help
āyo	,, came	*jasto*	same as
usle diī	she gave	*dos̲h̲*	blame
u bhaī	,, was	*na*	not
garn̲u	to do	*pani*	also, even
garyena	(he) did not	*pari*	way, manner
garun̲	(I) may do	*pāp*	sin
din̲nu	to give	*bābu*	father
diyena	(he) gave not	*bālakha*	child
dekhyena	,, saw ,,	*bibād*	argument
dekhyo	,, ,,	*bishwās*	faith
bhayena	,, was not	*byāhā*	marriage
hun̲da chha	(he, she) is	*bhāg*	share
hun̲nu	to be	*bhed*	difference
adhikār	inheritance	*mān̲thi*	upon
ani	and	*ra*	and
āimāi	woman	*rāt*	night
ān̲mā	mother	*logne*	husband
āsāmi	debtor	*lugā*	clothes
ekā arkā	one another	*sab*	all
ki	or	*swāmī*	master
-ko bis̲h̲aymān̲	concerning	*swāsnī*	wife
ks̲h̲amā	forgiveness	*ho*	is, yes
khet	field	*hoina*	is not, no, not.]
khetālā	,, labourer		

u gothālākī arkī chhorīkī mitranī bhaī.
उ गोठालाकी अर्कीं छोरीकी मित्रनी भई।
She was the friend of the shepherd's other daughter.

mainle tyo uslāi diyen: terā bhāīharu mero bābuko
मैंले त्यो उस्लाइ दियें. तेरा भाईहरु मेरो बाबुको
I gave it to him (or her): thy brothers are in my father's

gharmān chhan.
घर्मां छन्।
house.

hānmiharu ra timiharukī ānmāharumān bhed chha.
हांमिहरु र तिमिहरुकी आंमाहरुमां भेद् छ।
There is a difference between our mothers and yours.

e tan yesle tanlāi kye diyo.
ए तं येस्ले तंलाइ क्ये दियो
O thou, what did this one give thee?

e chhorā kye yes mānchhele tanlāi kyei diyo.
ए छोरा क्ये येस् मान्छेले तंलाइ क्येइ दियो।
O son, did this person give thee anything?

e timi chorharu ho yo timiharuko kyā ho.
ए तिमि चोर्हरु हो यो तिमिहरुको क्या हो।
O you thieves, what is this of yours?

timile aru kattilāi āphnu bhāg dinnu hunda chha.
तिमिले अरु कत्तिलाइ आफ्नु भाग् दिंनु हुंद छ।
Thou (hon.) art giving thy share to some others.

timi koī na koī parile arkāharuko adhikārmān
तिमि कोई न कोई परिले अर्काहरुको अधिकार्मां
Thou (hon.) camest in some way or other into the inheritance

āyau.
आयौ।
of the others.

āphu hānmi khetālāharukā swāmī hunnu bhayo.
आफु हांमि खेतालाहरुका स्वामी हुंनु भयो।
Thou (hon.) wast us labourers' master.

he īshwar tapāṉile hāṉmiharulāi kshamā garnu bhayo.
हे ईश्वर् तपांइले हांमिहरुलाइ क्षमा गर्नु भयो ।
O God, Thou didst forgive us.

timiharule āphnā āsāmiharulāi kshamā garyau.
तिमिहरुले आफ्ना आसामिहरुलाइ क्षमा गर्‍यौ ।
You forgave your debtors.

taiṉle āphnai hoina usaiko āsāmi kshamā garis.
तैंले आफ्नै होइन उसैको आसामि क्षमा गरिस् ।
Thou forgavest, not thine own, (but) his debtor.

usle āphnu chhorolāi kyei roṭi diyo.
उस्ले आफ्नु छोरोलाइ क्येइ रोटी दियो ।
He gave his (own) son some bread.

usle usko chhorolāi kyei roṭi diyo.
उस्ले उस्को छोरोलाइ क्येइ रोटी दियो ।
He gave his (another's) son some bread.

yinale āphai maṉlāi ti diye.
यिनले आफै मंलाइ ति दिये ।
These themselves gave me them.

ti sabai hāṉmiharu sabaikā sabai khetamāṉ āye.
ति सबै हांमिहरु सबैका सबै खेतमां आये ।
These all came into all the fields of us all.

jasle yo garyo tyesle kasko pāp garyo.
जस्ले यो गर्‍यो त्येस्ले कस्को पाप् गर्‍यो ।
Against whom did he sin who did this ?*

jo josukai āye tiniharule kasai kasailāi kyei kyei diye.
जो जोसुकै आये तिनिहरुले कसै कसैलाइ क्येइ क्येइ दिये ।
Whosoever came, they gave certain things to certain (persons).

---

* Notice the order : (1) relative clause, (2) antecedent.

koīṇi timro gharmān̲ chha.
कोईनि तिम्रो घर्मां छ।
Is there some one in thy (hon.) house ?

timiharukā gharamān̲ kun chain̲ āye yini ki tini.
तिमिहरुका घरमां कुन् चइं आये यिनि कि तिनि।
Which (hon.) came into your houses ? This, or that ?

he prabhu ani uni ko hun ra man̲ uni mān̲thi bishwās garun̲.
हे प्रभु अनि उनि को हुन् र मं उनि मांथि बिश्वास् गरुं।
And who is he (hon.), Lord, that I should believe on him ?

jas jasle tyeslāi dosh diye tinailāi dosh chha.
जस् जस्ले त्येस्लाइ दोष् दिये तिनैलाइ दोष् छ।
The blame is to them that blamed him.

jye jye usle garyo ti kasaile dekhyo ki dekhyena.
ज्ये ज्ये उस्ले गर्‍यो ति कसैले देख्यो कि देख्येन।
Did any one see the things he did, or not ?

kye aruharule arkālāi kyei diye hoina ekāle arkālāi diye.
क्ये अरुहरुले अर्कालाइ क्येइ दिये होइन एकाले अर्कालाइ दिये।
Did others give the others anything ? No ; (they) gave to one another

tyo sabai āpastamān̲ bhāg bhāg garye.
त्यो सबै आपस्तमां भाग २ गर्‍ये।
(They) shared it all amongst themselves.

kye koī āyo. koī āyena. koī panī āyena.
क्ये कोई आयो। कोई आयेन। कोई पनि आयेन।
Did any one come ? No one came. No one at all came.

tain̲le ti kaslāi dius. āphailāi hoina tara āphu-
तैंले ति कस्लाइ दिइस्। आफैलाइ होइन तर आफु
To whom didst thou give them ? (I) gave them, not to myself,

harukana diyen̲.

हरुकन दिये .

but to you (hon.)

kas kasle yo garye; hān̲miharu āphaile garyūn̲.

कस् कस्ले यो गर्‍ये. हांमिहरु आफैले गर्‍यूं।

Who (plu.) did this? We did (it) ourselves.

āphule āphai yes kāmko bis̲haymān̲ gohār garnu bhayo

आफुले आफै येस् काम्को बिषयमां गोहार् गर्नु भयो।

Thou (hon.) thyself didst help concerning this work.

kasaile pani gohār garyena timiharu āphu āphaile garyau.

कसैले पनि गोहार् गर्‍येन तिमिहरु आफु आफैले गर्‍यौ।

No one at all helped, you did (it) your very selves.

yo kasko ho. merā bābu ān̲māko jasto chha.

यो कस्को हो। मेरा बाबु आंमाको जस्तो छ।

Whose is this? It is like my parents'.

tinale āpastamān̲ yesai bis̲haymān̲ bibād garye.

तिनले आपस्तमां येसै बिषयमां बिबाद् गर्‍ये।

They argued among themselves concerning this very matter.

timiharule āphai uslāi usaikā lugā diyau.

तिमिहरुले आफै उस्लाइ उसैका लुगा दियौ।

You gave him his own clothes yourselves.

tyesai āimāile katti bālakhalāi kati kati dān dīī.

त्येसै आइमाइले कत्ति बालखलाइ कति कति दान् दिईं।

The same woman gave some children some gifts.

timiharulāi kye kyei pani bal bhayena.

तिमिहरुलाइ क्ये क्येइ पनि बल् भयेन।

Had you no strength at all?

hān̲mi kāṭhmāṇḍūkāharulāi āphu āphumān̲ bal chha.

हांमि काठमाण्डूकाहरुलाइ आफु आफुमां बल् छ।

We Kāṭhmāṇḍū (people) have strength in ourselves.*

---

* Notice 'have' made by the D. and *chha*: 'there is to us.'

tyo kaskī swāsnī bhaī. kye ti sabaikī ki.

त्यो कस्की स्वास्नी भई। क्ये ति सबैकी कि।

Whose wife was she? Of all those, or (what)?

yesai rātmān yinalāi dinnu bhayo ani tinalāi dinnu bhayena

येसै रात्मां यिनलाइ दिंनु भयो अनि तिनलाइ दिंनु भयेन।

This very night (thou) (hon.) gavest to these, and not to those.

usle kunai parile kassai arulāi kyei diyena.

उस्ले कुनै परिले कस्सै अरुलाइ क्येइ दियेन।

He by no means gave anything to any more.

aru kasle kati diyo. mero chain [See p. 38.] *arko jasto chha.*

अरु कस्ले कति दियो। मेरो चइं अर्को जस्तो छ।

Who else gave some? Mine is like the other.

timro bibādko bishay kyā ho. kyei pani hoina.

तिम्रो विबाद्को विषय् क्या हो। क्येइ पनि होइन।

What is your matter of dispute? Nothing at all.

kye bibādko kunai bishay chha. kunai pani chhaina.

क्ये विबाद्को कुनै विषय् छ। कुनै पनि छैन।

Is there any matter of dispute? None at all.

āphuharuni yinai gharakā swāmī hunnu hunda chha.

आफुहरुनि यिनै घरका स्वामी हुंनु हुंद छ।

Are you (hon.) the masters of these very houses?

junharule yo garye merā āsāmi tinai hun.

जुन्हरुले यो गर्‍ये मेरा आसामि तिनै हुन्।

(They) who did this, *they* are my debtors.

gharko swāmī uinai ho arko chain hoina.

घर्को स्वामी उइनै हो अर्को चइं होइन॥

He, not the other, is the master of the house.

THE ADJECTIVE.

Inflexion.

Adjectives ending in an unvocalised consonant do not, as a rule, undergo any change for gender or number; but there are exceptions: *abyāhit* (m.), *abyāhitā* (f.), 'unmarried'; *nirdosh* (m.), *nirdoshinī* (f.), 'guiltless.'

Those ending in a vocalised consonant change, as a rule, the inherent *a* to *ā* for the fem.: *yogya* (m.), *yogyā* (f.), 'worthy'; *bhakta* (m.), *bhaktā* (f.), 'pious.'

Those ending in *ā* change this, as a rule, to *ī* for the fem.: *baulāhā* (m.), *baulāhī* (f.), 'mad'; *bhalāchangā* (m.) *bhalīchangī* (f.), 'healthy' [the latter, a compound adjective, inflects both parts].

Those ending in *i* or *ī* change this, as a rule, to *inī* or *iṇī* for the fem.: *aṭṭeri* (m.) *aṭṭerinī* (f.), 'obstinate'; *pāpī* (m.), *pāpinī* (f.), 'sinful'; *byabhichārī* (m.), *byabhichāriṇī* (f.), 'adulterous.' A notable exception is *jāti*, 'good,' which does not change, as a rule.

Those ending in *e* change this, as a rule, to *ī* or *enī* for the fem.: *alchhe* (m.), *alchhī* (f.), 'lazy'; *upakāre* (m.), *upakārenī* (f.), 'helpful'; *rupwante* (m)., *rupwantī* (f.), 'shapely.'

Those ending in *o* or *u* (except those in *ālu* or *elu*) change this, as a rule, to *ī* for the fem., sing. and plu., and to *ā* for the masc. plu.: *baṛo* (m. s.), *baṛī* (f. s. and p.), *baṛā* (m. p.) 'great'; *sānnu* (m. s.), *sānnī* (f. s. and p.), *sānnā* (m. p.), 'small.' There is a considerable number of exceptions, however: *pragaṭo*, 'manifest'; *dherjaso*, 'several'; *aru*, 'other,' which do not change.

Exceptions to the above rules—the sing. masc. form used for both genders and numbers—are especially frequent when the adjective stands in the predicate: *uskā mārga sojo pāra*, 'make his paths straight'; *usle strīlāi niko pāryo*, 'he healed the woman.'

For honorific purposes, the masc. plu. is used for the masc. sing.: *baṛo ājñā* (आज्ञा, pronounced *āg-yā*), 'a great commandment'; *baṛā ājñā*, 'THE GREAT commandment.'

The above rules (disregarding exceptions) are exemplified in the following table of typical adjectives:—

Masc.		Fem.		
Sing.	Plu.	Sing.	Plu.	
assal	*assal*	*assal*	*assal*	first-rate
pavitra	*pavitra*	*pavitrā*	*pavitrā*	holy
andhā	*andhā*	*andhī*	*andhī*	blind
aṭṭeri	*aṭṭeri*	*aṭṭerinī*	*aṭṭerinī*	obstinate
pāpī	*pāpī*	*pāpinī*	*pāpinī*	sinful
ṭhulo	*ṭhulā*	*ṭhulī*	*ṭhulī*	big
sānnu	*sānnā*	*sānnī*	*sānnī*	little
alchhe	*alchhe*	*alchhī*	*alchhī*	lazy
jhagare	*jhagare*	*jhagarenī*	*jhagarenī*	quarrelsome
dayālu	*dayālu*	*dayālu*	*dayālu*	merciful

Nouns and Pronouns as Adjectives

this usage has already been noted (pp. 15, 23, 24, 25, 27, 29).

Possessive Adjectives.

are of course just the G. of the pronouns: *mero*, 'my'; *āphnu*, 'own.'

Quantitative Adjectives.

sab (emphat., *sabai*) 'all,' 'every,' precedes its noun in the sing., but may follow it in the plu.: *sabai keṭolāi* 'to every boy'; *sab keṭāharulāi*, or *keṭāharu sabailāi*, 'to all boys.'

sab, 'all,' *katti*, 'some,' 'how many?' *dherai*, 'many,' *thorai*, 'few,' may take the word *janā* before nouns of person, and the affix *waṭā* (ī) before nouns of person or thing: *sabai janā rājāharulāi*, or *rājāharu sabai janālāi*, 'to all kings'; *dherai janā*, or *dheraiwaṭī*,, *bidhuwīharu*, 'many widows'; *katti janā*, or *katiwaṭā*, *rājāharu*, 'some (or, how many ?) kings'; *thoraiwaṭā roṭī*, 'a few loaves'; *timiharu sabai janāko*, 'of you all.'

Distributive Adjectives.

janange (before persons), and *goṭā* or *goṭai pichchhe* (before not-persons), 'each,' 'every,' usually precede their noun in the sing., and follow it in the plu. They are really adverbs in Nepāli, though representing adjectives in English, and do not affect the syntax: *timiharu janangele āphnu bhāīlāi kshamā garyau*, 'you each forgave your brother'; *tiniharu janangele uslāi bhannu lāgye*, 'they each began to say to him'; *janange āsāmilāi*, 'to each debtor'; *āsāmiharu janangelāi*, 'to every debtor'; *sabai āsāmiharu janangeko*, 'of all the debtors severally;' *gotai pichchhe hāngāmān*, 'on each branch'; *hāngāharu gotai pichchhemān*, 'on every branch'; *gotā ser*, 'a (=each) seer'; *jiundāharu janange jantulāi* (idiomatic, for *jiundā jantuharu janangelāi*), 'to every living thing.'

Even in the sing. *janange* follows its noun when that is formed from the Infinitive of a verb: *bishwās garne janangelāi*, 'to each (or every) believer,' where *garne* is the noun of *garnu*, 'to do.'

Even in Nepālī *janange* is sometimes used as a true adjective: *timiharumānko janangelāi*, 'to each among you.'

'Either (one)' is *koī pani*; 'neither (one),' *koī pani*, with the verb in the negative: *tinamānko koī pani hunchha* (or, *hundaina*), 'either of them (or neither of them) will do.'

Distinguishing Adjectives, or Articles.

See pp. 13, 23, 26.

Distinguishing Particle.

This is the word *chain*. Translated 'as for,' it might be considered a preposition; but translated 'the..one,' it may be classified as an adjective. It follows what it qualifies: *keto chain*, 'the boy one'; *ketolāi chain*, or (qualifying only the noun itself, not also the relationship indicated by the case ending) *ketochainlāi*, 'to the boy one'; *yo chain*, 'this one'; *kun chain*, 'which one?'; *timiharulāi chain*, or *timiharuchainlāi*, 'to the you ones.' It does not always require or admit of translation (see p. 35). Notice that when it falls between the noun and its case affix, it is written as one word with them: *yeschainlāi*, but *yeslāi chain*, 'to this one.'

The distinguishing conjunction *tā*, 'indeed,' has much the same force as *chain*: *keto tā*, 'the boy, indeed'; *ketolāi tā*, 'to the boy, indeed.'

Comparison

is indicated by *bhandā* for the Comparative, and *sabai bhandā* for the Superlative, when the object with which the comparison is made is expressed; when this object is not expressed, the Positive stands for all three degrees; *dekhi* is sometimes used instead of *bhandā* :—

keṭi sāṉnī chha { ‘the girl is small’ (Pos.)
„ „ „ smaller’ (Comp.)
„ „ „ smallest’ (Sup.)

keṭo bhandā / „ *dekhi* } *keṭi sāṉnī chha*, ‘the g. is smaller than the boy.’

sabai bhandā / „ *dekhi* } „ „ „ ‘the g. is the smallest.’

Comparison may be expressed by the L. case : *keṭo ra keṭīmāṉ keṭī sāṉnī* : ‘the girl (is) smaller than the boy’ ; *sabaimāṉ keṭī sāṉnī*, ‘the girl (is) the smallest.’

bhandā is the Imperfect participle of *bhannu*, ‘to say’; *dekhi* the Conjunctive partic. of *dekhnu*, ‘to see,’ is the preposition ‘from.’ Both are translatable as ‘than.’

NUMERAL ADJECTIVES.

The student need not master these, or the immediately following tables, right off, but should rather refer to them on occasion.

The Cardinals are, of course, translated ‘one,’ ‘two,’ ‘three,’ etc. ; the Ordinals, ‘first,’ ‘second,’ ‘third,’ ‘fourth,’ ‘fifth,’ etc.

The Devanāgarī Figures have already been given, on p. 10.

	Cardinal.		Ordinal.	
0	सुन्	*sun*	सुन्ने	*sunnye*
1	एक्	*ek*	पहिलो (-ी,-ा)	*pahilo* (-ī, -ā)
2	दुइ	*dui*	दोस्रो (-ी,-ा)	*dosro* (-ī, -ā)
3	तीन्	*tīn*	तीस्रो (-ी,-ा)	*tīsro* (-ī, -ā)
4	चार्	*chār*	चौथो (-ी,-ा)	*chautho* (-ī, -ā)
5	पांच्	*pāṉch*	पांचौं	*pāṉchauṉ*
6	छ	*chha*	छैठो (-ी,-ा)	*chhaiṭho*
7	सात्	*sāt*	सातौं	*sātauṉ*
8	आठ्	*āṭh*	आठौं	*āṭhauṉ*
9	नौ	*nau*	नवं	*nawaṉ*
10	दस्	*das*	दसौं	*dasauṉ*

11	एघारह्	*eghārah*	एघार्हौं	*eghārhauṉ*
12	बारह्	*bārah*	बार्हौं	*bārhauṉ*
13	तेरह्	*terah*	तेर्हौं	*terhauṉ*
14	चौदह्	*chaudah*	चौधौं	*chaudhauṉ*
15	पन्द्रह्	*pandrah*	पन्द्र्हौं	*pandrhauṉ*
16	सोरह्	*sorah*	सोर्हौं	*sorhauṉ*
17	सत्रह्	*satrah*	सत्र्हौं	*satrhauṉ*
18	अठारह्	*aṭhārah*	अठार्हौं	*aṭhārhauṉ*
19	उनीस्	*unīs*	उनीसं	*unīsaṉ*
20	बीस्	*bīs*	बीसं	*bīsaṉ*
21	एक्काईस्	*ekkāīs*	एक्काईसं	*ekkāīsaṉ*
22	बाईस	*bāīs*	बाईसं	*bāīsan*
23	तेईस्	*teīs*	तेईसं	*teīsaṉ*
24	चौबीस्	*chaubīs*	चौबीसं	*chaubīsaṉ*
25	पचीस्	*pachīs*	पचीसं	*pachīsaṉ*
26	छब्बीस्	*chhabbīs*	छब्बीसं	*chhabbīsaṉ*
27	सताईस्	*satāīs*	सताईसं	*satāīsaṉ*
28	अठाईस्	*aṭhāīs*	अठाईसं	*aṭhāīsaṉ*
29	उनन्तीस्	*unantīs*	उनन्तीसं	*unantīsaṉ*
30	तीस्	*tīs*	तीसं	*tīsaṉ*
31	एकतीस्	*ektīs*	etc.	etc.
32	बतीस	*batīs*		
33	तेंतीस्	*teṉtīs*		
34	चौंतीस्	*chauṉtīs*		
35	पैंतीस्	*paiṉtīs*		
36	छतीस्	*chhattīs*		

37	सैंतीस्	*sain̲tīs*		
38	अड़तीस्	*arṭīs*		
39	उनन्चालीस्	*unanchālīs*		
40	चालीस्	*chālīs*		
41	एक्चालीस्	*ekchālīs*		
42	बयालीस्	*bayālīs*		
43	तेंतालीस्	*tentālīs*		
44	चौआलीस्	*chauālīs*		
45	पैंतालीस्	*pain̲tālīs*		
46	छियालीस्	*chhiyālīs*		
47	सैंतालीस्	*sain̲tālīs*		
48	अड़तालीस्	*arṭālīs*		
49	उनन्चास्	*unanchās*		
50	पचास्	*pachās*		
51	एकावन्	*ekāwan*		
52	बावन्	*bāwan*		
53	तिर्पन्	*tirpan*		
54	चौवन्	*chauwan*		
55	पच्पन्	*pachpan*		
56	छप्पन्	*chhappan*		
57	सतावन्	*satāwan*		
58	अठावन्	*aṭhāwan*		
59	उन्सठ्	*unsaṭh*	उन्सठौं	*unsaṭhaun̲*
60	साठि	*sāṭhi*	साठौं	*sāṭhaun̲*
61	एक्सठ्	*eksaṭh*	etc.	etc.
62	बासठ्	*bāsaṭh*		
63	तिर्सठ	*tirsaṭh*		

64	चौंसठ्	*chaunsaṭh*		
65	पैंसठ्	*painsaṭh*		
66	छियासठ्	*chhiyāsaṭh*		
67	सरसठ्	*sarsaṭh*		
68	अड्सठ्	*aṛsaṭh*		
69	उनहत्तर्	*unahattar*		
70	सत्तर्	*sattar*		
71	एकहत्तर्	*ekhattar*		
72	बहत्तर्	*bahattar*		
73	तिहत्तर्	*tihattar*		
74	चौहत्तर्	*chauhattar*		
75	पचहत्तर्	*pachhattar*		
76	छिहत्तर्	*chhihattar*		
77	सत्हत्तर्	*sathattar*		
78	अठ्हत्तर्	*aṭhhattar*		
79	उनासी	*unāsī*		
80	अस्सी	*assī*	अस्सीवं	*assīwan*
81	एकासी	*ekāsī*	एकासीवं	*ekāsīwan*
82	बयासी	*bayāsī*	etc	etc.
83	तिरासी	*tirāsī*		
84	चौरासी	*chaurāsī*		
85	पचासी	*pachāsī*		
86	छियासी	*chhiyāsī*		
87	सतासी	*satāsī*		
88	अठासी	*aṭhāsī*		
89	उनानब्बे	*unanabbe*		
90	नब्बे	*nabbe*		
91	एकानबे	*ekānabe*		
92	बानबे	*bānabe*		

93 तिरानबे *tirānabe*

94 चौरानबे *chaurānabe*

95 पचानबे *pachānabe*

96 छियानबे *chhiyānabe*

97 सतानबे *satānabe*

98 अठानबे *aṭhānabe*

99 उनन्सै *unansai* उनन्सैवं *unansaiwan̲*

100 (एक्) सै, सये (*ek*) *sai, saye* सैयं *saiyan̲*

101 एक् सै एक् *ek sai ek* एक् सै पहिलो *ek sai pahilo*

102 एक् सै दुइ *ek sai dui* एक् सै दोस्रो *ek sai dosro*

1,000 (एक्) हजार् (*ek*) *hajār* हजारौं *hajāraun̲*

10,000 दस् हजार् *das hajār* दस् हजारौं *dashajāraun̲*

1,00,000 (एक्) लाख् (*ek*) *lākh* लाखौं *lākhaun̲*

10,00,000 नियुत् *niyut* नियुतौं *niyutaun̲*

100,00,000 करोड़्* *karoṛ* करोड़ौं *karoṛaun̲*

1,000,00,000 अर्ब् *arb* अर्बौं *arbaun̲*

100,000,00,000 खर्ब् *kharb* खर्बौं *kharbaun̲*

100,00,000,00,000 नील् *nīl* नीलं *nīlan̲*

100,00,00,000,00,000 पद्म् *padm* पद्मौं *padmaun̲*

100,00,00,00,000,00,000 शंख् *shan̲kh* शंखौं *shan̲khaun̲*

153 एक् सै तिर्पन् *ek sai tirpan* सै तिर्पनं *sai tirpanan̲*

Remarks on the Numerals.

Ordinals are really demonstrative adjectives, and follow adjective rules : final *o* becomes *ī* for the fem., sing. and plu. ; and *ā*, for the masc. plu. Final *an̲* and *wan̲* may become *in̲* and *wīn̲* for the fem. Final *aun̲* does not seem to change.

---

* Or करवर् *karawar.*

In numbering persons the word *janā*, and in numbering either persons or not-persons the affix *waṭā*, may be added to the number, except with collective nouns: *pāṉch janā mālīharule chārwaṭā bārī lagāye*, '5 gardeners planted 4 gardens'; *tin janā kaptānale bīsai kampūlāi* (or *kampanilāi*) *chha bagāl bheṉṛā bakshi diye*, '3 captains presented the 20 companies with 6 flocks of sheep'; *nau janāni kahāṉ chhan*, 'where are the 9 (persons)?'

Except in its emphatic form (*ekaiwaṭā*) the word *ekwaṭā* is not used, but, instead, the word *yeuṭā*, 'one': *yeuṭā* (or *ek janā*) *keṭo*, 'one boy,' 'a boy.' '70' is, not *sattarwaṭa*, but *sattariwaṭa*.

The form *ekā*, 'one,' is used, not only in the phrase *ekā arkā*, 'one another' (p. 27), but also in the sense of 'a single': *ekā ṭhāṉumāṉ*, 'in a single place.'

euṭā or *ewaṭā* for *yeuṭā*, *tin* for *tīn*, *tesro* for *tīsro*, *saye* for *sai*, are examples of the innumerable variants of the various numerals.

SOME PHRASES.

ek ek gari	one by one, each
dui dui gari	two by two
ekai	the one
duwai	the two, both
dui ek	one or two
dui chār	'two or three'
āṭh ek	about eight
saikaṛā	per cent.
lākh lākh (or *lākhauṉ lākh*)	'hundreds of thousands'

DENOMINATIVES

In multiplication the denominative, or multiplicand, is in several cases modified :—

ekaṉ	1	*paṉje*	5
duaṉ	2	*chhakkā*	6
tīnaṉ	3	*satte*	7
chāraṉ	4	*āṭhaṉ*	8

nawan	9	*bīsāsai*	120
dasan	10	*chhabbīsāsai*	126
ekāsai	101	*tīsāsai*	130
duwāsai	102	*nabbesai*	190

Examples: *dui ekan dui*, '2 (times) 1 (is) 2'; *chār duwāsai chār sai āṭh*, '4 (times) 102 (is) 408.'

Collectives

in several cases add *ā* to the cardinals:—

bīsā	a twenty	*batīsā*	a thirty-two
tīsā	a thirty	*chālīsā*	a forty.

This may explain the form *ekā* (p. 44).

The following special collectives are used:—

joṛā	a two, couple, pair
gaṇḍā	a four, quartette
panjā	a five, quintette
korī	a twenty, score
saikaṛā	a hundred, per cent.

Fractions

are scarcely known. They are therefore, with a few exceptions, but cumbrously expressed:—

ādhā	½	
ek ra ādhā	1½	
dui ,, ,,	2½	
chār hissāmān ek hissā	¼	*lit.* 'in 4 parts 1 part'
tīn ,, ,, ,,	⅓	,, ,, 3 ,, ,, ,,
chār ,, *tīn* ,,	¾	,, ,, 4 ,, 3 ,,
ek ra dosroko chautho	1¼	,, '1 and ¼ of a second'

In place of *hissā*, 'a part,' *bhāg*, *khaṇḍa* and *ansha* are also used, all with the same meaning: *ek ra ṭrikhaṇḍa*, '1¾'; *dasaun ansha* '1/10'; '*chautho bhāg*, '¼'; *tihāī* '⅓'; *chauthāī*, '¼' occur.

The Hindī *sāṛhe*, 'and a half,' is already much used in money counting; *sāṛhe pānch rupiyā*, '5½ rupees'; *sāṛhe sai*, '150' = 100 + ½ (100).

Proportionals

are expressed by the affix *guṇā*, '-fold':—

duguṇā	two-fold	*tiguṇā*	three-fold

chauguṇā	four-fold	*āṭhguṇā*	eight-fold
paṉchguṇā	five ,,	*nanguṇā*	9 ,,
chhaguṇā	six ,,	*dasguṇā*	10 ,,
satguṇā	seven ,,	*saiguṇā*	100 ,,

It is obvious that they may be used for multiplication purposes: *ekguṇā ek ek*, '1 time 1 (is) 1'; *duguṇā tīn chha*, '2 times 3 (is) 6.'

For *duguṇā* other words are also used: *doharo, dohoro, dobar, ḍabal*, all meaning 'double'; and for *tiguṇā*,—*ṭriguṇā, teharo*, all meaning 'triple.'

MONEY TABLES (*rupiyā paisāko hisāp*).

There are two systems current; the Mohar and the Paisā; and it is necessary, on each occasion, to state whether the amount is *moharko hisāpmāṉ*, 'on the Mohar system,' or *paisāko hisāpmāṉ*, 'on the Paisā system.'

1. The Móhar [or Ānā] System Table.

8 *phukādāmko* / 4 *dām* ,,	1 *paisā*		8 *phukādām* / 4 *dām*	= 1 *paisā*
6 *paisā* ,,	1 *ānā*		etc.	
2 *ānā* ,,	1 *suki*			
4 ,, ,,	1 *sukā*			
8 ,, ,,	1 *mohar*			
16 ,, ,, / 2 *mohar* ,,	1 *rupiyā*.			

2. The Paisā [or Gaṉḍā] System Table.

8 *phukādāmko* / 4 *dām* ,,	1 *paisā*
4 *paisā* ,,	1 *gaṉḍā*
11 ,, ,,	1 *suki*
22 ,, ,,	1 *sukā*
11 *gaṉḍā* ,,	1 *mohar*
22 ,, * ,, / 2 *mohar* ,,	1 *rupiyā*
25 *rupiyā* ,,	1 *sunko* ('gold') *asarphī*.

The *asarphī* (असर्फी) varies in value with the price of gold.

There is also a measure called *paisāko ṭoṛā*, 'a talent of paisā' (or copper), which may contain paisā to any amount.

* There is also a 24 *gaṉḍāko* "*rupiyā*."

but generally 50 or 60 rupees worth ; and another called *rupiyā-ko toṛā*, 'a talent of rupiyā' (or silver), which may contain rupiyā to any amount, but generally 500 or 1000 rupees worth.

The British India Table,

however, is gradually superseding the native Nepālī tables, and, as everybody knows, is as follows :—

3 *pāī* ('pie') *ko*		1 *paisā* ('pice')
12 ,,	,,	1 *ānā* ('anna')
4 *paisa*	,,	
16 *ānā*	,,	1 *rupiyā* ('rupee')
16 *rupiyā*	,,	1 *sunko mohar* ('gold mohur').

[Dr. Daniel Wright's valuable "History of Nepal," in a table of 'Nepalese Coinage,' enumerates, besides the *asarphī*, mentioned above, the following other gold coins :—

a gold	*pātle* (?),	worth	$\frac{2}{5}$	of the	*asarphī*
,, ,,	*sukā*	,,	$\frac{1}{2}$	,, ,,	*pātle*
,, ,,	*suki*	,,	$\frac{1}{2}$	,, ,,	*sukā*
,, ,,	*ānā*	,,	$\frac{1}{2}$	,, ,,	*suki*
,, ,,	*dām*	,,	$\frac{1}{4}$	,, ,,	*ānā*.]

MONEY NOTATION (*rupiyā paisāko lekhāī*).

The following is the usual way of writing sums of money :—

'Rupees'	'Annas'	'Pie'				
		3	is written	)।	*i.e.*,	1 paisā
		6		)॥		2 ,,
		9		)।॥		3 ,,
	1			’)		1 ānā
	2			•)		2 ,,
	3			••)		3 ,,
	4			।)		1 4-ānā
	5			।’)		1 ,, + 1 ānā
	6			।•)		1 ,, + 2
	7			।••)		1 ,, + 3 ,,

'Rupees'	'Annas'	'Pie'			
	8	is written	॥)	*i.e.*, 2 4-ānā	
	9		॥/)	2 ,,	+ 1 ānā
	10		॥//)	2 ,,	+ 2 ,,
	11		॥///)	2 ,,	+ 3 ,,
	12		॥।)	3 ,,	
	13		॥।/)	3 ,,	+ 1 ,,
	14		॥।//)	3 ,,	+ 2 ,,
	15		॥।///)	3 ,,	+ 3 ,,
1			१)	1 rupiyā	
301	15	3	३०१॥।///)॥		

The) merely marks the division between paisā and the larger denominations. To the right of it, each stroke (perpendicular) marks 1 'pice'; to the left of it, each horizontal stroke marks 1 'anna,' each perpendicular stroke, 1 'four-anna.' To the left of all, the 'rupees' are written in the ordinary figures: १।/)। 1 rupee + 1 four-anna + 1 anna + 1 pice.

Measures Table (*bharāīko hisāp*).

10 *muṭhiko*	1 *mānā*	(= ½ 'seer')
8 *mānā* ,,	1 *pāthī*	(= 4 ,,)
20 *pāthī* ,,	1 *murī*	(= 2 'maunds')

muṭhi means literally 'a handful.'

Weights Table (*jokhāīko hisāp*).

4 *ḍoleko*	1 *ganḍā*	(or *chār ḍole goṭā ganḍā*)
28½ *ganḍāko*	1 *bisaulī*	
2 *bisaulīko*	1 *dhārnī*	

There are other sub-divisions called *boṛī*, *pol*, *nauboṛī*, *hamālī*, *sāser*, which, however, are only names to the present writer.

ganḍā, the weight of 4 *ḍole*, or 'dumpy pice,' = about 3¼ 'tolas' = about 1½ oz.

Ratti, corresponding to the English 'grain,' seems to be the smallest Nepālī weight.

The commonest British India Weights are

4 *chauannī* (4 '4-anna bits')	= 1 *tolā*	written	
5 *tolā*	= 1 *chhaṭāṉk*	,,	
4 *chhaṭāṉk*	= 1 *pāwa* ('¼')	,,	
4 *pāwa*	= 1 *ser* ('seer')	,,	
5 *ser*	= 1 *paṉserī*	,,	
8 *paṉserī*	= 1 *man* ('maund')	,,	

"The Laws of Manu," VIII, 132—("Sacred Books of the East" series) gives a table of Sanskrit weights and measures, which may be worth consulting.

Wright's "History of Nepal" gives the following tables, quoted verbatim et literatim :—

"Weights used in weighing gold.

10 rattīs or lāls	= 1 māsā
10 māsās	= 1 tolā.

"Weights used in weighing silver.

8 rattīs or lāls	= 1 māsā
12 māsās	= 1 tolā.

"Weights used in weighing utensils.

4½ tolās	= 1 kanwā
4 kanwās	= 1 tukn *or* pāo
4 tuknīs	= 1 ser
3 sers	= 1 dhāranī = 5 lbs. avoirdupois.

"Dry measure.

2 manās	= 1 kurwā
4 kurwās	= 1 pāthī = 8 lbs. avoird.
20 pāthīs	= 1 murī.

"Liquid Measure.

4 dīyās	= 1 chauthāī
2 chauthāīs	= 1 ādh tuknī
2 ādh tuknīs	= 1 tuknī
4 tuknīs	= 1 kurwā = 1 ser
4 kurwās	= 1 pāthī."

TIME TABLES (*dinko hisāp*).

1. Hours of the Day.

60 *bipalā*	= 1 *palā*	('minute')
60 *palā*	= 1 *gharī*	('hour')
7½ *gharī*	= 1 *pahar*	('watch')
4 *pahar*	= 1 *din*	('day')
4 *pahar*	= 1 *rāt*	('night')

In the English day of 24 hours there are thus 216,000 'seconds' (*bipalā*), or 3,600 'minutes,' or 60 'hours,' or 8 'watches.'

The 'hours' are measured by water-clocks. A copper vessel, called *gharī*, is placed in a water-vessel, called *ārhi*; and the time it takes to fill, through a hole in its base, and sink and strike a metal plate, called *ghanṭā*, is one *gharī*, or 'hour.'

'Daylight,' *ujiyālo*, begins when a man can see the hairs on the back of his hand: 'dark,' *andhyāro*, when he can no longer do so.

'Midday,' *maddheni din*, and 'midnight,' *maddheni rāt*, are both called *dui pahar* (adverb, *dopahari*), 'two watches.'

'Midforenoon' is *din ek pahar gayo*, 'midafternoon,' *din ek pahar rahyo*.

As English time-pieces make their way, English time is kept, of course, and read as follows, as a rule:—

12	o'clock	= 12 *baji*					
12·5	„	= „	*bajyera*	5	*miliṭ*	*bhayo*	
12·10	„	= „	„	10	„	„	
12·15	„	= „	„	15	„	„	
12·30	„	= „	„	*ādhā*		„	
12·35	„	= 1	*bajnulāi*	25	„	*chha*	
12·53	„	= „	„	7	„	„	
1		= 1 *baji*					

baji is short for *baji gayo*. *bajyo* also is used. *baji, bajyera* and *bajyo* are parts of *bajnu*, 'to strike' (as a clock). *Miliṭ* is the Nepālī attempt at 'minute.'

2. Days of the Week (*sātākā din*).

āitabār	Sunday	*budhbār*	Wednesday
saumbār	Monday	*bihibār*	Thursday
mangalbār	Tuesday	*sukrabār* (or *shukrabar*)	Friday
	sancharabār (or *sanishcharbār*)	Saturday	

In letter-writing, instead of the name of the day, its number in the week is often given : *din* 1 (or *roj* 1), 'Sunday.'

sātā, 'week,' is really the Collective form of *sāt*, 'seven.'

3. Days of the Month (*mahīnākā din*).

For these special ordinals are used. The month is reckoned in two parts of 15 lunar days each : (1) *kṛishṇapakshe*, or *badī*, 'the waning half of the moon'; (2) *shuklapakshe*, or *sudī*, 'the waxing half of the moon.' The 15 days of the first half run *purne dekhi auṉsi samma*, 'from full to new moon'; of the second half, *auṉsi dekhi purne samma*, 'from new to full moon.'

The 15 days of the first half are as follows, with *tithi*, 'lunar day,' understood after each :—

1st	*parewā*		8th	*ashṭamī*
2nd	*dutiyā*		9th	*nawamī*
3rd	*tṛitiyā*		10th	*dasamī*
4th	*chauthī*		11th	*ekādasī*
5th	*paṉchamī*		12th	*dwādasī*
6th	*khashṭī*	(षष्ठी)	13th	*tridasī*
7th	*saptamī*		14th	*chaturdasī*

15th *auṉsi*.

The 15 days of the second half are the same as above, except that the 15th is, not *auṉsi*, but *purne*.

Example : *baishākh sudī ashṭamī* (or *baishākh sudī* 8) is 'the 8th (day) of the (month) Baishākh, the waxing half of the moon.'

When the English method is followed, the usage is, for example : *jūnko pāṉchauṉ tithi* (or *jūnko pāṉch din jāṉdo*), 'the 5th June.' *jāṉdo* means 'going.'

4. Months of the Year (*barshakā mahīnā*).

baishākh	= (approximately)	April-May
jeṭh	=	May-June
ashāṛh (or *asār*)	=	June-July
sāhun	=	July-August
bhādoṉ (or *bhadau*)	=	August-September
asauj	=	September-October
kāttik (or *kārttik*)	=	October-November
moṉsīr (or *maṉsīr*)	=	November-December

pūs	= (approximately)	**December-January**
māgh	=	**January-February**
phāgun	=	**February-March**
chait	=	**March-April.**

5. Seasons of the Year (*barshakā ritu*)

basanta	'Spring'	
grīshma	'Summer'	
barsāt (or *barkhā* बर्खा)	'The Rains'	(Baish.—Asauj)
sharad	'Autumn'	
hemanta (or *hiun*, or *hiundo*)	'Winter,'	(Kātt.—Chait)

6. Nepāl Eras (*nepāl sambat*).

Eras—	Commencing on—	Dating from—
sambat	1*st baishākh badī*	57 B.C.
sāke	,, ,, ,,	78 A.D.
nepāl sambat	,, *kāttik* ,,	880 A.D.
kaligat		3101 B.C. (?)

Example: '1886 A.D.', 1886 *sambat yīshwī* (*i.e.*, 1886 of the Christian Era), is *sambat* 1943 *sāl*, or *sāke* 1808, or *nepāl sambat* 1006 *sāl*, or *kaligat* 4987. [*sāl* means 'year.']

7. Ages of the World (*jagatkā yug*).

satyayug	'the Golden Age'	(or 'Age of Truth')
tretā	,, Silver ,,	
dwāpar	,, Brazen ,,	
kaliyug (or *kaligat*)	,, Iron ,,	(or 'Age of Sin').

V. Exercise.

[Vocabulary.

anugrah	grace	*kshimeki*	neighbour
anyadesī	foreign	*gayo*	(he) went
āntyo	(he) was about to	*gara*	do (2nd plu.)
ughāryo	,, opened	*gari*	doing, having [done
kannye	maiden	*gāī*	cow
kaptān	captain	*guru*	religious teacher
kam	less, minus	*gorkhālī*	Gorkhā (adj.)
kisāni	husbandman	*ghatī*	diminution
kuro	word, thing	*gharī*	hour
kos	kos (2 miles)	*ghorā*	horse

chaṛhyo	(he) ascended	*pun̲ṛo*	about, nearly
chākare	servant	*prabhu*	lord
chhoṭo	small	*bajnu*	to strike
jatan	effort	*baṛo*	great
janan̲ge	each, every	*balliyo*	strong
jaba	when	*bidhuwī*	widow
jāti	good	*baidya*	doctor
jhain̲	like as	*bhani*	that (conj.)
ṭhulo	big	*bhanye*	(they) said
ḍhīlo	slow, slack	*bhanyo*	(he) ,,
ṭulyāun̲chhu	(I) shall make	*bhaye*	(they) were
thor, thorai	few, little	*bhayo*	(he) was
din	day	*bhalāchan̲gā*	in good health
diyo	(he) gave	*bhalo*	good
dekhi	from, than	*bhen̲ṛā*	sheep
dailo	door	*madhauro*	sick
dhan	riches	*mān*	honour
dher, dherai	many, much,	*miliṭ*	minute
dherjaso	several [enough	*rahan̲ḍā*	remaining
niko	well, healthy	*rāt*	night
paṭhāye	(they) sent	*lagāyo*	(he) planted
pahar	watch	*lyā*	bring (2nd s.)
pāpī	sinful	*shiksh̲e*	disciple
pāyo	(he) found	*sañа*	with
pāyau	(you) ,,	*samet*	with
parewā	dove	*sān̲nu*	little
pāryo	(he) made	*seto*	white.]

भलो तिलंगाका भला छोराहरुले पापिनी जिमिदार्नीको पापी छोरोलाइ धेर्‌जसो भला कुरा भन्ये।	*bhalo tilan̲gākā bhalā chhorāharule pāpinī jimidārnīko pāpī chhorolāi dherjaso bhalā kurā bhanye.*	The good soldier's good sons said several good words to the sinful Jimidār woman's sinful son.
बड़ा बैद्‌ले बड़ो जतन्‌ले सांनी मधौरी केटीलाइ निको पार्‍यो।	*baṛā baidyale baṛo jatanle sān̲nī mādhaurī keṭīlāi niko pāryo.*	The great doctor with great efforr made the little sick girl whole.

मेरी दुवै बैनीहरू भलीचंगी (or निको, or निकी, or जाति) छन्।	*merī duwai bain̲nīharu bhalīchan̲gī* (or *niko*, or *nikī*, or *jāti*) *chhan*	My two younger sisters are well.
यस्ले येस् चाकरेलाई भन्यो मं तं छोटोलाई बड़ा तुल्याउंछु भनि।	*yesle yes chākarelāi bhanyo man̲ tan̲ chhoṭolāi baṛā tulyāun̲chhu bhani.*	This one said to this servant, (that) I shall make thee, a small (person), great.
जुन् (or जस्) मान्छेले यि सांना केटाहरूलाई ठुलो मान् गर्यो त्यस्ले आफ्ना लोगको राजा देखि धेरै धन् र येउटा ठुलो घर् पायो।	*jun* (or *jas*) *mānchhele yi sān̲nā keṭāharulāi ṭhulo mān garyo tyesle āphnā logako rājā dekhi dherai dhan ra yeuṭā ṭhulo ghar pāyo*	The person who did these little boys great honour, received from the king of his people much riches and a big house.
सबै जना केटाहरूले (or केटाहरू सबै जनाले) तिनिहरूका सबै छिमेकिहरूलाई आफ्ना धेर् (or धेरै, or धेरैवटा) रोटी दिये।	*sabai janā keṭāharule* (or *keṭāharu sabai janāle*) *tiniharukā sabai ks̲h̲imekiharulāi āphnā dher* (or *dherai*, or *dheraiwaṭā*) *roṭī diye.*	All the boys gave all their (others') neighbours their (own) many loaves.
कत्ति (or कति कति, or कत्ति जना, or कतिवटी, or कत्तिवटी) अन्यदेसिनी आइमाइहरू र धेरै गोर्खालिनी बिधुवीहरू आफ्नी थोरैवटी कन्ये केटीहरू समेत् गोटै पिच्छे घरमां छन्।	*katti* (or *kati kati*, or *katti janā*, or *katiwaṭī*, or *kattiwaṭī*) *anyadesinī āimāiharu ra dherai gorkhālinī bidhuwīharu āphnī thoraiwaṭī kannye keṭīharu samet goṭai pichchhe gharmān̲ chhan.*	Some foreign women, and many Gorkhā widows, with their few maiden daughters, are in each house.
प्रभुको अनुग्रह तिमिहरू सबै जना सङ्ग भयो।	*prabhuko anugrah timiharu sabai janā sañā bhayo.*	The grace of the Lord was with you all.

गुरुले आफ्ना बाह्र गोर्खाली शिष्यहरुलाई एक् एक् वस्त्र दियो।	*gurule āphnā ḇār-hai gorkhālī shiks̲h̲e-harulāi ek ek bastra diyo.*	The guru (religious teacher) gave his 12 Gorkhā disciples a garment each.
तिनमांको कोई पनि धेरै छैन।	*tinamān̲ko koī pani dherai chhaina.*	None (or neither) of them is sufficient.
तिमिहरु (or तिमिहरुमांको) जनंगेलाई एक् (or येउटा, or एक् एक्, or एक् २) घोड़ा र पांच् (or पांच्वटा, or पांच् २ वटा) गाई छन्।	*timiharu* (or *timiharumān̲ko*) *janan̲gelāi ek* (or *yeuṭā*, or *ek ek*, or *ek 2*) *ghoṛā ra pān̲ch* (or *pān̲chwaṭā*, or *pān̲ch 2 waṭā*) *gāī chhan.*	There are to each (or every) one of you 1 horse and 5 cows.
येस्ले ता होइन तर ठुलो चइं केटोले सेतो चइं दैलो उघार्यो।	*yesle tā hoina tara ṭhulo chain̲ keṭole seto chain̲ dailo ughāryo.*	Not this one, but the big boy, opened the white door.
तिमिहरुचइंले तिनिहरुले झैं न गर॥	*timiharuchain̲le tiniharule jhain̲ na gara.*	Do not you do like as they (do).
उनिहरुचइंमां ठुला ठुला कुन् चइं भये।	*uniharuchainmān̲ ṭhulā ṭhulā kun chain̲ bhaye.*	Who were the biggest of them?
उ मं भन्दा (or देखि) बलियो भयो।	*u man̲ bhandā* (or *dekhi*) *balliyo bhayo.*	He was (or became) stronger than I.
चारै कप्तानले तिलंगालाई बीस् २ गरि पठाये।	*chārai kaptānale tilan̲gālāi bīs 2 gari paṭhāye.*	The four captains sent the soldiers by twenties.
मेरो चइं घरी ३ मिलिट्को ढीलो छ।	*mero chain̲ gharī 3 miliṭko ḍhīlo chha.*	As for my watch, it is 3 minutes slow.
नवं चइं आइमाईलाई बीस् एक् कोस् पठाये।	*nawan̲ chain̲ āimāilāi bīs ek kos paṭhāye.*	(They) sent the ninth woman some 20 kos.

तिनै दस् जना राजाले एकै दिन्मां सैवटा तरवार् पठाये ।	*tinai das janā rājāle ekai dinmā̱n saiwaṭā tarawār paṭhāye.*	The same ten kings sent 100 swords on the one day.
कस् (or कुन्) किसानिले येउटा बारी लगायो ।	*kas* (or *kun*) *kisānile yeuṭā bārī lagāyo.*	Which husbandman planted a garden?
दुइ कोरी दस् भेंड़ा र एकावन् जोड़ा परेवा चौंसठौं दिन्मां ल्या ।	*dui korī das bhe̱nṛā ra ekāwan joṛā parewā chau̱nsaṭhau̱n dinmā̱n lyā.*	Bring, on the 64th day, two-score-and-ten sheep and 51 pair doves.
उस्ले आफैलाइ रोटीका चार् हिस्सामां एक् हिस्सा दियो ।	*usle āphailāi roṭikā chār hissāmā̱n ek hissā diyo.*	He gave himself ¼ of the loaf.
चार् सै र पचास् एक् बर्ष भयो ।	*chār sai ra pachās ek baṟsha bhayo.*	About 450 years ago.
यिहूदा (इस्करयोती चइं होइन) रात्को चौथो पहर्मां आयो ।	*yihūdā* (*iskaryotī chai̱n hoina*) *rātko chautho paharmā̱n āyo.*	Judas (not the Iscariot one) came in the 4th watch of the night.
जब पहर् एक् दिन् चढ़्यो ।	*jaba pahar ek din chaṛhyo.*	About the third hour of the day (*lit.*, 'when the day had ascended about a watch').
उ दोस्रो अनि तीस्रो पहर् दुवै पुङ़ो गयो ।	*u dosro ani tīsro pahar duwai pu̱nṛo gayo.*	He went both about the 6th and the 9th hour (*lit.*, 'both about the 2nd and 3rd watch.')
घरी एक् दिन् रहंदा भयो ।	*gharī ek din rahaṉdā bhayo.*	(It) was about the 11th hour of the day (*lit.*, the day about an hour remaining').

दुइ बज्नु आंट्यो।	*dui bajnu āntyo.*	It is about 2 o'c.
५ बज्नुलाइ २० मिलिट् छ।	5 *bajnulāi* 20 *milit chha.*	It is 20 minutes to 5.
अनि ति जनंगे आफ्नु २ घर्मां गये।	*ani ti janange āphnu* 2 *gharmān gaye.*	And they went each to his own house.
नेपाल् संबत् १०१६ चैत् बदी रोज ३।	*nepāl sambat* 1016 *chait badī roja* 3	The 3rd Chait, waning half, 1016 N.S.
ख्रीष्ट संबत् (or यीश्वी, contracted यी°) १८९६ जुलाय् ५ दिन् जांदो (or जुलायको पांचौं तिथि, or simply जुलाय् ५)।	*khrisht sambat* (or *yīshwī*, contracted *yī.*) 1896 *julāy* 5 *din jāndo* (or *julāyko pānchaun tithi*, or simply *julāy* 5).	The 5th July, 1896, A.D.
दस् रुपिया र बारह् आना कम् (or घटी) दुइ सै।	*das rupiyā ra bārah ānā kam* (or *ghatī*) *dui sai.*	Rs. 189-4-0 (*lit.*, 'Rs. 10-12-0 less, 200').
४६७॥ ॥॥ मां॥	*chār sai sarsath rupiyā pandrah ānā tīn paisāmān.*	At Rs. 467-15-9.

THE VERB

is of one conjugation and regular, except the following, which are more or less irregular :—

hunnu	to be	*dinnū*	to give
dhunnu	,, wash	*linnu*	,, take
chhunnu	,, touch	*jānnu*	,, go
runnu	,, weep	*laijānnu*, or *lānnu*	,, take away

These vary their stem in certain parts.

THE STEM OF VERBS

is got by dropping the Infinitive termination *nu* : *gar*, the stem of *garnu*, 'to do'; *hun*, of *hunnu*, 'to be.'

From the stem all the parts of regular verbs are formed; but (what deserves the student's best attention) the Perfect parts of those whose stem ends in *ṉ*, *aṉ*, *uṉ*, drop this ending: *garyo*. Indef. Perf. of *garnu*, 'to do'; *aṛīyo*, *aṛīṉnu*, 'to halt'; *bahyo*, of *bahaṉnu*, 'to flow'; *garāyo*, of *garāuṉnu*, 'to cause to be done'; *duhyo*, of *duhuṉnu*, 'to milk.'

It will be found that (dropping *ṉ*, *aṉ*, *uṉ*, as above directed) the stem is identical (in reg. verbs) with the 2nd sing. Imperative: *gar*, *aṛī*. *bah*, *garā*, *duh*.

Causal Verbs.

Many primitive verbs, which may be either intransitive, or active or (in form) passive, have a causal form derived from them, by, as a rule, shortening their stem vowel (if that be long) and adding *āu* (or *āuṉ*), or by simply lengthening their stem vowel (if that be short); *īṉ* in the stem is shortened to *y* or *iy*. Causal. are to be distinguished from Second Causal verbs (afterwards referred to). The former express *immediate* causation. the latter. the *mediate* causation of the act or state of the primitive.

The following are some examples of Causal derivatives:—

uṭhnu	to rise	*uṭhāuṉnu*	to cause to rise
maṉrnu	,, die	*māṉrnu*	,, ,, ,, die = kill
maṉrnu	,, die	*maṉrāuṉnu*	,, ,, ,, be put to death
jīuṉnu	,, live	*jiyāuṉnu*	,, ,, ,, live
bahaṉnu	,, flow	*bahāuṉnu*	,, ,, ,, flow
boknu	,, carry	*bokāuṉnu*	,, ,, ,, be carried
khāṉnu	,, eat	*khuwāuṉnu*	,, give ,, eat
pīuṉnu	,, drink	*piyāuṉnu*	,, ,, ,, drink
garnu	,, do	*garāuṉnu*	,, cause ,, be done
chhāpnu	,, print	*chhapāuṉnu*	,, ,, ,, be printed
aṛīṉnu	,, stop, halt	*aṛyāuṉnu*	,, ,, ,, stop = stop (trans.)
banīṉnu	,, become	*banāuṉnu*	,, ,, ,, become = make
niklaṉnu	,, come out	*nikālnu*	,, ,, ,, come out
balnu	,, burn	*bālnu*	,, ,, ,, burn = kindle
biknu	,, be sold	*bechnu*	,, ,, ,, be sold = sell
būjhnu	,, understand	*bujhāuṉnu*	,, ,, ,, be understood

Where no causal form exists, the causal sense may be obtained by the use of *garāi dinnu* after the primitive: *dinnu garāi dinnu*, 'to cause to be given'; or by a paraphrase: ***dinos bhannye** ājñā garnu*, 'to cause to be given' (*lit.*, 'to order that (it) be given'); or by a paraphrastic use of the Second Causal idiom: *pāunnu lāunnu*, 'to cause to be given' (*lit.*, 'to cause to receive').

Compound Verbs

are an idiomatic combination of verbs with another verb, following them, to modify their meaning. It is only the modifying verb that is conjugated. The following table of the various combinations of *boknu*, 'to carry' (for which any other verb, primitive or causal, might be substituted) exemplifies this usage. The first column gives the different kinds of compound verbs :—

1.	Second Causal	*boknu lāunnu*	
		bokne garāunnu	to cause (another) to [carry
2.	Intensive	*boki dinnu*	,, carry away
3.	Potential	*boknu saknu*	,, be able to carry
4.	Completive	*boki* ,,	,, finish carrying
5.	Frequentative	*bokne garnu*	
		bokdai ,,	,, carry habitually
6.	Inceptive	*boknu lāgnu*	
		,, *thālnu*	,, begin to carry
		,, *āntnu*	,, be about to ,,
7.	Desiderative	,, *khojnu*	
		bokne ichchhe garnu	
		,, *man* ,,	,, desire to ,,
8.	Permissive	*boknu dinnu*	,, permit to ,,
9.	Acquisitive	,, *pāunnu*	,, be permitted to ,,
10.	Continuative	*bokdai rahannu*	
		boki ,,	,, be engaged in [carrying
11.	Progressive	*bokdai jānnu*	,, go on ,,
12.	Statical	,, *āunnu*	,, come ,,
13.	Reiterative	*boknu tā boknu*	,, indeed carry

Compound verbs are conjugated as active or intransitive, according as the first verb is such, except Nos. 1, 7, 8, 9, which are always active: (1) *usle timilāi premmāṉ parasasta huṉnu lāwas*, 'may he cause thee to abound in love'; *kasaile timilāi phūlpāti gumāuṉne na garāwas*, 'may no one cause thee to forfeit the prize'; (2) *usle tinalāi chhoi dewas*, 'let him touch them,'; *u majhuwā bhai diyo*, 'he intervened'; (3) *u āuṉnu sakchha*, 'he will be able to come'; *usle māṉrnu sakchha*, 'he will be able to kill'; (4) *u āi sakyo*, 'he has quite (or already) come; *usle māṉri sakyo*, 'he has quite (or already) killed'; (5) *tyo āuṉne* (or *āuṉdai*) *garyo*, 'he came habitually'; *tyesle bokne* (or *bokdai*) *garyo*, 'he carried habitually'; (6) *tyo āuṉnu lāgyo* (or *thālyo*, or *āṉṭyo*), 'he began to come'; *tyesle garnu lāgyo*, etc., 'he began to do'; (7) *tyesle āuṉnu khojyo* (or *āuṉne ichchhe*, or *man*, *garyo*), 'he sought (or wished, or was minded) to come'; (8) *tyesle maṉlāi āuṉnu diyo*, 'he let me come'; (9) *tyesle āuṉnu pāyo*, 'he was permitted to come' (*lit.*, 'he found to come'); (10) *tyo āuṉdai* (or *āi*) *rahyo*, 'he was engaged in (or he continued) coming'; *tyesle bhandai* (or *bhani*) *rahyo*, 'he continued saying'; (11) *tyo jāṉdai gayo*, 'he went on going'; *tyesle bhandai gayo*, 'he went on saying'; (12) *tyo bahaṉdai āyo*, 'it came flowing'; *usle bhandai āyo*, 'he came saying'; (13) *timiharule piuṉnu tā piyaulā*, 'you will indeed drink'; *timiharu āuṉnu tā āyau*, 'you did indeed come.'

(2) In the formation of Intensives other verbs than *diṉnu* also are used, and in the same way: *rākhnu*, 'to keep,' *basnu*, 'to stay,' *āuṉnu*, 'to come,' *jāṉnu*, 'to go,' *uṭhnu*, 'to rise,' *hālnu*, 'to cast,' *parnu*, 'to happen,' *liṉnu*, 'to take,' *rahaṉnu*, 'to continue,' '*lāgnu*,' 'to get home, hit.' *E.g.*, *āphāli rākhnu*, 'to throw away'; *birsi hālnu*, 'to forget'; *āi lāgnu*, 'to come upon'; and so on.

(5) The form *bokne garnu*, in the sense of 'to carry habitually,' is not sanctioned by the Kāṭhmāṇḍū authorities, who say it means 'to see that (one) carries'—is, in a word, a Second Causal; but it is not only in general currency at Darjeeling, but, meaning literally, as it does, 'to play the carry-er,' grammatically natural. The Kāṭhmāṇḍū usage as well, however, is not unknown at Darjeeling: *tiniharu āphnu 2 man pherne gari manāīye*, 'they were persuaded into changing their minds' (*lit.*, 'they causing their own minds to change.

were persuaded'). *āi jāi garnu*, 'to habitually come and go,' is a Frequentative, adopted from Hindī.

(6) The form represented by *boknu ān̲ṭnu*, 'to be about to carry,' 'to be on the point of carrying,' is, like the Greek μέλλειν *mellein*, also used to express a settled futurity: *bishwās garnu ān̲ṭneharulāī*, 'to them who shall hereafter believe.'

(13) *rahi rahan̲nu*, 'to remain'; *khān̲dai pani na khāwas*, 'neither let him eat,' are examples of other Reiterative forms.

Classification of Verbs.

Verbs are **Transitive** or **Intransitive.** *boknu*, 'to carry,' is Trans.; *āun̲nu*, 'to come,' Intrans. Some, which may be Trans. in English, are Intrans. in Nepālī: *bolnu*, 'to speak'; *pachhtāun̲nu*, 'to repent'; *karāun̲nu*, 'to cry.'

The nominative to trans. verbs (active voice, of course) is put in the **Agent** case, except in the first pers. sing. and plu. of the indefinite and imperfect tenses. (See p. 98.)

Inflexion of Verbs.

Verbs are changed or modified for voice, mood, tense, gender, number, person and negation. This is done, partly by inflexion, partly by the use of the auxiliary verb, *hun̲nu*, 'to be.'

Voice.

Trans. verbs have 2 Voices, **Active and Passive.**

The **Passive** is formed from the Act., by insert. .g, after the stem, *ī* before nothing, vowels and semi-vowels, and *īn̲* before consonants, except that where the stem ends in *āu*, the *ī* takes the place of the *u*: *gar* (act.) *garī* (pass.)

gar (act.)	*garī* (pass.)
garī	*garīī*
garun̲	*garīun̲*
garyo	*garīyo*.
garda	*garīn̲da*
garāun̲nu	*garāīn̲nu*.

The *ī*, or *īn̲*, corresponds to the Braj *i*, or *ij*, and the Mārwāṛī *īj*. Its pronunciation is often like *īi*, or *iya*, but the only way of reducing its use to rule seems to be to write it invariably *ī*, *īn̲*.

Mood.

Verbs have five Moods: Indicative, Subjunctive, Conditional, Imperative (used also as an Optative and a Potential) and Infinitive.

Tense

Verbs have fifteen Tenses: three groups of four each, centering round the three chief tenses, Present, Past and Future, with one extra tense added to the second group, and two to the third :—

I. Present—
1. Indefinite
2. Imperfect
3. Perfect
4. ,, Continuous

II. Past—
5. Indefinite
6. Imperfect
7. Perfect
8. ,, Continuous
9. Indefinite Perfect

III. Future—
10. Indefinite
11. Imperfect
12. Perfect
13. ,, Continuous
14. Contingent
15. Perfect Contingent.

Nos. 4, 8, 11, 13 are of comparatively rare occurrence.

Gender, Number, Person.

The changes of the verb in these respects will be shewn in the detailed examples that follow.

Negation.

The modification of verbs for Negation is one of the most important peculiarities of Nepālī. It consists, generally speaking, in the addition or insertion of *na* in the Positive form, and of course makes Conjugation doubly long.

PARADIGM.

The following general paradigm of the terminations of the various moods, tenses (1st pers. masc. sing.) and participles (masc. sing.), positive and negative, of every verb, shews that Nepālī conjugation, though extended, is not really difficult.

The hyphen in the Paradigm marks where the stem (act. or pass.) comes in.

The first line opposite each tense is the positive form; the second, the negative.

Fill in the stem of any verb, and the other persons, number and gender, and you have the conjugation of that verb (regular) complete.

Tenses.	Indicative.	Subjunctive.
Pres. Ind.	*-ne chhu*, or *huṉ*	Same as the Indicative, with *bhanye dekhi*, or *ta*, added.
	,, *chhuiṉna* or *hu-iṉna*	
,, Imp.	*-da chhu*	
	-dīṉna	
,, Per.	*-yeko chhu*	
	,, *chhuiṉna*	
,, ,, Con.	*-ne bhayeko chhu*	
	,, ,, *chhuiṉna*	
Past Ind.	*-thyeṉ*	*-do huṉ*
	-daina thyeṉ	*na -do* ,,
,, Imp.	*-da thiyeṉ*	Same as
	-daina ,,	Past Ind.
,, Per.	*-yeko thiyeṉ*	*-yeko bhaye dekhi*
	,, *thiiṉna*	*na* ,, ,, ,,
,, ,, Con.	*-ne bhayeko thiyeṉ*	*-ne bhayeko* ,, ,,
	,, ,, *thiiṉna*	,, *na* ,, ,, ,,
,, Ind. Per.	*-yeṉ*	Same as Indicative,
	-iṉna	with *ta* added.
Fut. Ind.	*-chhu*	*-yeṉ bhanye dekhi*
	-dīṉna	*-iṉna* ,, ,,
,, Imp.	*-dai huṉchhu*	*-dai bhayeṉ* ,, ,,
	-daina ,,	*-daina* ,, ,, ,,
,, Per.	*-yeko* ,,	*-yeko* ,, ,, ,,
	,, *huṉdīṉna*	,, *bhaiṉna* ,, ,,
,, ,, Con.	*-ne bhayeko huṉchhu*	*-ne bhayeko bhayeṉ* ,, ,,
	,, ,, *huṉdīṉna*	,, ,, *bhaiṉna* ,,
,, Conting.	*-uṉlā*	Same as the Indicative with *ta* added.
	-oiṉna, or *-waiṉna*	
,, Per. ,,	*-yeko houṉlā*	
	,, *howaiṉna*	

Conditional.	Imperative.	Infinitive.	Participles.
	-un	*-nu*	**Imperfect.**
	na -un	*na* ,,	
	-da houn	*-dai hunnu*	*-do*
	-daina ,,	*-daina* ,,	*na* ,,
	-yeko houn	*-yeko* ,,	*-dā*
	- ,, *na* ,,	,, *na* ,,	*na* ,,
		-ne bhayeko ,,	*-dāhunni*
		,, ,, *na* ,,	*na* ,,
			-dākheri
			na ,,
			-dai gardākheri
			-daina ,,
			-dāmān
			na ,,
			Perfect.
			-dai garyeko
			-daina ,,
-ne thiyen			*-yeko*
,, *thiinna*			
			na ,,
			Conjunctive.
		-nu ānṭnu	
		,, *na* ,,	*-i*
	-yes	*-nu ānṭyeko hunnu*	*na* ,,
	na -yes	,, ,, *na* ,,	*-ikana*
			na ,,
			-yera
			na ,,

CONJUGATION.

In the following detailed examples of conjugation, (I) that of the irregular intransitive verb *hu̱nnu*, 'to be,' or 'to become,' is given in full ; (II) that of the regular transitive verb *garnu*, 'to do,' or 'to make,' and of the other irregular verbs is only sufficiently indicated.

I. *hu̱nnu*, 'TO BE,' 'TO BECOME.'

This verb, like its English equivalent, is used (1) as a notional or principal verb: *īshwar chha*, 'God is,' where 'is' means 'exists'; *īshwar ho*, 'it is God,' *īshwar sṛishṭikarttā ho*, 'God is Creator,' 'it is the Creator God,' where 'is' is merely a copula or joiner; (2) as an auxiliary to a principal verb, or to an adjective, viewed as a principal verb: *īshwarle garda chha*, 'God is doing,' *īshwar pavitra chha*, 'God is holy.'

In the following conjugation, the feminine, where it differs from the masc., is indicated parenthetically. In the following paragraphs the Kāthmāṇḍū variations are indicated thus: [K..].

INDICATIVE MOOD.

PRESENT INDEFINITE TENSE.

Positive.

मं	छु	or	हुं	*ma̱n*	*chhu*	or	*hu̱n*	I am
तं	छस्	,,	होस्	*ta̱n*	*chhas*	,,	*hos*	thou art
उ	छ	,,	हो	*u*	*chha*	,,	*ho*	he, she, it, is
हामिहरु	छौं	,,	हौं	*hā̱nmiharu*	*chhau̱n*	,,	*hau̱n*	we are
तिमिहरु	छौ	,,	हौ	*timiharu*	*chhau*	,,	*hau*	you ,,
उनिहरु	छन्	,,	हुन्	*uniharu*	*chhan*	,,	*hun*	they ,,

As the personal pronouns are the same throughout the conjugation, they will not be again expressed, though always understood. *tyo*, *tiniharu*, may be used instead of *u*, *uniharu*, and must be used for English neuters (p. 21).

The colloquial *chhes, chhe, chheu, chhin,* as feminines of *chhas, chha, chhau, chhan,* should not be countenanced, though they are found in frequent use.

Negative—' I am not,' etc.

छुइँन	or	हुइँन	*chhuin̲na*	or	*huin̲na*
छैनस्	,,	होइनस्	*chhainas*	,,	*hoinas*
छैन	,,	होइन	*chhaina*	,,	*hoina*
छौंन	,,	हौंन	*chhaun̲na*	,,	*haun̲na*
छौन	,,	हौन	*chhauna*	,,	*hauna*
छैनन्	,,	होइनन्	*chhainan*	,,	*hoinan*

The colloquial *chhinas, chhina, chheuna, chhinan,* as feminines of *chhainas, chhaina, chhauna, chhainan,* should not be countenanced, though they are found in frequent use.

[K.—*chhaina,* for *chhuin̲na*; *hoina,* for *huin̲na*; *chhainau,* for *chhaun̲na* and *chhauna*; *hoinau,* for *haun̲na* and *hauna.*]

Emphatics: *chhunai, chhasnai,* etc. A strong form of *chhaina* is *chhan̲dai chhaina*; and of *hoina, hun̲dai hoina.* These express absolute certainty.

How *chhu* and *hun̲* are used *

The alternative forms *chhu* and *hun* are not used indifferently, and their right use is for the foreigner somewhat difficult. The following rules will be found helpful.

1. The general rule has been already incidentally indicated (p. 66). *chhu* is used as a notional, when the sense is ' exist,' and also as an auxiliary to a notional verb or adjective: *īshwar chha,* ' God is (exists),' ' there is a God '; *īshwar chhaina,* ' God is not (does not exist),' ' there is not a God '; *īshwarle garda chha,* ' God is doing '; *īshwar apavitra chhaina,* ' God is not unholy.'

* **Note.— Compare what Wenger says in his Bengali Grammar on *āchhi* and *haon*: " *āchhi* (*chhu*) has exclusive reference to the subject indicated " by the nominative, and describes its existence, presence, or state, at a " particular time or place; while *haon* (*hun̲nu*) which properly means ' to " become,' usually describes what the subject is to others, and is used in " the sense of ' to turn out,' ' to prove oneself,' being generally accom- " panied by an adjective, participle, etc.."**

Huṉ also is used as a notional, but only as a formal copula or connective, and as an auxiliary, but only in the Past Ind. and Imp. Subjunctive: *īshwar ho*, '(it) is God'; *īshwar sṛishṯikarttā ho*, 'God is the Creator,' '(it) is the Creator God'; *īshwar apavitra huṉdo ho*, 'if God were unholy.'

2. A special rule is that *huṉ* has always the implicit sense of (and, especially in the third sing. (*ho, hoina*), is often used expressly for), 'yes,' 'it is so,' 'is it so?', 'no,' 'it is not so,' 'is it not so?': *īshwar sṛishṯikarttā ho*, 'God the Creator,—yes'; *īshwar apavitra hoina pavitra chha*, 'God unholy,—no; (he) is holy,' 'God is, not unholy, (but) holy.'

3. The foregoing rules point to the distinction, that *chhu* expresses more a quality or action of the subject spoken of; *huṉ*, more an assertion on the part of the subject speaking,—a distinction which explains many apparent exceptions.

The above abstract, may now be reduced to the following mechanical rules:—

4. *chhu* is used, as a NOTIONAL, whenever the sense is 'exist,' so that the verb stands alone, a verb of complete predication: *īshwar chha*, 'God is (exists),' 'there is a God'; *kye koī chha ki chhaina*, 'is there any one or not?'; *maṉ rājā chhu*, 'I, the king, am.'

5. *chhu* is further used, as an AUXILIARY, with whatever is, or is syntactically equivalent to, an ADJECTIVE, that is to say:—

with an adjective: *pavitra chhu*, 'I am holy';

,, a participle, which is really an adjective: *maṉ āyeko chhu*, 'I have come'; *maṉ āuṉda chhu*, 'I am coming'—[except in the two cases given below (7) in which *huṉ* is used];

,, an indefinite noun or pronoun in the nominative (in verb-apposition to the subject), which, being indefinite, is really equivalent to an adjective: *maṉ rājā chhu*, 'I am a king,' 'I am of the quality of a king'; *tyo koī chha*, 'he is some one';

,, a noun or pronoun in the dative, which involves the idea of a participle of existence, 'belonging': *maṉlāi chha*, '(it) is (belongs) to me,' 'I have..';

with an indefinite noun or pronoun in the agent case: *rājāle chha*, 'it is by a king';

„ a noun or pronoun in the genitive, when this states the relation of the possessor: *rājāko ghar chha*, 'the king has a house'; or when it is indefinite (in which case it is equivalent to an adjective): *rājāko ghar chha*, '(it) is a king's house,' 'it is the house of a king,' 'it is a house such as a king has';

„ a noun or pronoun in the locative, which involves the idea of a participle of existence, 'resting in': *gharmāṉ chha*, '(it) is in the house';

„ an adverb of rest in a place, which is equivalent to a noun in the locative: *kahāṉ chha*, 'where is (it)?';

„ a preposition (except of source or agency): *mero lāgi chha*, '(it) is for me,' which is equivalent to a dative.

6. *huṉ* is used, as a NOTIONAL, with whatever is, or is syntactically equivalent to, a NOUN, that is to say:—

with a definite noun or pronoun in the nominative (in verb-apposition to the subject): *ishwar ho* 'it is God'; *ishwar srishtikarttā ho*, 'God is the Creator,' 'it is the Creator God'; *maiṉ huṉ*, 'it is I'; *maṉ rājā huṉ*, 'I am the king'; *shabda yei ho*, 'this is the word'; *timro nāṉu kyā ho*, 'what is your name?';

„ a definite noun or pronoun in the agent case: *rājāle ho*, 'it is by the king';

„ a definite noun or pronoun in the genitive when this states the relation of the possessed, *rājāko ho*, 'it is the king's'; '*mero ghar ho*,' 'it is my house'; *ghar merai ho*, 'the house is mine'; *jati mero chha sabai tero ho*, 'as much as I have is thine';

„ an adjective used as a definite noun; *ti bishwāsyogya hun*, 'they are the faithful';

„ an infinitive, which is really a noun: *dharmma dharmma garnu ho*, 'righteousness is to do righteousness';

„ an adverb (except of rest in a place): *u katā ho*, where (*lit.*, whither) is he?'; *abasse ho*, 'it certainly is'; *āiu ho*, 'it is to-day'; *kasogari ho*, 'how is it?'

with a preposition of source or agency : *ti sabai ekai dekhi hun*, 'they are all of (from) the one' ; *rājāko kāraṇle ho*, 'it is because of the king.'

7. *huṉ* is further used, as an AUXILIARY, with a participle, in the past indefinite and imperfect subjunctive only : *maṉ hundo huṉ*, 'if I were' ; *īshwarle bhando ho*, 'did God say.'

Apparent exceptions will be found but to prove the seven rules given above. For example :—

(1) *jaslāi maiṉlei sirjyeko ho*, 'whom I myself have created.' Here *ho* has the force of '**yes**' (rule 2), and *chhu* is understood before it (rule 5) : 'whom I myself have, it is true, created.'

(2) *jasori jīu ātmā binā murdā chha tyesairi bishwās pani karmma binā murdā ho*, 'as the body is dead without the spirit, so also is faith dead without works.' Here *ho* is an **assertion**, on the part of the subject speaking (rule 3), and *chha* is understood before it (rule 5).

In many other cases, **indefiniteness** will explain a *chhu*, where the rules seem to require a *huṉ* ; and **assertion**, a *huṉ*, where a *chhu* seems required.

How the use of *chhu* or *huṉ* affects the sense is well exemplified in these sentences : *merī swāsnī chhaina*, 'I have not a wife' ; *merī swāsnī hoina*, 'she is not my wife' : *timro nāṉu kyā ho*, 'what is your name ?' ; *timro nāṉu kye chha*, 'have you a name' ?

An emphatic form of the Pres. Ind.

having the sense of **ascertainment** on enquiry, is current at Darjeeling [though it seems unknown at K.]. It is probably a corruption of *rahye chhu* the pres. perf. Indic. of *rahaṉnu*, 'to remain,' and may be translated literally 'I am, after all,' etc. :—

Positive.

रांछु	or	हो रांछु	*rāṉchhu*	or	*ho*	*rāṉchhu*
रैछस्	,,	,, रैछस्	*raichhas*	,,	,,	*raichhas*
रछ	etc.		*rachha*		etc.	
रांछौं			*rāṉchhauṉ*			
राछौ			*rāchhau*			
राछन्			*rāchhan*			

Negative.

रैनछु	or	होइन रांछु	*rainachhu*	or	*haina rān̲chhu*
रैनछस्	,,	,, रैछस्	*rainachhas*	,,	,, *raichhas*
रैनछ		etc.	*rainachha*		etc.
रैनछौं			*rainachhaun̲*		
रैनछौ			*rainachhau*		
रैनछन्			*rainachhan*		

rān̲chhu corresponds to *chhu*; and *ho ran̲chhu*, to *hun̲*.

The forms *rahechhu*, etc., *rahenachhu*, etc. are also found.

rān̲chhu, etc., may be used with any part of any verb, in the same way as with *ho* and *hoina*: *gard̲a rān̲chhu*, 'I am, after all, doing'; *gardaina rān̲chhu*, 'I am not, after all, doing'; *garẏeko raichhas*, 'thou hast after all done'; *garyeko rainachhas*, 'thou hast not, after all, done'; *tapān̲i īshwarko pat̲t̲i bāt̲o niskan̲nu bhayeko ho rachha*, 'Thou hast, after all, come forth from God.'

Such idioms as *chhu ra*, *chhas ra*, 'I am,' 'thou art,' are common, at the end of a sentence, and are elliptical for 'I am, and [therefore so and so, understood, follows],' 'am I, that [therefore so and so, understood, should follow]'? *ra*, which means 'and,' may follow any part of any verb in the same way: *garyo ra*, 'he did, and [so and so, understood, follows]'; *rot̲ī lyāyekā chhaun̲na ra*, 'we have not brought bread and [therefore he has said that to us]' (Matt. xvi. 7).

PRESENT IMPERFECT.

Pos.

हुंद छु	*hun̲da chhu*	I am	being, I am	
,, छस्	,, *chhas*	thou art	,,	etc.
,, छ	,, *chha*	he, she, it, is	,,	
,, छौं	,, *chhaun̲*	we are	,,	
,, छौ	,, *chhau*	you ,,	,,	
,, छन्	,, *chhan*	they ,,	,,	

For the above, when the tense if unmistakable, the fut. ind., *hun̲chhu*, etc., may be used, for brevity.

Neg.—' I am not being', etc.

हुंदीन	or	हुंन्न	*hundīnna*	or	*hunnna*
हुंदैनस्	,,	हुंन्नसं्	*hundainas*	,,	*hunnas*
हुंदैन	,,	हुंन्न	*hundaina*	,,	*hunna*
हुंदैांन	,,	हुंन्नैां	*hundaunna*	or	*hunnnaun*
हुंदौन	,,	हुंन्नौ	*hundauna*	,,	*hunnnau*
हुंदैनन्	,,	हुंन्नन्	*hundainan*	,,	*hunnan*

The second form, though given here, is mainly used in the fut. indef. tense, which see (p. 77).

The same contraction takes place in other verbs whose stem ends in a vowel and anusvār: *dinnna*, of *dinnu*, 'to give'; *jānnna*, of *jānnu*, 'to go'; and occasionally also in other verbs: *garnna* of *garnu*, 'to do,' but not as a rule.

hunnna is formally correct, but in practice the *n* is usually dropped, and the word written *hunna*, the same as the third sing.

hunnnaun and *hunnnau* are K. forms, but may well be adopted as standard.

[K. for *hundaunna* is *hundainaun*; and for *hundauna*, *hundainau.*]

In honorific speech it is the short form, *hunna*, that is used; *āphule yo garnu hunna*, 'thou art not doing this.' The reason is that the long form, *hundaina*, often has the imperative force, 'it won't do,' which would not be respectful.

The emphatic of *hunda* is *hundai*, or *hundainai* (to be carefully distinguished from *hundaina*).

When the meaning is 'exist,' *chhandai* is substituted for *hunda*, and, generally, the form *chhand-*, for *hund*: *chhandai chhaun*, 'we have our being.'

This tense is often made by the compound inceptive (p. 59); *hunnu lāgyen* 'I have begun to be,' which is of course a very expressive imperfect.

PRESENT PERFECT.

Pos.

भयेको (ी) छु	*bhayeko* (ī) *chhu*	I	have been
,, ,, छस्	,, ,, *chhas*	thou hast	,,
,, ,, छ	,, ,, *chha*	he has	,,
भयेका ,, छौं	*bhayekā* ,, *chhauṉ*	we have	,,
भयेका (ी) छौ	*bhayekā* (ī) *chhau*	you have	been
,, ,, छन्	,, ,, *chhan*	they ,,	,,

[Here, as throughout after this, 'he' stands for 'he, she, it.']

Neg.—'I have not been,' etc.

भयेको (ी) छुइँन	*bhayeko* (ī) *chhuiṉna*
,, ,, छैनस्	,, ,, *chhainas*
,, ,, छैन	,, ,, *chhaina*
भयेका ,, छौंन	*bhayekā* ,, *chhauṉna*
,, ,, छौन	,, ,, *chhauna*
,, ,, छैनन्	,, ,, *chhainan*

When the nom. is fem., *bhayekī* is used; when masc. plu., *bhayekā*. In other words, *bhayeko*, which is the perf. participle, follows the rule of adjectives. [K., strangely, makes the fem. plu. the same as the masc. plu.]

bhayeko (ī, ā) may be shortened to *bhaye*, especially when used as a sort of Historical pres. perf.: *bhaye chha*, 'he has been.'

A colloquial form is *bhāko*; another is *bhayāko*.

In the above tense the word 'have' is used as an AUXILIARY. When it is used as a NOTIONAL, it is translated by the verb 'to be,' with the dat., or gen., or gen.-loc.: *uslāi adhikār chha*, 'he has authority'; *usko yeuṭā chhoro chha*, 'he has a son'; *uskāṉ dhan chha*, 'he has riches'; *merāṉ gāīgoru thiyo*, 'I had cattle.' [*-kāṉ* = *-komāṉ*; *merāṉ* = *meromāṉ*: a combination of the gen. and loc. affixes.]

10

So, 'having': *dhan hunne mānchhe*, 'a person having wealth'; *ānkhā hundā hundai*, 'while (though) having eyes'; *gangā nānu bhayeko ek janā newār*, 'a Newar having the name (named) Ganga.'

Present Perfect Continuous.

Pos.

हुंने भयेको (ी) छु	*hunne bhayeko* (ī) *chhu*	I have	been being
,, ,, ,, छस्	,, ,, ,, *chhas*	thou hast ,,	,,

etc.

Neg.—'I have not been being,' etc.

हुंने भयेको (ी) छुइंन	*hunne bhayeko* (ī) *chhuinna*
,, ,, ,, छैनस्	,, ,, ,, *chhainas*

etc.

An alternative form is the compound continuative (p. 59), *hundai rahyeko chhu*, etc., 'I have continued being'; *rahyeko* being the perf. partic. of *rahannu*, 'to continue.'

Past Indefinite.

Pos.

थियें	*thiyen*	I was
थिइस	*thiis*	thou wast
थियो (थिई)	*thiyo* (*thiī*)	he was
थियूं	*thiyūn*	we were
थियौ	*thiyau*	you ,,
थिये (थिइन्)	*thiye* (*thiin*)	they ,,

Notice the change of termination in the 1st plu. The rule is: *-aun*, after a consonant (except in fut. conting., and pres. imperat.); *-ūn*, after a vowel, or after the semi-vowel, *y*.

[Throughout conjugation, final *e* is often written *ā*: *thiyān*, for *thiyen*; *thiyā*, for *thiye*; *bhayā*, for *bhaye*; *bhayāko*, for *bhayeko*; *hunyā*, for *hunne*; and so on.]

A very common abbreviation is to drop the first *i*: थें *thyen*, etc.

The forms in parentheses are the feminine, of course.

Neg.—' I was not,' etc.

थिइंन	*thiinna*
थिइनस्	*thiinas*
थियेन (थिईन)	*thiyena* (*thiīna*)
थियूंन	*thiyūnna*
थियौन	*thiyauna*
थियेनन् (थिइनन्)	*thiyenan* (*thiinan*)

[K. for *thiyauna*, *thiyenau*.]

PAST IMPERFECT.

Pos.

हुंद् थियें	*hunda thiyen*	I	was	being
,, थिइस्	,, *thiis*	thou	wast	,,

etc.

Neg.—' I was not being,' etc.

हुंदैन थियें	*hundaina thiyen*
,, थिइस्	,, *thiis*

etc.

Abbreviations: *thyen*, for *thiyen*, *this* for *thiis*, etc.; *hunthyen*, for *hunda thiyen*; *hunthis*, for *hunda thiis*, etc. [K., *hunthen*, *hunthis*, etc.]

hundaina thiyen, etc., must be carefully distinguished from *hundainai thiyen*, which is, not neg., but pos., and means 'while I was in the act of being.'

This tense, like the pres. imperf. (p. 71), is sometimes made by the compound inceptive: *hunnu lāgyeko thiyen*, 'I had begun to be.' 'Was existing' is *thindai thiyen*, etc.

PAST PERFECT.

Pos.

भयेको (ी) थियें	*bhayeko* (*ī*) *thiyen*	I	had	been
,, ,, थिइस्	,, ,, *thiis*	thou	hadst	,,

etc.

Neg.—'I had not been,' etc.

भयेको (ी) थिइंन	*bhayeko*	(ī)	*thiin̲na*
,, ,, थिइनस्	,,	,,	*thiinas*

etc.

[K. fem. plu. same as masc. plu.]

Past Perfect Continuous.

Pos.—'I had been being,' etc.

हुंने भयेको (ी) थियें	*hun̲ne bhayeko*	(ī)	*thiyen̲*
,, ,, ,, थिइस्	,,	,,	,, *thiis*

Neg.—'I had not been being,' etc.

हुंने भयेको (ी) थिइंन	*hun̲ne bhayeko*	(ī)	*thiin̲na*
,, ,, ,, थिइनस्	,,	,,	,, *thiinas*

Alternative: the compound continuative form (p. 59), *bhai rahyeko thiyen̲*, 'I had continued being.'

Indefinite Perfect.

Pos.

भयें	*bhayen̲*	I	was,	or	have been	
भइस्	*bhais*	thou	wast	,,	hast	,,
भयो (भई)	*bhayo (bhaī)*	he	was	,,	has	,,
भयूं	*bhayūn̲*	we	were	,,	have	,,
भयौ	*bhayau*	you	,,	,,	,,	,,
भये (भइन्)	*bhaye (bhain)*	they	,,	,,	,,	,,

Neg.—'I was not, or have not been,' etc.

भइंन	*bhain̲na*
भइनस्	*bhainas*
भयेन (भईन)	*bhayena (bhaīna)*
भयूंन	*bhayūn̲na*
भयौन	*bhayauna*
भयेनन् (भइनन्)	*bhayenan (bhainan)*

Students who do not know the Devanāgarī must note that *bhais, bhain* are words of two syllables (*bha-is, bha-in*): *bhaiṉ-na, bhainas, bhainan*, of three.

bhayeu is sometimes written for *bhayau*, especially in the fem., and also as the plu. fut. perf. imperat.

Emphatic forms add *nai*: *bhayeṉnai, bhaisnai*, etc.

Colloquial for *bhayo* is *bho*.

[K.: *bhayenauṉ, bhayenau*, for *bhayūṉna, bhayauna*; and 3rd. plu. fem. same as 3d. plu. masc.]

Future Indefinite.

Pos.

हुंछु	*huṉchhu*	I	shall,	or	will	be
हुंछस्	*huṉchhas*	thou	wilt	,,	shalt	,,
हुंछ	*huṉchha*	he	will	,,	shall	,,
हुंछौं	*huṉchhauṉ*	we	shall	,,	will	,,
हुंछौ	*huṉchhau*	you	will	,,	shall	,,
हुंछन्	*huṉchhan*	they	,,	,,	,,	,,

Neg.—'I shall, or will, not be,' etc.

हुंदैन or हुन्न *huṉdīṉna* or *huṉnna*

etc.

The negative is the same as of Pres. Imperf., which, with the notes thereon, see (p. 71).

In honorific address, the Fut. Conting. *holā* is sometimes, when modesty requires, used instead of *huṉchha*; *āphule tyo garnu holā*, 'thou wilt do that'; and for the negative the short form, *hunna* is always used, not *huṉdaina*, which has an authoritative force inconsistent with respectfulness: *āphule tyo garnu hunna*, 'thou wilt not do that.'

Distinguish *hunnan* of this tense from *hunan* of the Fut. Conting. (p. 80).

The tense, as the translation of it shews, is used, not only to express simple **futurity** ('I shall,' 'thou wilt,' etc.,) but **also determination** ('I will,' 'we will') and **authority** ('thou shalt,' 'he shall,' etc.)

When '**will**' means 'WISH,' it is rendered by the compound desiderative (p. 59) : *hun̲ne ichchhe garda chhu*, 'I wish to be.'

When '**shall**' expresses COMMAND, it is best made by the imperative: *jhūṭho na ho*, 'thou shalt not be false,' 'be not false.'

hun̲chha has sometimes the sense of **permission or approval**; and *hun̲daina*, of **prohibition** or disapproval: *hun̲chha*, 'it will do,' 'you have permission,' 'yes'; *hun̲daina*, 'it won't do,' 'you shan't,' 'it is impossible,' 'no'; *hun̲dai hun̲daina*, 'it won't do at all.'

'**I won't be**' is *hunna* (short for *hun̲nna*); 'I won't go,' *jāṅna*; 'I won't give,' *dinna*; and so on with other verbs whose stem ends in a vowel and anusvār.

'**must**' may be made by the fut. and *abasse*, 'necessarily'; *abasse hun̲chhu*, 'I must be'; or by the fut. of *parnu*, 'to happen,' and the infinitive : *man̲ hun̲nu parchha*, 'I must be.'

Besides the regular fut. indef., there is also the **logical future** and **settled futurity** form, *hun̲ne chhu*, which is the full pres. indef. form, and, indeed, is the unabridged form of *hun̲chhu* itself. It means 'I am a be-er' 'a be-er now and always, and therefore also at the future time in question' (logical future); or 'I am the be er,' 'the one who is to be' (settled futurity). So with other verbs; *āun̲ne chhu*, 'I shall come'; 'I am the coming one'; *tyesle garne chha*, 'he shall do'; 'he is the doing one.' [This is the explanation of the K. fut. indef., *hunyāchhu*.]

FUTURE IMPERFECT.

Pos.

हुँदै हुँछु	*hun̲dai*	*hun̲chhu*	I shall, or will, be being,
,, हुँछस्	,,	*hun̲chhas*	thou wilt, ,, shalt ,, ,,

etc.

Neg.—'I shall, or will, not be being,' etc.

हुंदैन हुंछु *hundaina hunchhu*
,, हुंछस् ,, *hunchhas*
etc.

FUTURE PERFECT.

Pos.—'I shall, or will, have been,' etc.

भयेको (ी) हुंछु *bhayeko (i) hunchhu*
,, ,, हुंछस् ,, ,, *hunchhas*
etc.

Neg.—'I shall, or will, not have been,' etc.

भयेको (ी) हुंदीन *bhayeko (i) hundinna* or (p. 72).
,, ,, हुंदैनस् ,, ,, *hundainas*
etc.

This tense may sometimes be translated as if it were the fut. indef., regarding the *bhayeko*, not as a part of the verb, but as an adjective, pure and simple: 'I shall be a been one.'

FUTURE PERFECT CONTINUOUS.

Pos.—'I shall, or will, have been being,' etc.

हुंने भयेको (ी) हुंछु *hunne bhayeko (i) hunchhu*
,, ,, ,, हुंछस् ,, ,, ,, *hunchhas*
etc.

Neg.—'I shall, or will, not have been being,' etc.

हुंने भयेको (ी) हुंदीन *hunne bhayeko (i) hundinna* or (p. 72).
,, ,, ,, हुंदैनस् ,, ,, ,, *hundainas*
etc.

Alternative: *hundai rahyeko hunchhu*, 'I shall have continued being,' etc.

Future Contingent.

Pos.

होउंला (ी)	*houn̲lā* (*ī*)	I shall be
होलास् (ीस्)	*holās* (*īs*)	thou will ,,
होला (ी)	*holā* (*ī*)	he will ,,
होऊंला ,,	*hoūn̲lā* ,,	we shall ,,
होऔला ,,	*hoaulā* ,,	you will ,,
हुनन् (हुनिन्)	*hunan* (*hunin*)	they ,, ,,

Neg.—' I shall not be,' etc.

होवैंन	*howain̲na*
होवैनस्	*howainas*
होवैन	*howaina*
होवैनौं	*howainaun̲*
होवैनौ	*howainau*
होवैनन् (होवैनिन्)	*howainan* (*howainin*)

This tense is used when the event is deemed, not certain, but contingent, and is sometimes translated 'may be,' or as present ('is,' etc.): *jahān̲ loth holā tyahān̲ giddha bhelā hun̲chhan*, 'where the carcase is, there will the vultures be gathered together.' Here there is an element of uncertainty or contingency in the first clause ('is' being equivalent to 'may be'), but a declaration of certainty in the second.

holā is used after any part of any verb to express probability: *chha holā*, 'it probably is'; *garyo holā*, 'he probably did'; *hun̲chhu holā*, 'I shall probably be'; *hun̲daina holā*, 'it probably will not be'; *holā ho* is a strong form of *holā*.

In honorific speech *holā*, as already noted (p. 77), is often preferable to *hun̲chha*, for the fut. indef.

The l of this tense should properly be n (as seen in the 3rd plu.); but the substitution is characteristic of Indian. Ask a Native to say 'number,' and he will probably say 'lumber' His word for 'blue' is as often *līl* as, the correct form, *nīl*.

[K. substitutes *o* for *a* in the second syllable of the negative : *howoinna, howoinas*, etc. For the standard rule, see note on the fut. conting. of *garnu*.]

FUTURE PERFECT CONTINGENT.

Pos.—' I shall have been,' etc.

भयेको (ी) होउंला (ी)	*bhayeko*	(ī)	*hounlā*	(ī)
,, ,, होलास् (ीस्)	,,	,,	*holās*	(īs)

etc.

Neg.—' I shall not have been,' etc.

भयेको (ी) होवैंन	*bhayeko*	(ī)	*howainna*
,, ,, होवैनस्	,,	,,	*howainas*

etc.

Example: *jye jye bhūl bhayekā hunan*, ' whatever mistakes there will (or may) have been.'

[K. has, for plu. of neg., *huoyinaun, huoyinau, huoyinan*.]

SUBJUNCTIVE MOOD.

The PRESENT group of tenses is the same as for the Indicative, with *bhanye dekhi*, ' if,' or *ta*, ' then,' ' therefore,' added.

The PAST and FUTURE groups are different from the Indicative; except the indef. perf., which is the same as for the Indicative, with *ta* added; but these also, if they are, or are equivalent to quotations, may be the same as the Indic., with the conjunction added. See EXERCISE VIII. 17.

bhanye dekhi is short for *bhanyeko* (partic. of *bhannu*, ' to say') *dekhi*, lit., ' from having said ' = ' if you say ' = ' if.' The *dekhi* is frequently omitted; *chhu bhanye*, ' if I am.' [K. : *bhane*, for *bhanye dekhi*.]

ta, ' then,' ' therefore,' is the conjunctive adverb, and indicates that the statement it follows is subjunctive, or subjoined to the principal statement.

[Such ENGLISH Subjunctive usages as (1) Oh! that he were, (2) ' lest thou be poor,' (3) ' whoever he be,' are respectively rendered: (1) *nāy u buddhimān bhaye dekhi tā hunthyo* (lit., 'Oh! had he indeed been wise, it should have been [all right]'); (2) *na bhaye tā tan kangāli holās* (lit., 'otherwise indeed thou mayest be poor'), or *tan kangāli na hunnulāi* (lit., 'in order to thy not being poor'), or *tan kangāli na ho bhani* (lit., 'saying, be thou not poor'), or *ra tan kangāli na ho* (lit., 'in order that thou be not poor'); (3) *u junsukai hawas* (lit., 'let him be whosoever').]

PRESENT INDEFINITE.—'If I am, or be,' etc.

Pos.	Neg.
chhu, or *hun* { *bhanye dekhi* / *ta*	*chhuinna*, or *huinna* { *bhanye dekhi* / *ta*

PRESENT IMPERFECT.—'If I am, or be, being,' etc.

hunda chhu { *bhanye dekhi* / *ta*

PRESENT PERFECT.—'If I have been,' etc.

bhayeko (ī) *chhu* { *bhanye dekhi* / *ta*

PRESENT PERFECT CONTINUOUS.—'If I have been being,' etc.

hunne bhayeko (ī) *chhu* { *bhanye dekhi* / *ta*

For the rest of these tenses, see the corresponding Indicative, Positive and Negative (pp. 66—74).

On 'if I am,' 'if I be,' see p. 85, on the fut. indef. of this mood.

PAST INDEFINITE AND PAST IMPERFECT.

Pos.

हुंदो	(ी)	हुं	*hundo*	(ī)	*hun*	if I	were,	or	were	I
,,	,,	होस्	,,	,,	*hos*	,, thou	wert	,,	wert	thou
,,	,,	हो	,,	,,	*ho*	,, he	were	,,	were	he
हुंदा	,,	हौं	*hundā*	,,	*haun*	,, we	,,	,,	,,	we
,,	,,	हौ	,,	,,	*hau*	,, you	,,	,,	,,	you
,,	,,	हुन्	,,	,,	*hun*	,, they	,,	,,	,,	they

Neg.—' If I were, or were I, not,' etc.

न हुंदो (ी) हुं   *na hundo* (ī) *hun*

" " " होस्   " " " *hos*

etc.

[K. translates: ' I may or might have been'; and, for the neg., gives: *hundaina hun*, *hundaina hos*, etc.]

PAST PERFECT.

Pos.—' If I had, or had I, been,' etc.

भयेको भये देखि   *bhayeko bhaye dekhi*

Neg.—' If I had, or had I, not been,' etc.

न भयेको भये देखि   *na bhayeko bhaye dekhi*

This tense is really impersonal, and does not vary for person, number or gender.

Sometimes it is shortened to *bhaye*, *na bhaye* (dropping the *-ko bhaye dekhi*) with the distinguishing conjunctive adverb *tā*, ' indeed,' added.

It is sometimes used for the indef. perf. tense, ' if I was, or have been.'

It has an alternative form, viz.—

Pos.

भयेको (ी) हुंदो (ी) हुं   *bhayeko* (ī) *hundo* (ī) *hun*

" " " " होस्   " " " " *hos*

etc.

Neg.

" " न " " "   " " *na* " " "

etc.

PAST PERFECT CONTINUOUS.

Pos.—' If I had been being,' etc.

हुंने भयेको भये देखि   *hunne bhayeko bhaye dekhi*

Neg.—'If I had not been being,' etc.

हुंने न भयेको भये देखि *hunne na bhayeko bhaye dekhi.*

Or *hundo hun*, etc., may be substituted for *bhaye dekhi*, as in past per.

Indefinite Perfect.

Pos.

भयें त	*bhayen ta*	if I was,	or have been
भइस् ,,	*bhais* ,,	,, thou wast ,,	hast ,,

etc.

Neg.—'If I was not, or have not been,' etc.

भइंन त	*bhainna ta*
भइनस् ,,	*bhainas* ,,

etc.

This is just the Indic. tense, with *ta* added.

Future Indefinite.

Pos.—'If I shall, or should, or were to, be,' etc.

भयें भन्ये देखि	*bhayen bhanye dekhi*
भइस् ,, ,,	*bhais* ,, ,,

etc.

Neg.—'If I shall not be,' etc.

भइंन भन्ये देखि	*bhainna bhanye dekhi*
भइनस् ,, ,,	*bhainas* ,, ,,

etc.

See note on the fut. perf., below.

This is the same form as the preceding, with *bhanye dekhi*, instead of *ta*. The Nepālī throws himself, in imagination, forward into the future, and supposes it already past: 'supposing it to be said, when the time has passed, that I was,' or 'supposing the time to have passed, and that I was,' *i.e.*, 'if I shall be.'

It is obvious that the above form can only express simple futurity, not determination or authority, etc., (p. 78). To express these the fut. indef. INDICATIVE form must be used, with *ta* added; or recourse must be had to some periphrasis.

When the English 'if I am,' 'if I be,' have a future sense, as they often have, they are of course rendered in Nepālī, not by the pres. indef., but by the fut. indef.

FUTURE IMPERFECT.

Pos.—'If I shall, or should, or were to, be being,' etc.

हुंदै भयें भन्ये देखि	*hu͟ndai bhaye͟n bhanye dekhi*
,, भइस् ,, ,,	,, *bhais* ,, ,,

etc.

Neg.—'If I shall, etc., not be being,' etc.

हुंदैन भयें भन्ये देखि	*hu͟ndaina bhaye͟n bhanye dekhi*
,, भइस् ,, ,,	,, *bhais* ,, ,,

etc.

FUTURE PERFECT.

Pos.—'If I shall, or should, or were to, have been,' etc.

भयेको (ी) भयें भन्ये देखि	*bhayeko* (ī) *bhaye͟n bhanye dekhi*
,, ,, भइस् ,, ,,	,, ,, *bhais* ,, ,,

etc.

Neg.—'If I shall, etc., not have been,' etc.

भयेको (ी) भइंन भन्ये देखि	*bhayeko* (ī) *bhai͟nna bhanye dekhi*
,, ,, भइनस् ,, ,,	,, ,, *bhainas* ,, ,,

etc.

The fut. indef. is often used loosely for this form.

FUTURE PERFECT CONTINUOUS.

Pos.—'If I shall, or should, or were to, have been being,' etc.

हुंने भयेको (ी) भयें भन्ये देखि	*hu͟nne bhayeko* (ī) *bhaye͟n bh. d.*
,, ,, ,, भइस् ,, ,,	,, ,, ,, *bhais* ,, ,,

etc.

Neg.—'If I shall, etc., not have been being,' etc.

हुंने भयेको (ी) भइंन भन्ये देखि *hunne bhayeko* (ī) *bhainna bh. d.*

,, ,, ,, भइनस् ,, ,, ,, ,, ,, *bhainas* ,, ,,

etc.

FUTURE CONTINGENT.

FUTURE PERFECT CONTINGENT.

Properly speaking, the Subj. Mood has no fut., or fut. perf.. conting.; but, if necessary, they can always be formed by merely adding *ta*, 'then,' to the Indic. forms.

CONDITIONAL MOOD.

This mood has only one tense: the English "Future Subjunctive," without its conjunction:—

Pos.—'I should, or would, be, or should, or would, have been,' etc.

हुंने थियें *hunne thiyen*

,, थिइस् ,, *thiis*

etc.

Neg.—'I should, etc., not have been,' etc.

हुंने थिइंन *hunne thiinna*

,, थिइनस् ,, *thiinas*

etc.

This is the same form as the past indef. Indicative, with *hunne* before it (p. 74), and is subject to the same abbreviations as the past imperf. Indic.: *hunthyen*, etc.

Of course, when 'should' means 'ought,' or 'would' means 'could wish,' they cannot be rendered simply as above: 'you should be,' *timiharu hunnu parda chha* (or *parchha*); 'you should have been,' *timiharu hunnu parthyo* (or *paryo*,); 'you would not' *timiharule ichchhe garyauna*; 'would that ye were,' *timiharu bhaye tā hunthyo*; 'I would all were like me,' *ichchhe garne thiyen sabai man jastai houn bhani*; and so on. (See EXERCISE VIII. 22, 34).

'Might' in the Conditional sense would require some such contingent word as *holā* or *koni* to be added to the Conditional tense; 'I might be,' *hunne thiyen holā*, or *koni hunne thiyen*; or, changing to direct speech, simply *hounlā*, 'I shall possibly be.' For 'might' in other senses, see under IMPERATIVE MOOD, p. 88.

'Could' in the Conditional sense would require the Conditional tense of the compound potential (p. 59): 'I could be,' *hunnu sakne thiyen*; or, in direct speech, *hunnu sakunlā*, 'I likely shall be able to be.'

What has been said of 'should,' 'would,' 'might,' 'could,' applies equally to 'should have,' etc.

IMPERATIVE, OPTATIVE AND POTENTIAL MOOD.

PRESENT INDEFINITE AND IMPERFECT.*

Pos.

होउं	*houn*	let me be;	may I be;	(that) I may or might be
हो	*ho*	be thou	mayest thou ,, ,,	thou ,, might- ,, mayest est
हवस्	*hawas*	let him be	may he ,, ,,	he may ,, might ,,
होऊं	*hoūn*	,, us ,,	,, we ,, ,,	we ,, ,, ,, ,,
हव	*hawa*	be you	,, you ,, ,,	you ,, ,, ,, ,,
होउन्	*houn*	let them be	,, they ,, ,,	they ,, ,, ,, ,,

Neg.—'Let me, etc., not be,' etc.

न होउं	*na houn*
,, हो	,, *ho*

etc.

houn, hoūn are sometimes written *houñ, hoūñ.*

ho is often lengthened to *hou*, as a respectful form, and *hou* is not infrequently lengthened out to *houna.* So also with other verbs: *deu, deuna*, 'give'; *jāu, jāuna*, 'go'; *garauna*, 'do.'

hawas is often contracted to *hos.*

---

* The formal Impf., *hunda* (Neg., *hundaina*) *houn*, occurs.

'That' with this part, is translated by *ra* before the verb, or *bhani*, or *bhanyera*, or *bhannye khātirle*, after the verb: *ra man houn*, or *man houn bhani* (or *bhanyera*, or *bhannye khātirle*), 'that I may be.' [The same sense may be rendered by the Infinitive: *man hunnulāi, or man hunnuko lāgi*, or *man hannu bhani*, or *man hunnu bhanyera*, 'that I may be.'] See on SUBORDINATIVE CONJUNCTIONS.

'Let,' when it means 'allow,' requires the compound permissive form (p. 59): *manlāi hunnu deu*, "allow me to be.'

On **'may'** in the contingent sense, see p. 80. When it means 'can,' it is of course rendered by the compound potential (p. 59): *hunnu sakda chhu* 'I may (can) be.' When **'can'** means 'may,' it is rendered by the Potential Mood: 'you can go,' *jāu, jāwa, jānnu, jānnu hawas, jānnu hunchha.*

How it is that properly 'may' tenses may, as here, be rendered **'might,'** is, that what in English is INDIRECT, is often in Nepālī changed into DIRECT speech: *u bhāīharu jasto hunnu paryo dayāwanta hawas bhannye khātirle*, 'he had to be like the brethren that he might (*lit.*, may) be merciful' [notice the rendering of **'had to'** by *paryo* (*lit.*, 'it was necessary,' etc.)]; *sodhye yo kye holā bhani*, 'they asked what this might (*lit.*, may) be'; *manlāi nirbhay chha ra pani*, 'though I might be bold' (*lit.*, to me is [= I have] boldness'). [In other senses, 'might' is rendered in other ways: *tyesle u saña hunnulāi u sita binti garyo*, 'he besought him that he might be (*lit.*, to be) with him.'] See p. 87.

This idiom of direct, for indirect speech, that is, of present, for past tenses, is all-pervasive in Nepālī, and should be kept in mind by the student. See the paragraph on the subject under SYNTAX.

The form *hounjyāl* [K., *hunjyāl*] is from this tense. It is combined with the word *samma*, 'level with,' **'till'**: *man hounjyāl samma*, 'till I am not,' *lit.*, 'as long as I am (may be)'; *man na hounjyāl samma*, 'till I am,' *lit.*, 'as long as I am not (may not be).' [So with other verbs: *garunjyāl*, of *garnu*, 'to do'; *banāunjyāl*, of *banāunnu*, 'to make.'] When the sense is 'exist,' the form *chhaunjyāl* छउंज्याल is substituted for *hounjyāl*: *man chhaunjyāl samma*, 'as long as I exist.' Observe that when the proper translation is 'till,' the negative Nepālī stands for the positive English, and vice versâ; but that when the proper translation is 'as long as', the negative or positive is the same in both languages.

The honorific form of the Imperative is:—

houn
hou, houna, hunnu, hunnu hawas
houn
houn
hunnu, hunnu hawas
houn

So with other verbs: *āphule garnu hawas*, 'do thou'; etc. For the pronouns of the form, see p. 21.

Present Perfect.

Pos.—'Let me, may I, (that) I may or might, have been,' etc.

भयेको (ी) होउं	*bhayeko (ī) houn*
,, ,, हो	,, ,, ,,

etc.

Neg.—'Let me, etc., not have been,' etc.

भयेको (ी) न होउं	*bhayeko (ī) na houn*
,, ,, हो	,, ,, ,, *ho*

etc.

Future Perfect.

Pos.—'Thou shalt, or shouldst, be, or have been.'

भयेस्	*bhayes*

Neg.—'Thou shalt, etc., not be, or have been.'

न भयेस्	*na bhayes*

bhayes is probably a contraction of *bhayeko hunchhas* (fut. perf Indic.), 'thou shalt have been,' and it may be called the Completive Imperative. Its emphatic is भयेस्है *bhayes-hai*? Its plu. is *bhayeu*, p. 77.

INFINITIVE MOOD.

Present Indefinite.

Pos.—'To be.'

हुनु *hun̲nu*

Neg.—'Not to be.'

न हुनु *na hun̲nu*

Present Imperfect.

Pos.—'To be being.'

हुंदै हुनु *hun̲dai hun̲nu*

Neg.—'Not to be being.'

हुंदैन हुनु *hun̲daina hun̲nu*

Present Perfect.

Pos.—'To have been.'

भयेको (ी) हुनु *bhayeko* (ī) *hun̲nu*

Neg.—'Not to have been.'

भयेको (ी) न हुनु *bhayeko* (ī) *na hun̲nu*

The *na* may also precede the *bhayeko*, if the sense require. So, in the tenses that follow.

Present Perfect Continuous.

Pos.—'To have been being.'

हुने भयेको (ी) हुनु *hun̲ne bhayeko* (i) *hun̲nu*

Neg.—'Not to have been being.'

हुने भयेको (ी) न हुनु *hun̲ne bhayeko* (ī) *na hun̲nu*

Future.

Pos.—'To be about to be.'

हुनु आंट्नु *hun̲nu ān̲ṭnu*

Neg.—'Not to be about to be.'

हुंनु न आंट्नु — *hun̲nu na ān̲ṭnu*

This is really one of the compound Inceptive forms (p. 59).

Future Perfect.

Pos.—'To have been about to be.'

हुंनु आंट्येको (ै) हुंनु — *hun̲nu ān̲ṭyeko* (ī) *hun̲nu*

Neg.—'Not to have been about to be.'

हुंनु आंट्येको (ै) न हुंनु — *hun̲uu ān̲ṭyeko* (ī) *na hun̲nu*

The Infinitive is really a verbal noun, used and declined as such: *hun̲nu kaṭhin chha*, 'to be is difficult'; *hun̲nu khān̲cho chha*, 'to be is necessary'; *usle hun̲nu khojyo*, 'he sought to be'; *hun̲nuko lāgi*, 'for the sake of being.'

As gerund, *hun̲nu* usually takes the form *hun̲nā*: *dharmmī hunnāle jiun̲chhu*, 'I shall live by being righteous.'

The gerundial infinitive is made by adding *-lāi* or *-ko lāgi*: *u baptismā hun̲nulāi* (or *hun̲nuko lāgi*) *āyo*, 'he came to be baptized'; but these, as also other affixes, may be dropped, though understood: *u baptismā hun̲nu āyo*, 'he came to be baptized'; *hun̲nu kaṭhin*, 'difficult to be'; *boknu kaṭhin bhayekā bojhā*, 'burdens difficult to carry.' See on "Gerundial Infinitive," under Syntax.

By changing the final *u* to *e* its adjective is formed: *hun̲ne*, 'a being (one)' (or, used as a noun, a 'be-er'); *dhanna naram hun̲neharu*, 'blessed (are) the meek'; *dhan hun̲ne āimāi*, 'a woman having riches' (p. 73).

The Infinitive may be used as a mild or respectful Imperative (see p. 89): *timi hun̲nu*, 'be thou'; *bhalā hun̲nu*, 'be good.' Doubtless the construction is elliptical, as in Greek.

hun̲na, for *hun̲nu*; and *hun̲nye*, *hunnye*, *hunyā*, for *hun̲ne*, often occur. So with all other verbs: *garna*, for *garnu*; *garnyā*, for *garne* (see p. 74).

PARTICIPLES.

Imperfect.

Pos.—'Being.'

1.	हुंदो	*hun̲do*	(local)
2.	हुंदा (ी)	*hun̲dā* (ī)	(modal)
3.	हुंदाहुंनि	*hun̲dāhun̲ni*	(temporal)
4.	हुंदाखेरि	*hun̲dākheri*	,,
5.	हुंदै गर्दाखेरि	*hun̲dai gardākheri*	,,
6.	हुंदामां	*hun̲dāmān̲*	,,

Neg.—'Not being.'

1.	न हुंदो	*na hun̲do*
		etc.
5.	हुंदैन-गर्दाखेरि	*hun̲daina gardākheri*
6.	न हुंदामां	*da hun̲dāmān̲*

1 is mostly of place: *bāṭo hun̲do*, 'in the way'; *parbat hun̲do*, 'through the mountains'; *yahān̲ hun̲do*, 'about here'; *yetā hun̲do holā*, 'it will be hereabouts'; *utai hun̲do pāīn̲chha*, 'thereabouts will it be found': *hun̲do ani āun̲do jīun̲ni*, 'the life here and hereafter'; *yo hun̲do barttamān dushṭa jagat*, 'this present evil world.'

It is also used to form the past indef. and imperf. subjunctive: *ui hun̲do ho ta ān̲dhī hun̲ne thiyena*, 'were it that (person), then there would not be a storm.'

2 is mostly of manner or circumstance: *jatane hun̲dā āyen̲*, 'I came with diligence'; *alchhe na hun̲dā*, 'not being slothful'; *alchhe hun̲dā āin̲na*, 'I did not come lazily'; *phalānī āimāi byāulākān̲ byāulī hun̲dā* (or -ī) *āī*, 'a certain (such-and-such a) woman came to (chez) the bridegroom as bride'; *shaitān hawwā thān̲i sāpko jīumān̲ pasyeko hun̲dā āyo*, 'Satan came to Eve enclosed in the body of the serpent'; *īshwar putra autārī hun̲dā san̲sār saña bolyo*, 'God the Son, being incarnate, spake to the world.'

3–6 are mostly of time, 'while being.' 5 means 'while in the act of being' · *maṉ girjākā pāṭh chhāndai huṉdāhuṉni* (or *huṉdākheri*, or *huṉdāmān*) *maṉlāi na chalā na bolā*, 'while I am selecting the church lessons, do not disturb me'; *maṉ māṉsuko dokānmāṉ huṉdāhuṉnī*, etc., *timi yeso bajār tira āyau*, 'while I was in the butcher's shop, you came on towards the Bazar'; *tyesle lekhyeko huṉdai gardākheri*, etc., *maiṉle tyeslāi hallāi diyeṉ*, 'when he was engaged in writing I shook him.'

3–6 are often shortened to *huṉdā*, the same form as 2: *maṉ pāṭh chhāndai huṉdā*, 'while I am (or was) selecting the lessons.' When *huṉdā* is thus short for *huṉdāhuṉni*, etc., it does not change for the feminine, as, indeed, 2 itself sometimes does not do.

The emphatics are formed by changing *-do*, *-da*, to *-dai*, and have the force of greater definiteness or completeness.

The form *huṉdā huṉdai* is used in a concessive sense, 'although being, or having': *kye āṉkhā huṉdā huṉdai pani dekhdauna*, 'even with eyes, do you not see?' The form *huṉdai* is used as the primitive in four of the compounds (p. 59).

When the sense is 'exist' the *chhaṉ-* forms are used: *tyesle jīuṉdo chhaṉdākheri bhanyo*, 'he, while he was yet alive, said.'

These participles can be used only as qualifying the subject. To qualify the object, one of the Perfect participles must be used. No. 1, however, when used purely as an adjective, may be used also with the object, of course.

PERFECT.

Pos.—'Having been, or being.'

1.	हुंदै गर्‍येको (ी, ा)	*huṉdai garyeko* (*ī*, *ā*)
2.	भयेको (ी, ा)	*bhayeko* (*ī*, *ā*)

Neg.—'Not having been, or not being.'

1.	हुंदैन गर्‍येको (ी, ा)	*huṉdaina garyeko* (*ī*, *ā*)
2.	न भयेको (ी, ा)	*na bhayeko* (*ī*, *ā*)

1 is really past imperfect in meaning: *11 bajyeko na huṉdā kheri rel jāṉdai garyeko dekhyeṉ*, "11 o'clock yet unstruck, I saw the train go'; *chaurastā jāṉdā dawāīko bikri huṉdai*

garyeko dekhye<u>n</u>, 'while going to the Chaurasta, I saw the sale of medicine taking place'; *tero byāhā hu<u>n</u>dai garyekomā<u>n</u> a<u>n</u>dhyāro thiyo*, 'on the occasion of thy wedding, it was dark'; *kinabhanye tyesle tyeslāi nikānandai* (pronounced *nikāndai*) *hu<u>n</u>dai garyeko pheri pāyo*, 'because he recovered him safe and sound'; *su<u>n</u>gurharule khā<u>n</u>dai garyekā kosā*, 'the husks which the swine did eat.'

In any of the above examples the *garyeko* might be left unexpressed, though understood.

2 is a true perfect, and, as such, is used in the perfect tenses of the various moods. As participle, it is a most useful form: *timiharu bhandā agāṛi bhayekā agambaktāharu*, 'the prophets which were before you'; *jaba yi sabai bhayekā dekhaulā*, 'when ye will see all these things come to pass'; *yeti bhayekomā<u>n</u> ma<u>n</u> āu<u>n</u>chhu*, 'when so much has come to pass (= thereupon) I shall come'; *dushṭa bhayekole*, 'by being wicked,' 'because of (his) wickedness'; *uslāi gharmā<u>n</u> bhayekī dekhda chhu*, 'I see her in the house.'

In any of the above examples the form may be shortened to *bhaye*; *bhayekā* may further be shortened to *bhayā*. So *hirkāye*, *hirkāā*, for *hirkāyekā*; etc.

These participles can be used as qualifying either subject or object; and, like other adjectives, may of course be used as nouns.

CONJUNCTIVE.

Pos.—'Being, or having been.'

1.	होइ	or	होइकन	*hoi*	or	*hoikana*	(concurrent)
2.	भइ	,,	भइकन	*bhai*	,,	*bhaikana*	
3.	भयेर			*bhayera*			(preliminary)

For the NEG. put न *na* before each of the above.

They are called conjunctive, because used as verbal conjunctions, rather than as verbal adjectives. They imply a logical or moral connection between the fact stated by the participle and that stated by the principal verb, which is absent in the case of the other participles.

They can be used only with the subject

With the first two, the statements conjoined are concurrent; with the third, the one statement is preliminary to the other. The first is imperfect, the second perfect, the third past perf.

Examples: *tainle mānchhe hoi* (or *hoikana*) *īshwar hun bhanda chhas*, 'thou, being a man, sayest thou art (*lit.*, 'I am') God'; *tinale nirdayālu bhai* (or *bhaikana*) *ayogya kām garda chhan*, 'they being (*lit.*, 'been') merciless do unworthy works'; *tiniharu tripta bhayera ghar gaye*, 'they, having been (= 'when they had been') satisfied, went home,' or 'they were satisfied, and went home'; *u shokit bhai royo*, 'he wept in sorrow'; *u shokit bhayera royo*, 'he was sorry, and wept'; *dhanna tyo dās jaslāi tyesko prabhule āyera yeso gardai garyeko bheṭāulā*, 'blessed (is) the servant (slave) whom his Lord will come and find so doing.'

hoi and *bhai* are also used with *jānnu*, 'to go,' or *āunnu*, 'to come,' to form a compound verb meaning 'to become'. *hoi* is so used in the present and imperfect tenses: *bhai*, in the past and perfect: *tyo mūrkha hoi jānda chha, bhai gayo, bhai gayeko chha, hoi jānchha, bhai gayeko hunchha*, 'he is becoming, became, has become, will become, will have become foolish'; *bhasma hoi jā*, 'become thou ashes,' 'be consumed'; *shaitānko kshay ho jāwas*, 'may the destruction of Satan come about'; *dukha pāunne gat hoi āundā mati beglai hunchha*, 'as the state of suffering comes on, your opinion will be different'; *uṛāū putrale harikangāl hoi jāndā pashchāttāp garyo*, 'the prodigal son, as he became destitute, repented.'

hoi and *bhai* are also used as the primitive in three of the compound verbs (Nos. 2, 4, 10, p. 59); *tyo jhan chāmchum bhai diyo*, 'he was all the quieter'; *tyo hoi na sakunjyāl samma*, 'till it be accomplished'; *bhai sakyo*, 'it is completed'; *bhai rahyena*, 'he did not continue to be.'

hoi is also used in a locative sense, like *hundo*, but while the latter signifies 'being in,' *hoi* signifies 'being at,' a place: *phāgu kamān jāndā relmān gayau bhanye dekhi jalpāigaṛi hoi baṭāigol niski sāinli hāṭ dekhi ukālo lāgnu parchha*, 'if, going to Phagu tea-garden, you go by rail, you must, arriving at Jalpaiguri and coming out at Bataigol, begin the ascent at Sylee Bazar.'

The emphatics are formed by adding *ai* or *nai*: *hoinai, hoikanai*, etc.

VI. EXERCISE.

1. Name and complete, with personal pronouns and meaning, the tenses beginning, respectively, *chhu, hun̲, chhuin̲na, huin̲na, hun̲dīn̲na, thiyen̲, thiin̲na, bhayen̲, bhain̲na hun̲chhu, houn̲lā, hun̲nna, howain̲na, hun̲do hun̲, bhayeko bhaye dekhi, bhayeko na hun̲do hun̲, bhayen̲ ta, bhayen̲ bhanye dekhi, hunne thiyen̲, houn̲, bhayes.*

2. What, with meaning, are *hun̲nu ān̲tnu, hun̲dā, hun̲dāhun̲ni, chhan̲dākheri, chhan̲dai gardākheri, hun̲dai garyekī, bhayekā?*

3. What is the difference between *chhu* and *hun̲, hunnan* and *hunan, bhayo ta* and *bhayo bhanye dekhi, hun̲daina* and *hun̲dainai, hun̲dā* and *hundākheri, hun̲do* and *hoi, hoi* and *bhai, bhai* and *bhayera*; *ho, hou* and *houna*; *hos* and *hawas*?

4. Write out in full the honorific forms of the Indef. Perf. Indic. and Pres. Imp. Imperative.

5. Translate: *rājākān̲, rājākana, hun̲ne chhu, hoi jān̲nulāi, bhai gayen̲, bhai diis, bhai sakyau, bhaī rahan̲daun̲na, hoi sakun̲jyāl samma, uthāun̲nu, mān̲rnu, khuwāun̲nu, hun̲nu lāun̲nu, hun̲nu saknu, hun̲dai garnu, hun̲nu thālnu, hun̲ne tchchhe garnu, hun̲nu din̲nu, hun̲nu pāun̲nu, hun̲dai rahan̲nu, hun̲dai jān̲nu, hoi āun̲nu, hun̲dai āun̲nu, hun̲nu tā hun̲chhas, bhayo ra, bho, bhāko, hun̲this*

6. Translate: he will be able to come, he will be able to kill, neither let him *eat*, there is a house, it is the house, it is not my house, I have not a house, the house is *mine*, he is (after all) the king, he has a son, he has riches, I have cattle, a person having riches, though having eyes, a certain woman named Sukhmāyā, in the act of being, while he was in the act of being, I won't be, it won't do, no, it won't do at all, he must be, I probably was, Oh! that he were not foolish (*mūrkha*), lest he be foolish, whoever he was, if I be foolish, (pres. and fut.), if I had been here I should have been foolish, you should (ought to) be, that I may not be foolish, let me be (Imperat.), let me be (permissive), he had to be, they asked (*sodhye*) what this might be, till I am, as long as I have being, difficult to be, it is necessary to be, for the sake of becoming

the meek (verbal, plu.), in the mountains, thereupon, the prophets which were before you, I saw the sale of medicine taking place, he came in sorrow (partic.), he was sorry (partic.) and came, when in the Bazar I was foolish, till I be king, that I may be king, it is the king's, it is a king's, what is your name? have you a name?

7. Which of the participles are imperfect, as to tense? Which, perfect? Which, past perfect? Which can be used with either subject or object? Which, only with the subject?

8. What is the essential distinction between the Conjunctive and the other participles?

II. *garnu*, 'TO DO,' 'TO MAKE.'

As the inflexion endings are the same as of ***hu͟nnu***, 'to be,' only the 1st pers. sing. masc. of each tense need now be shewn.

With each part, the corresponding part of other two representative regular verbs, ***jānnu***, 'to know,' and ***garāu͟nnu***, 'to cause to be done,' and of each of the irregular verbs, ***hu͟nnu***, 'to be,' *dhu͟nnu*, 'to wash,' *di͟nnu*, 'to give,' *jā͟nnu*, 'to go,' and *laijā͟nnu* (or *lā͟nnu*), 'to take away,' is indicated.

Of the other irregulars, on p. 57, *chhu͟nnu*, 'to touch,' and *ru͟nnu*, 'to weep,' are conjugated like *dhu͟nnu*; and *li͟nnu*, 'to take,' like *di͟nnu*.

For the slight irregularity of verbs like *duhu͟nnu*, 'to milk,' and *tuhu͟nnu*, 'to miscarry,' see the rule on p. 58.

The subject of an INTRANSITIVE verb (as already seen in the conjugation of *hu͟nnu*), or of a transitive in the PASSIVE voice, is put in the nominative case :—

mānchhe chha	the person is
ko āyo	who came?
koi garīyo	'some one was made'

ma͟n	*āyen*	I came	*hā͟nmiharu*	*āyū͟n*	we came.
ta͟n	*āis*	thou camest	*timiharu*	*āyau*	you ,,
u	*āyo* (*āi*)	he (she) came	*uniharu*	*āye* (*āin*)	they ,,

The subject of a transitive verb in the ACTIVE voice is put in the Agent case :—

mānchhele garyo	the person did.
kasle ,,	who ,, ?
kasaile ,,	some one ,,

mainle garyen	I did	*hānmiharule*	*garyūn*	we did.
tainle garis	thou didst	*timiharule*	*garyau*	you ,,
usle garyo (rī)	he (she) did	*uniharule*	*garye (rin)*	they ,,

To this rule there is in Nepali as spoken in Darjeeling a notable exception. The 1st pers., sing. and plu., of the Indefinite and Imperfect tenses [marked in what follows with an asterisk before and after the name of the tense], even of active transitives, is as a rule, in the nominative :—

man garne chhu	I do	*man garchhu*	I shall do.
,, *garda* ,,	I am doing	,, *gardai hunchhu*	,, ,, be doing.
,, *garthyen*	I did	,, *garunlā*	,, ,, do.
,, *garda thiyen*	I was doing		

That the fut. indef. Subj. is *mainle garyen bhanye dekhi* is an exception that proves the rule, for it is really the indef. perf. Indic., with *bhanye dekhi* added.

The 2nd pers. is sometimes made to follow the above rule of the 1st, but not usually.

It must be recorded, however, that very frequently Nepali follows the usual custom of the Hindi languages and puts the 1st person also in the Agent case.

In the Infinitive mood, and with the participles, the subject of an active transitive is always in the **Agent** case : *mainle garnu, mainle gardā*, etc.

Moreover, in the Inf. mood, and with the partic. of any verb, the subject must always be expressed, because otherwise, seeing that these parts are uninflected, the subject could not be known. The subject of *hunchhu*, though unexpressed, will be understood to be *man*, from the form ; but the subject of *hunnu*, to be known, must be expressly stated, unless, of course, it can be gathered from the context.

The rule for the formation of the passive voice of trans. verbs is so simple and regular (except of *laijānnu*, or *lānnu*, 'to take away')—see p. 61—that the single example of its conjugation furnished in what follows is all that is needed.

To each tense, in the following examples of conjugation, the respective notes already given in the conjugation of *hunnu* apply, *mutatis mutandis*, and ought to be referred to.

INDICATIVE MOOD.

Pres. Indef.

'I am a doer'; 'I do.'

Pos.— मं गर्ने छु or हुं *man̲ garne chhu* or *hun̲*
Neg.— ,, ,, छुइंन ,, हुइंन ,, ,, *chhuin̲na* ,, *huin̲na*
Pass.—*garīn̲ne chhu* or *hun̲*, etc.

garne chhu is sometimes shortened to *garchhu*, and *garne chhuin̲na*, to *gardīn̲na*, the fut. indef. forms (see p. 102).

garne is sometimes written *garnyā*.

When the form is *garne hun̲*, the subject is nom. case throughout.

So—*jānne*, *garāun̲ne*, *hun̲ne*, *dhun̲ne*. *din̲ne*, *jān̲ne*, *laijān̲ne* or *lān̲ne* (Pass. *lagīn̲ne*) *chhu* or *hun̲*.

Pres. Imperf.

'I am doing'; 'I do'; lit. 'I am a-doing.'

Pos.— मं गर्दै छु *man̲ garda chhu*
Neg.— ,, गर्दीन ,, *gardīn̲na*

tain̲le or *tan̲ garda chhas*; *tyesle garda cha*, etc.

Pass.—*garīn̲da chhu*, *garīn̲dīn̲na*

garda chhu is sometimes shortened to *garchhu*.

So—*jānda*, *garāun̲da*, *hun̲da*, *dhun̲da*, *din̲da*, *jān̲da*, *laijān̲da* or *lān̲da* (Pass. *lagīn̲da*) *chhu*.

Pres. Perf.

'I have done.'

Pos.— मैंले गर्येको छु *main̲le garyeko chhu*
Neg.— ,, ,, छुइंन ,, ,, *chhuin̲na*
Pass.—*garīyeko chhu*, *chhuin̲na*

So—*jānyeko*, *garāyeko*, *bhayeko*, *dhoyeko*, *diyeko*, *gayeko*, *lagyeko* (Pass. *lagīyeko*) *chhu*.

For the meaning of the * * see p. 98.

PRES. PERF. CONTINUOUS.

'I have been doing.'

Pos.— मं गर्ने भयेको छु *man garne bhayeko chhu*

Neg.— ,, ,, ,, छुइंन ,, ,, ,, *chhuinna*

Pass.—*garīnne bhayeko chhu, chhuinna*

Alternative form : *man gardai rahyeko chhu* (p. 59).

So—*jānne, garāunne, hunne, dhunne, dinne, jānne, laijānne* or *lānne* (Pass. *lagīnne*) *bhayeko chhu.*

PAST INDEF.

'I was doing'; 'I did.'

Pos.— मं गर्थें *man garthyen*

Neg.— ,, गर्दैन थें ,, *gardaina thyen*

tainle or *tan garthis, tyesle garthyo,* etc.

Pass.—*garīnthyen, garīndaina thyen*

So—*jānthyen* (Pass. *jānīnthyen*), *garāunthyen, thiyen, dhunthyen, dinthyen, jānthyen, laijānthyen* or *lānthyen* (Pass. *lagīnthyen*).

PAST IMPERF.

'I was doing.'

Pos.— मं गर्द थियें *man garda thiyen*

Neg.— ,, गर्दैन ,, ,, *gardaina* ,,

tainle or *tan garda thiis, tyesle garda thiyo,* etc.

Pass.—*garīnda thiyen, garīndaina thiyen*

Sometimes it is shortened to the past indef. forms.

So—*jānda, garāunda, hunda, dhunda, dinda, jānda, laijānda* or *lānda* (Pass. *lagīnda*) *thiyen.*

PAST PERF.

'I had done.'

Pos.— मैंले गरयेको थियें *mainle garyeko thīyen*

Neg.— ,, ,, थिइंन ,, ,, *thiinna.*

Pass.—*garīyeko thiyen, thiinna*

So—*jānyeko, garāyeko, bhayeko, dhoyeko, diyeko, gayeko, lagyeko* (Pass. *lagīyeko*) *thiyen.*

PAST PERF. CONTINUOUS

'I had been doing.'

Pos.— मं गर्ने भयेको थियें   m̄an̲ garne bhayeko thiyen̲

Neg.— „ „ „ थिइंन   „ „ „ thiin̲na

Pass.—garīn̲ne bhayeko thiyen̲, thiin̲na

Alternative form : man̲ gari rahyeko thiyen̲ (p. 59).

So—jānne, garāun̲ne, hun̲ne, dhun̲ne, din̲ne, jān̲ne, laijān̲ne or lān̲ne (Pass. lagīn̲ne) bhayeko thiyen̲.

INDEF. PERF.

'I did'; 'I have done.'

Pos.—	मैंले गर्यें	main̲le garyen̲
	तैंले गरिस्	tain̲le garis
	त्यसले गर्यो (गरी)	tyesle garyo (garī)
	हामिहरूले गर्युं	hān̲miharule garyūn̲
	तिमिहरूले गर्यौ	timiharule garyau
	तिनिहरूले गर्ये (गरिन्)	tiniharule garye (garin)
Neg.—	मैंले गरिंन	main̲le garin̲na
	तैंले गरिनस्	tain̲le garinas
	त्यसले गर्येन (गरीन)	tyesle garyena (garīna)
	हामिहरूले गर्यूंन	hān̲miharule garyūn̲na
	तिमिहरूले गर्यौन	timiharule garyauna
	तिनिहरूले गर्येनन् (गरिनन्)	tiniharule garyenan (garinan)

Pass.—garīiyen̲, garīin̲na

[K. : elide the y in 1st sing. and 3rd plu. pos., and 3rd sing. and plu. neg.]

garyen̲, garye, are often garyān̲, garyā.

So—jānyen̲, garāyen̲, bhayen̲, dhoyen̲, diyen̲, gayen̲, lagyen̲ (Pass. lagīyen̲). Neg.—jānin̲na (P. jānīin̲na), garāin̲na (P. garāīin̲na), etc.

FUT. INDEF.

'I shall do'; 'I will do.'

Pos.— मं गर्छु *maṉ garchhu*

Neg.— „ गर्दिन „ *gardiṉna*

taiṉle or *taṉ garchhas*, *tyesle garchha*, etc.

This form is often used for the Present Indefinite also. See p. 99.

Pass.—*garīṉchhu*, *garīṉdīṉna*

So—*jānchhu*, *garāuṉchhu*, *huṉchhu*, *dhuṉchhu*, *diṉchhu*, *jāṉchhu*, *laijāṉchhu* or *lāṉchhu* (Pass. *lagīṉchhu*). Neg.—*jāndīṉna*, *garāuṉdīnna* or *garāunna*, *huṉdīṉna* or *hunna*, *dhuṉdīṉna* or *dhunna*, *diṉdīṉna* or *dinna*, *jāṉdīṉna* or *jānna*, *laijāṉdīṉna* or *laijānna* or *lāṉdīṉna* or *lānna* (Pass. *lagiṉdīṉna* or *lagīnna*. See note on pp. 77, 72).

FUT. IMPERF.

'I shall, or will, be doing.'

Pos.— मं गर्दै हुंछु *maṉ gardai huṉchhu*

Neg.— „ गर्दैन „ „ *gardaina* „

taiṉle or *tāṉ gardai huṉchhas*, *tyesle gardai huṉchha*, etc.

Pass.—*garīṉdai*, *garīṉdaina huṉchhu*

So—*jāndai*, *garāuṉdai*, *hundai*, *dhuṉdaī*, *diṉdai*, *jāṉdai*, *laijāṉdai* or *lāṉdai* (Pass. *lagiṉdai*) *huṉchhu*.

FUT. PERF.

'I shall, or will, have done.'

Pos.— मैंले गर्येको हुंछु *maiṉle garyeko huṉchhu*

Neg.— „ „ हुंदैन „ „ *huṉdīṉna* or (p. 71)

Pass.—*garīyeko huṉchhu*, *huṉdīṉna*

So—*jānyeko*, *garāyeko*, *bhayeko*, *dhoyeko*, *diyeko*, *gayeko*, *lagyeko* (Pass. *lagīyeko*) *huṉchhu*.

FUT. PERF. CONTINUOUS.

'I shall, or will, have been doing.'

Pos.— मं गर्ने भयेको हुंछु *maṉ garne bhayeko huṉchhu*

Neg.— „ „ „ हुंदैन „ „ „ *huṉdīṉna* or (p. 71)

Pass.—*garīṉne bhayeko huṉchhu*, *huṉdīṉna*

Alternative : *maṉ gardai rahyeko huṉchhu*

So—*jānne*, *garāuṉne*, *huṉne*, *dhuṉne*, *diṉne*, *jāṉne*, *laijāṉne* or *lāṉne* (Pass. *lagīṉne*) *bhayeko huṉchhu*.

FUT. CONTINGENT.

'I shall do.'

Pos.—	मं गरुंला (ी)	*man̲ garun̲lā* (ī)
	तैंले or तं गर्लास् (ीस्)	*tain̲le* or *tan̲ garlās* (īs)
	त्येस्ले गर्ला (ी)	*tyesle garā* (ī)
	हांमिहरु गरुंला ,,	*hān̲miharu garūn̲lā* (ī)
	तिमिहरुले or तिमिहरु गरौला (ी)	*timiharule* or *timiharu garaulā* (ī)
	तिनिहरुले गर्नन् (गर्निन्)	*tiniharule garnan* (*garnin*)
Pass.—	*garīun̲lā* (ī)	*garīūn̲la* (ī)
	garīlās or *garīyelās* (īs)	*garīaulā* ,,
	garīlā ,, *garīyelā* (ī)	*garīnan* (*in*)
Neg.—	मं गरोइंन	*man̲ garoin̲na*
	तैंले or तं गरोइनस्	*tain̲le* or *ta garoinas*
	त्येस्ले गरोइन	*tyesle garoina*
	हांमिहरु गरोइनौं	*han̲miharu garoinaun̲*
	तिमिहरुले or तिमिहरु गरोइनौ	*timiharule* or *timiharu garoinau*
	तिनिहरुले गरोइनन् (गरोइनिन्)	*tiniharule garoinan* (*garoinin*)
Pass.—	*garīwain̲na*	*garīwainaun̲*
	garīwainas	*garīwainau*
	garīwaina	*garīwainan* (*in*)

The forms *garīlās*, *garīlā*, though more regular, are not so popular as the more euphonious *garīyelās*, *garīyelā*.

So—*jānun̲lā*, *jānlās* .. *jānnan*
garāun̲lā, *garāulās* .. *garāunan*
houn̲lā, *holās* .. *hunan*
dhoun̲lā, *dholās* .. *dhunan*
diun̲la, *delās*, *delā*, *diūn̲lā*, *deaulā*, *dinan*
jāun̲lā, *jālās*, *jālā*, *jāūn̲lā*, *jāaulā*, *jānan*
laijāun̲la, *laijālās* .. *laijānan*

Neg.—*jānoin̲na*, *garāwain̲na*, *howain̲na*, *dhowain̲na*, *diwain̲na*, *jāwain̲na*, *laijāwain̲na*.

Pos. Pass.—*jānīuṉla*, *jānilās* or *jānīyelās* ..
garāīuṉlā, *garāilās* or *garāiyelās* ..
dhoīuṉlā, *dhoīlās* or *dhoīyelās* ..
dīīuṉlā, *dīīlas* or *dīīyelās* ..
lagīuṉlā, *lagīlās* or *lagīyelās* ..

Neg. Pass.—*jānīwaiṉna*, *jānīwainas* ..
garāīwaiṉna ..
dhoīwaiṉna ..
dīīwaiṉna ..
lagīwaiṉna ..

It will be observed that the rule for the neg. of this form is that after a stem ending in a consonant the termination runs *oiṉna*, *oinas*, etc.; after a vowel: *waiṉna*, *wainas*, etc. It follows that the Pass. must always take the *waiṉna* termination

FUT. PERF. CONTING.

'I shall have done.'

Pos.— मैंले गर्येको होउंला *maiṉle garyeko houṉlā*
Neg.— ,, ,, होवैंन ,, ,, *howaiṉna*
Pass.—*garīyeko houṉlā*, *howaiṉna*

So—*jānyeko*. *garāyeko*, *bhayeko*, *dhoyeko*, *diyeko*, *gayeko*, *lagyeko* (Pass. *lagīyeko*) *houṉlā*.

SUBJUNCTIVE MOOD.

PRES. INDEF.

'If I am, or be, a doer'; 'If I do.'

Pos.—*maṉ garne chhu*, or *huṉ*, *bhanye dekhi*, or *ta*
Neg.— ,, ,, *chhuiṉna* ,, *huiṉna* ,, ,, ,, ,,
Pass.—*garīṉne* ..

PRES. IMPERF.

'If I am, or be, doing'; 'If I do'

Pos.—*maṉ garda chhu bhanye dekhi*. or *ta*
Neg.— ,, *gardīṉna* ,, ,, ,, ,,
taiṉle or *taṉ garda chhas*, *tyesle garda chha*, etc.
Pass.—*garīṉda chhu*, *garīṉdīṉna* ..

PRES. PERF.

'If I have done.'

Pos.—*main̲le garyeko chhu* . *bhanye dekhi*, or *ta*.
Neg.— ,, ,, *chhuin̲na* ,, ,, ,, ,,
Pass.—*garīyeko chhu, chhuin̲na*..

PRES. PERF. CONTINUOUS.

'If I have been doing'

Pos.—*man̲ garne bhayeko chhu* *bhanye d̲ekhi*, or *ta*.
Neg.— ,, ,, ,, *chhuin̲na* ,, ,, ,, ,,
Pass.—*garīn̲ne*..
Alternative: *gardai rahyeko chhu bh. d.*, or *ta*.

The above four tenses being the same as the same tenses of the Indic. (p. 99), with *bhanye dekhi*, 'if,' or *ta*, 'then,' added, it is unnecessary to represent them here more fully.

PAST INDEF. AND PAST IMPERF.

'If I did'; 'Did I.'

Pos.— मं गर्दो हुं *man̲ gardo hun̲*.
Neg.— ,, न ,, ,, ,, *na* ,, ,,
Pass.—*garīn̲do, na garīn̲do hun̲*
So *jāndo, garāun̲do, hun̲do, dhun̲do, dindo, jān̲do, laijān̲do* or *lān̲do* (Pass. *lagīn̲do*) *hun̲*.

PAST PERF.

'If I had, or had I, done.'

Pos.— मैंले गर्‍येको भये देखि *main̲le garyeko bhaye dekhi*.
Neg.— ,, न ,, ,, ,, ,, *na* ,, ,, ,,
Pass.—*garīyeko, na garīyeko bhaye dekhi*

Alternative Form of Past Perf.

Pos.— मैंले गर्‍येको हुंदो हुं *main̲le garyeko hun̲do hun̲*.
Neg.— ,, ,, न ,, ,, ,, ,, *na* ,, ,,
Pass.—*garīyeko hun̲do, na hun̲do hun̲*
So—*jānyeko, garāyeko, bhayeko, dhoyeko, diyeko, gayeko, lagyeko* (Pass. *lagīyeko*) *bhaye dekhi*, or *hun̲do hun̲*.

Past Perf. Continuous.

'If I had, or had I, been doing.'

Pos.— मं गर्ने भयेको भये देखि *man̲ garne bhayeko bhaye dekhi.*

Neg.— ,, ,, न ,, ,, ,, ,, ,, *na* ,, ,, ,,

Pass.—*garīn̲ne..*

Alternative : *hun̲do hun̲, etc.*, in place of *bhaye dekhi.*

So—*jānne,* etc. (p. 102), *bhayeko bhaye dekhi,* or *hun̲do hun̲.*

Indef. Perf.

'If I did, or have done.'

Pos.— मैंले गर्‍यें त *main̲le garyen̲ ta.*

Neg.— ,, गरिंन ,, ,, *garin̲na* ,,

Pass.—*garīyen̲, garīin̲na ta.*

So—*jānyen̲,* etc. (see the indef. perf. Indic., p. 101, with which this part is the same, with *ta* added).

Fut. Indef.

'If I shall, or should, or were to, do'; 'If I do.'

Pos.— मैंले गर्‍यें भन्यें देखि *main̲le garyen̲ bhanye dekhi.*

Neg — ,, गरिंन ,, ,, ,, *garin̲na* ,, ,,

Pass —*garīyen̲, garīin̲na bhaye dekhi*

So—*jānyen̲,* etc. (see the preceding tense, with which it is the same, with *bhanye dekhi* instead of *ta*).

Fut. Imperf.

If I shall, or should, or were to, be doing'; 'If I be doing.'

Pos — मं गर्दैं भयें भन्ये देखि *man̲ gardai bhayen̲ bhanye dekhi.*

Neg.— ,, गर्दैंन ,, ,, ,, ,, *gardaina* ,, ,, ,,

Pass.—*garīn̲dai, garīn̲daina bhayen̲ bhanye dekhi*

So—*jāndai, garāun̲dai, hun̲dai, dhun̲dai, din̲dai, jān̲dai, lai-jān̲dai or lān̲dai* (Pass. *lagīn̲dai*) *bhayen̲ bhanye dekhi.*

Fut. Perf.

'If I shall, or should, or were to, have done.'

Pos.— मैंले गर्‍येको भयें भन्ये देखि *main̲le garyeko bhayen̲ bhanye dekhi*

Neg.— ,, ,, भइंन ,, ,, ,, ,, *bhain̲na* ,, ,,

Pass —*garīyeko..*

So - *jānyeko,* etc. (p. 105), *bhayen̲ bhanye dekhi.*

Fut. Perf. Continuous.

'If I shall, or should, or were to, have been doing.'

Pos.

मं गर्ने भयेको भयें भन्ये देखि *man garne bhayeko bhayen bhanye dekhi.*

Neg.

मं गर्ने भयेको भइंन भन्ये देखि *man garne bhayeko bhainna bhanye dekhi.*

Pass.—*garīnne..*
Alternative : *gardai rahyeko bhayen ..*
So—*jānne*, etc. (p. 102), *bhayeko bhayen bhanye dekhi.*

Fut. Conting., and Fut. Perf. Conting.

Where necessary, these are formed by adding *ta* to the Indic. form.

See note, p. 86.

CONDITIONAL MOOD.

'I should, or would, do'; 'I should, or would, have done.'

Pos.— मं गर्ने थियें *man garne thiyen.*

Neg.— „ „ थिइंन „ „ *thiinna.*

tainle or *tan garne thiis, tyesle garne thiyo*, etc.
Pass.—*garīnne thiyen, thiinna.*
So—*jānne*, etc. (p. 102), *thiyen.*

IMPERATIVE, OPTATIVE, AND POTENTIAL MOOD.

Pres. Indef. and Imperf.

'Let me do'; 'May I do'; '(That) I may, or might, do'

Pos.

मं गरुं	*man garun*	हांमिहरु गरूं	*hānmiharu garūn.*
तैंले or तं गर्	*tainle* or *tan gar*	तिमिहरुले or तिमिहरु गर	*timiharule* or *timiharu gara.*
त्येस्ले गरोस्	*tyesle garos*	तिनिहरुले गरुन्	*tiniharule garun.*

Neg.

न गरुं *na garun*, etc.

The Infinitive गर्नु *garnu* may also be used as a mild or respectful Imperative.

Alternative Imperf. : *man garda, gardaina houn*, etc.

Pass.—*garīun*	*garīūn.*
garī	*garīyau.*
garīos	*garīun.*

garun, garūn, are sometimes written *garuñ, garūñ.*

[K. : *garīis*, for *garī* ; *garīinas*, for *na garī* ; *garīenau*, for *na garīyau.*]

So—*jānun̲, jān, jānos, jānūn̲, jāna, jānun.*
garāun̲, garā, garāwas, garāūn̲, garāwa, garāun.
houn̲, ho, hawas, hoūn̲, hawa, houn.
dhoun̲, dho, dhowas, dhoūn̲, dhowa, dhoun.
diun̲, de, dewas, diūn̲, dewa, diun.
jāun̲, jā, jāwas, jāūn̲, jāwa, jāun.
laijāun̲, laijā

Pass.—*jānīun̲, jānī, jānīos, jānīūn̲, jānīyau, jānīun.*
garāīun̲, garāī, garāīos, garāīūn̲, garāīyau, garāīun.
dhoīun̲, dhoī, dhoīos, dhoīūn̲, dhoīyau, dhoīun.
diīun̲, diī, diīos, diīūn̲, diīyau, diīun.
lagīun̲, lagī, lagīos, lagīūn̲, lagīyau, lagīun.
le, the 2nd sing. Imperat. of *lin̲nu*, 'to take,' is sometimes written *li*.

The grammatical 2nd sing. and plu. Imperat. of verbs in—*an̲nu*, like *niskan̲nu*, 'to go out,' are respectively *nisk*; *niska*, etc., but are often written *niski*, which, however, is really the Conjunctive participle, with *jā* (sing.), or *jāwa* (plu.) understood: *nisk, niski, niski jā*, 'go thou out.' The 2nd sing. imperat. of *āun̲nu* is *ā*, or *āija*, 'come.'

See notes, pp. 88, 89.

PRES. PERF.

'Let me, may I, (that) I may or might, have done

Pos.— मैंले गर्येको होउं *mainle garyeko houn̲.*
Neg.— ,, ,, न ,, ,, ,, *na* ,,
Pass.—*gariyeko, gariyeko na houn̲.*
So—*jānyeko*, etc. (p. 105), *houn̲.*

FUT. PERF.

'Thou shalt, or shouldst, do, or have done.'

Pos.— तैंले गर्येस् *tāinle garyes.*
Neg.— ,, न ,, ,, *na* ,,
Pass.—*gariyes, na gariyes.*
Sometimes it is written *gares* (Pass. *garies*).
So—*jānyes, garāyes, bhayes, dhoyes, diyes, gayes, lagyes*, (Pass. *lagiyes*).

INFINITIVE MOOD.

Pres. Indef.

'To do.'

Pos.— गर्नु garnu.
Neg —न „ na „
Pass.—garinnu, na g.

Sometimes it is written garna, garinna.

So—jānnu (Pass. jāninnu), garāunnu (P. garāinnu), hunnu, dhunnu (P. dhuinnu), dinnu (P. diinnu), jānnu, laijānnu or lannu (P. laginnu).

The infinitive is sometimes used as a mild or respectful Imperative: and as a verbal noun or Gerund see p. 91.

Pres. Imperf.

'To be doing.'

Pos.—गर्दै हुनु gardai hunnu.
Neg.—गर्दैन „ gardaina „
Pass.—garindai, garindaina hunnu
So—jāndai, etc. (p. 106). hunnu.

Pres. Perf.

'To have done.'

Pos.—गर्येको हुनु garyeko hunnu.
Neg.— „ न „ „ na „
Pass.—gariyeko, gariyeko na hunnu
So—jānyeko, etc (p. 105), hunnu.

Pres. Perf. Continuous.

'To have been doing.'

Pos.—गर्ने भयेको हुनु garne bhayeko hunnu.
Neg.— „ „ न „ „ „ na „
Pass.—garinne..
Alternative: gardai rahyeko hunnu.
So—jānne, etc. (p. 102), bhayeko hunnu.

Future.

'To be about to do.'

Pos.— गर्नु आंट्नु garnu āntnu.
Neg.— „ न „ „ na „
Pass.—garinnu āntnu, na āntnu.
So—jānnu, etc. (p. 59), āntnu.

FUT. PERF.

'To have been about to do.'

Pos.— गर्नु थाल्येको हुनु	garnu	āṉṭyeko huṉnu.	
Neg.— ,, ,, न ,,	,,	,, na ,,	
Pass.—gariṉnu	āṉṭyeko huṉnu, na huṉnu.		
So—jānnu, etc. (p. 59),	,,	,, ,,	,,

VERBAL ADJECTIVE गर्ने garne, 'a doer.'

PARTICIPLES.

IMPERF.

'Doing, by doing, while doing, in doing,' etc.

Pos.—1.	गर्दो	gardo	Neg.—na	gardo.
2.	गर्दा	gardā	,,	gardā.
3.	गर्दाहुंनि	gardāhuṉni	,,	,, huṉni.
4.	गर्दाखेरि	gardākheri	,,	,, kheri.
5.	गर्दै गर्दाखेरि	gardai gardākheri	gardaina	,, ,,
6.	गर्दामां	gardāmāṉ		na gardāmāṉ.

The slight distinctions in the meanings of these six forms may be indicated thus:— (1) is used mostly of place; (2) of manner or circumstance; (3) and (4) of time; (5) really means 'in the very act of'; and (6) gives the actual time.

Pass.—gariṉdo, gariṉdā, gariṉdāhuṉni, gariṉdākheri, garīndai, gardākheri, gariṉdāmāṉ.

So—jāndo .... jāndai gardākheri..
garāuṉdo .... garāuṉdai ,,
huṉdo .... huṉdai ,,
dhuṉdo .... dhuṉdai ,,
diṉdo .... diṉdai ,,
jāṉdo .... jāṉdai ,,
laijāṉdo or lāṉdo .. laijāṉdai ,,

Pass.—jāniṉdo, garāiṉdo, dhuiṉdo, diiṉdo, lagiṉdo, etc.

huṉdo and jāṉdo are practically the only two of the above No. 1 forms that are used, except of course to form the Past Indef. and Imperf. Subjunctive (p. 105), for which purpose they are all used. jāṉdo is used principally in dating; julāy 5 din jāṉdo, 'on the 5th July.' maṉrdo, 'dying,' jiuṉdo, 'living,' āuṉdo, 'coming,' are other familiar examples, used mostly purely as adjectives.

See EXERCISE viii. 24 ; and all the notes, pp. 92, 93.

PERF.

'Having done'; 'Doing.'

1. गर्दै गर्‍येको *gardai garyeko* Neg.—गर्दैन गर्‍येको *gardaina garyeko.*
Pass.—*garīndai* ,, ,, *garīndaina* ,,
2. गर्‍येको *garyeko* ,, न गर्‍येको *na garyeko.*
Pass.—*garīyeko* ,, *garīyeko.*
So—1. *jāndai*, etc. (p. 106), *garyeko.*
2. *jānyeko*, etc. (p. 105).

1 is almost a Past Imperfect ; and 2 an actual Perfect.

CONJUNCTIVE.

'Doing'; 'Having done.'

1. गरि or गरिकन *gari* or *garikana.*
Neg.— न ,, ,, न ,, *na* ,, ,, *na* ,,
Pass.—*garīi* ,, *garīikana* ,, *garīi* ,, ,, *garīikana.*
2. गर्‍येर *garyera.*
Neg.— न ,, *na* ,,

1 is usually used of concurrent action ; and 2 of preliminary action.

Pass.—*garīyera* *na garīyera.*
[K.: no Pass.]

gari corresponds to *bhai* of *hunnu*. *āunnu, jānnu, laijānnu* are practically the only verbs which have parts corresponding to *hoi* (p. 94), namely, *āi, jāi, laijāi*

So—*jāni, jānikana, jānyera.*
garāi, garāikana, garāyera.
hoi, hoikana, bhai, bhaikana, bhayera.
dhoi, dhoikana, dhoyera.
dii, diikana, diyera.
jāi, jāikana, gai, gaikana, gayera.
laijāi, laijāikana, lagi, lagikana, laggera (Pass. *lagīi, lagīikana, lagīyera*).

VII. EXERCISE.

Translate—

1. I am a knower ; thou art not causing to be done.
2. He has been washed ; we have been doing (2 ways).

3. You were not giving ; they had not been taken away.
4. She had been going (2 ways) ; thou (fem.) didst not.
5. He will know ; he will go ; he can know ; he can go.
6. We shall not be causing to be done ; you will have been.
7. They will have been washed ; he will give (conting.).
8. Thou will not go (conting.) ; he will be taken away (conting.).
9. Ye will not be known (conting.) ; if we go [(1) pres., (2) fut.]
10 We shall not have been taken away (conting.).
11. If thou didst not know ; if thou do not know (fut.).
12. If thou hast been washing (2 ways) ; if he were to go.
13. If he went ; did he go ; did he go ? if he had gone (2 ways).
14. If she had been doing ; if thou gavest ; if she is doing.
15. If we shall wash ; if they (fem.) will not go (conting.).
16. If you should have been taking away.
17. Thou wouldst give (conditional) ; thou wouldst give (desiderat.).
18. Know thou (honorif.) ; let him know (imperat.) ; let him know (permiss.)
19. That we may give ; that it may be given.
20. Let them be taken away ; be thou known ; come out (sing.).
21. That they (fem.) may have taken away.
22. Thou shalt not have given (imperat.) ; to be washed.
23. To be about to be taken away ; going (modal).
24. Having gone (prelim.) ; not having washed (concurr.).
25. He must go ; he might go ; he ought to go.

Translate—

1. *janāuṉchhas ; huṉṉu lāuṉaa chhan ; diṉṉe garāī.*
2. *lagi diis ; dhoi sakyo : dhuṉṉu sakdaina.*
3. *garāuṉṉe garchha ; jāṉdai garyeko huṉdo hos.*
4. *diṉṉu khojne chha ; huṉne ichchhe na gara.*
5. *lāṉṉe man garyo holā ; laijāṉṉu lāglā.*
6. *lāṉṉu thālyo ta ; dhuṉṉu āṉtyo bhanye.*
7. *dhuṉṉu lāgnu de ; jāṉṉu pāṉṉu huṉdaina.*
8. *jāṉdai rahaṉṉu hawas ; gai rahyo ta.*
9. *diṉdai rahyeko bhaye dekhi tā huṉthyo.*
10. *gardai āis ; jānnu tā jānin ; jāṉṉu sakoina.*
11. *jāniṉṉe man garaulī ; garāiṉṉu āṉtyeṉ*
12. *diṉṉu lāyeko chha holā ho ; jāṉṉu khojdāmāṉ.*
13. *parbat huṉdo gayo ; gāṉu hoi niskyo.*

14. *jānikana diyo; dhoyera jānnu hawas.*

[But translation is much easier when there is a context.]

THE ADVERB.

is indeclinable, and practically a mere matter of vocabulary.

It is put, as near as possible, before the word it modifies: *aghor algo,* 'very high'; *chhiṭo jā,* 'go quickly.' But there are exceptions.

Any word or clause may be used adverbially by adding the word *gari* 'doing': *prem gari,* 'lovingly'; *rāmro gari,* 'beautifully.' The preposition *saña,* 'with,' is much used in the same way: *prem saña,* 'lovingly'; *kaṭhin saña,* 'hardly,' 'with difficulty.'

The concurrent conjunctive partic. of verbs is often best translated adverbially: *dugurikana,* 'at a run.'

Many adverbs are really adjectives as well: *chhiṭo,* 'quick,' 'quickly'; and those which are not also adjectives already, can always be turned into adjectives, as nouns are, that is, by adding the gen. affix: *aghar,* 'exceedingly'; *aghorko* (*ī, ā*), 'exceeding.' (See next paragraph.)

Emphasis is expressed by (1) doubling the central consonant, (2) *ai* or *nai,* (3) repeating the word, (4) other means: *aghor,*—*agghor, aghorai, agghorai, aghor aghor, agghor agghor*; *chhiṭo,*—*chhiṭṭo, chhiṭai, chhiṭṭai, chhiṭo chhiṭo chhiṭṭai chhiṭṭai*; *aba,* 'now,'—*abba, abanai, abbai*; *duguri,*—*dugurikanai, duguri duguri*; *prem gari,*—*premai gari, prem garikanai*; *na,* 'not,'—*nanai, nāhīn*; *tyahān,* 'there,'—*tihīn.*

Adverbs admit of comparison as adjectives do: . . *bhandā chhiṭo,* 'more quickly than . .'; . . *-mān chhiṭo,* 'most quickly of' . . 'Go more quickly' is *besi* (or *aru*) *chhiṭo jā,* or simply *chhiṭo jā.*

Adverbs are simple, merely modifying the words they go with: *aile,* 'now'; or conjunctive, also connecting one sentence or clause with another: *aba,* 'now.' The following are the only ones that call for any remark. For others see the VOCABULARY in the APPENDIX.

—*kaile,* when? ; *kaile kaile,* 'sometimes'; *kaile pani,* 'ever'—

kaile āyo, 'when did he come?'; *kaile kaile āyo* 'he sometimes came'; *kaile pani* (or *kailei*) *āyo,* 'did he ever come?'; *kaile pani āyena,* 'he never came.' 'When' is *jaba*: *jaba āyo taba gayen,* 'when he came then I went.'

—*jahān samma..ta tyahān samma*, '**inasmuch as**'—

jahān samma (or *jasogari*) *tyeslāi diyau ta tyahān samma* (or *ta yes ansār gari*) *manlāi diyau*, 'inasmuch as you gave (it) to him, you gave it to me.'

ajha, '**further**'

dherai log yahān samma gari bhelā bhaye ān duwārko chheumān pani ajha aṭāyenan, 'many people assembled, insomuch that, yea, round the door even, they no further (or longer) got in,'; *ajhai pani ṭhānu chha*, 'even still (further) there is room.'

jhan, '**the more**'

jati tinale tyeslāi hakārye tati tyo jhan sāro karāyo, 'the more they rebuked him, the more he cried aloud'; *ta tyesle kyei hunnu na sakyeko tara jhan khailābailā uṭhdai garyeko dekhyera hundaina holā bhanyera bhanyo*, 'so he, when he saw that it availed nothing, but that the tumult was the more rising, said, I am afraid it won't do'; *jahān pāp besi baniyo tyahān anugrah jhan besi gari parasasta bhayo*, 'where sin multiplied, there grace the more increasingly abounded'; *ta jhan kati jyāsti gari*, 'then how much the more greatly..?'

koni, '**who knows?**'; *katai*, '**someway**'

tara buddhimānharule uttar dii bhanin koni hānmi ra timiharuko lāgi pugoina baru bechneharukān gayera āphnu lāgi kini lyāwa bhani, 'but the wise (women) said in answer, Peradventure (who knows?) it will not suffice for us and you; rather go to the sellers and buy and fetch for yourselves'; *koni katai uslāi chhāmyera bheṭāunan*, 'haply (who knows?) they will someway grope after and find Him.' *katai* is often used in interrogative clauses as a mark of tone, expressing an intimation of the reality of the matter respecting which the question is asked, or the contrary; *kye katai khrisht yei ho*, 'can this be the Christ?' *kahīn* '**anywhere**,' is used in much the same way as *katai*, *kahīn* is the emphatic form of *kahān*, '**where?**'

khāli..māntrai, '**only**'

khāli man māntrai āyen, 'only I came'; *man khāli āyen māntrai*, 'I came only.' Either the *khāli* or the *māntrai* may be unexpressed: *khāli man*, or *man māntrai āyen*, 'only I came.'

tā, 'indeed'; ta, 'then,' 'therefore,' 'so'

tā follows its word or clause, and is frequently untranslatable, except by emphasis; *krodh gara tai pāp tā na gara*, 'be angry, yet do not *sin*.' It is a DISTINGUISHING adverb, and often best translated 'however.'

ta regularly precedes its clause: *manlāi ḍākyo ta gayen*, 'he called to me, so I went'; *āwa ta dekhchhau*, 'come, and you will see.' See also p. 81. It is sometimes extended to *ta taba tā*, 'so then,' 'it follows that.'

yeso, 'in this way'; tyeso, 'in that way'; tyahān, 'there'

are also written *yaso, taso, tahān*. The emphatic of *tyahān* is *tihīn*.

po, 'indeed'; hoina, 'no'

po follows its word or clause, and is almost untranslatable, though its general significance is that of 'indeed,' used RESTRICTIVELY: *yo tā kye po hunchha holā*, 'whatever, indeed, is this going to be?'; *yeso hoina tara phūṭphāṭ po*, 'not so, but, indeed, division'; *kye jhan tyesle tyeslāi mainle khāunjyāl piunjyāl samma kammar bāndhyera mero sewā gar ani tanchainle tyespachhi khānchhas piunchhas po bhandaina*, 'will he not rather (*jhan*) say to him, Till I have eaten and drunken, gird thyself and serve me; and as for thee, afterwards, indeed, thou shalt eat and drink?'; *yo tā kāmkājīnai gari usko gharmānnai tara tyo chain putrai gari usko ghar mānthinai po*, 'this one [was so and so] as a *servant in* his house, but that one, as a *son over* his house.' The right use of *po* and *tā*, as of *chhu* and *hun*, can only be learned from practice, not from rules. *hoina*, it will be observed, follows its (expressed or understood) word or clause.

yetā 'hither'; utā, 'thither'; 'yeso,' 'in this direction'; uso, 'in that direction'

These forms are worth noting. Another form of *utā* is *tyetā* or *tatā*: *yetā āu*, 'come hither'; *utā jāu*, 'go thither'; *yetā ra utā ḍula*, 'walk up and down'; *tan uso pulis lain tira jāndai gardā man yeso mānsuṭolā tira lāgyera mānsu kinnu lāgyen*, 'when thou (wast) going in the other direction towards the Police Lines, I set out in this direction towards the Fleshmarket (*lit.*, Flesh Quarter) and set about buying flesh.'

..bhari, 'throughout'

bhari, the conjunct. partic. of *bharnu*, 'to fill,' is a useful word. It is, when viewed as the partic., a separate word, but when viewed as an adverb, joined on to the word it modifies: *tyesle dinbharimān sāt khep tero pāp garyo bhanye dekhi tyeslāi kshamā garyes*, 'if he sin against thee seven times in the day' thou shalt forgive him; *barshabhari*, 'throughout the year'; *hātbhari de*, 'give a handful'; *hāt bhari de*, 'give with a full hand'; *hānmiharule garnu paryebhariko māntrai garyūn*, 'we have only done our duty' [*lit.*: 'the full of what was necessary (*parnu*) for us to do.' After *-ko*, understand *kām*].

jaso; *jhain*, 'as'

jaso precedes, *jhain* follows its word: *jaso usle garyo*, or *usle garyeko jhain*. 'as he did': *jaso lekhīyeko chha*, or *lekhīyeko jhain*, 'as it is written'; *jaso timiharu saña*, or *timiharu saña jhain tyeso hānmiharu saña*, 'as with you, so with us.' *jaso*, *tyeso*, are often written, in full, *jasogari*, *tyesogari*, or *jasori*, *tyesori*.

aile: *aba*, 'now'

aile is a simple, *aba* a conjunctive adverb. *aile*='at the present time,' 'already'; *aba*='this being the case,' 'after this': *aile āunchha*, 'he will come just now'; *aile āija*, 'come now'; *aba āija*, 'now come'; *aba hera*, 'now behold'; *aba yeutā rājā thiyo*; 'now there was a king.' 'already' is often expressed by the compound completive (p. 59): *gari sakyo*, 'he has already done it.'

THE PREPOSITION.

with one exception, follows its word: *mānchhe saña*, 'with the person': *mero pachhi*, 'after me'; *mero aghi*, 'before me.'

The measure of the relation expressed goes between the preposition and the word it governs: *mero alik aghi*, 'a little before me'; *yesko chār din agāri*, 'four days before this.'

The exception above referred to is *binā*, 'without,' which sometimes follows, sometimes precedes its word: *bastra binā*, 'without the garment'; *binā dawalko*, 'without form.' It generally follows when its word is a pronoun; *mero binā*, 'without me,' 'without mine'; but 'without mine' may also be *binā mero*. It always precedes when its word is a participle: *binā garikana*, 'without doing.'

Excepting the case endings, *lāi*, *le*, *ko*, *mān*, which are really prepositions, prepositions are written as a separate word: *man saña*, 'with me'; *mero saña*, 'with mine.' To this rule *kān*, 'in, or to, or at (the place, house, possessions) of,' and *kānto*, 'from (the place, etc.) of,' are only apparent exceptions; for

kā<u>n</u> is short for ***komā<u>n</u>***, and ***kā<u>n</u>to***, for ***komā<u>n</u> bāto*** : ***uskā<u>n</u>***, 'at his place'; ***uskā<u>n</u>to***, 'from his place'; ***merā<u>n</u>***, 'at my place' (p. 73); ***merā<u>n</u>to***, 'from my place.'

mā<u>n</u> is sometimes run into its word: *thāplā<u>n</u>* = *thāplomā<u>n</u>*, 'on the head'; *belā<u>n</u>* = *belāmā<u>n</u>*, 'at the time.' So also *ko*, *kā* ; *galāo* = *galāko* ; *galāā* = *galākā*, 'of the throat.'

The preposition can be used as an adjective, by throwing it into the form of a noun in the genitive; *bastra bināko mānchhe*, 'a garmentless person'; *agārikā dinamā<u>n</u>*, 'in the former days.'

Some prepositions govern the **genitive**; some, the **uninflected accusative** [some, indeed, really the **nom.**].

Some are really **nouns**, in the **ag.** or **loc.** case, and govern the gen.: (*-ko*) *sātomā<u>n</u>* 'instead of'; (*-ko*) *kāranle*, 'by reason of'; some, **verbs**: (*-ko*) *lāgi*, for the sake of': *dekhi*, 'from'; some, **adjectives**: (*-ko*) *yogya*, 'worthy of.'

Some Prepositions that govern the Genitive:

agāri	before	*bātole*	by means of
aghi	in front of	*bāto bāro* (*or bātāro*)	through (*viâ*)
ansārmā<u>n</u>	according to	*binā* (or *bin*)	without
uprānta	besides	*biblyā<u>n</u>to*	the opposite of
ultāulo	the reverse of	*biruddhamā<u>n</u>*	against
kāranmā<u>n</u>	in the cause of	*bishaymā<u>n</u>*	concerning
kāranle	because of	*bichmā<u>n</u>*	between
khātirle	for the purpose of	*bhitra*	inside of
chheumā<u>n</u>	at the side of	*mā<u>n</u>jhamā<u>n</u>*	in the middle of
najik	near	*mukhe<u>n</u>ji*	before the face of
nimitmā<u>n</u>	with a view to	*yogya* (*ā*) योग्य	worthy of
pachhāri	behind	*lāgi*	for the sake of
pachhi	after	*wāri*	on this side of
patti पट्टि	beside	*wārpār*	through and through
patti bāto	forth from	*waripari*	on all sides of
,, *bāro*	,, ,,	*sā<u>n</u>mu*	in presence of
pāri	on the other side of	*sā<u>n</u>munne*	opposite to
pu<u>n</u>ro	about (time)	*sātomā<u>n</u>*	in return for
bāira	outside of	*sathamā<u>n</u>*	in company of
bāto	from the direction of	*thā<u>n</u>umā<u>n</u>*	in place of .

Sometimes the genitive **affix is unexpressed;** *bidhi ansār*, for *bidhiko ansār*, 'according to the rule'; *ghar bhitra*, for *gharko bhitra*, 'inside the house'; *tyes samay punro*, for *tyes samayko punro*, 'about that season.'

Sometimes the case ending of the preposition itself is unexpressed; see *ansār*, for *ansārmān*, in the above paragraph; *mero kāraṇ*, for *mero kāraṇmān*, 'in my cause,' or *mero kāraṇle*, 'because of me'

Some of them (*uprānta, najik, pachhi, bāira, bhitra, biblyānto* बिबल्यांतो), instead of governing of genit. in *-ko* may also govern the accus. with *dekhi*; *ghar dekhi bāira* instead of *gharko bāira*, 'outside the house.' *punro*, with *dekhi*, means '**beyond**': *bābel dekhi punro*, 'beyond Babylon.'

Some of them, when they govern a demonstrative pronoun in the singular, form one word with it: *yeskhātirle*, 'for the purpose of this'; *yeskāraṇle*, 'because of this'; *yeslāgi*, 'for the sake of this'; *tyespachhi*, 'after that.' Others may form one word with the noun they govern; *dharmmānsār*, for *dharmmako ansārmān*, 'according to righteousness'; *bishwāsyogya*, 'trustworthy.'

Some are used with the participle or infinitive of verbs:—

garyeko ansār	according as ...	did
,, *agāri*	before ...	,,
,, *uprānta*	besides	doing
,, *kāraṇle*	because of	,,
,, *pachhi*	after	,,
,, *bāṭole*	through	,,
,, *biruddhamān*	against what ...	did
,, *sāṭomān*	in return for ,, ...	,,
garyekole	by	doing
garyekomān (or *garyemān*)	on	,,
garne khātirle	for the purpose of	,,
,, *nimtimān*	with a view to	,,
,, *yogya*	worthy of	,,
garnāle (or *garnule*)	by	,,
garnuko lāgi	for the sake of	,,
garnu bhandā agāri	before	,,
garnulāi	in order to	,,
binā garyekole	without	,,
,, *garikana*	,,	,,

Some Prepositions that govern the Accusative :—

**tala*	below	*māṉthi bāṭo*	off (from upon)
tira	towards	*māphikko* (*ī*, *ā*)	befitting
thāṉi	to, at (person)	**māstira*	upwards from
dekhi	from, since	**muni*	beneath
,, *ūṉdho*	down below	**muntira*	downwards from
,, *ūmbho*	up above	*rahit*	wanting
,, *bāhik*	besides	*saña*	(along) with
nira	beside	*samet*	including
bāṛo	*viâ*	*samma*	as far (or long) as, till
bittikai	immediately after	*sari*	like
bhayeṭhāṉu	to (the place of)	*sahit*	having
**māṉthi*	on, over, above	*sita*	with, at (person)

Those with an *asterisk may, like *ūṉdho*, etc., take *dekhi* before them, when the relation expressed includes comparison : *postak mej māṉthi chha*, 'the book is upon the table'; *chhoṭā girjā hāṉmro hātā dekhi māṉthi* (or *māstira*) *chha*, 'the Little Church is above our compound'; *kāgat āphālne ṭokarī mej muni chha*, 'the wastepaper basket is beneath the table'; *hāṉmro hātā chhoṭā girjā dekhi muntira* (or *tala*, or *tala tira*) *chha*, 'our compound is below the Little Church.' They are, indeed, really adverbs, but for the *dekhi* : *tyo ūṉdho gaī*, 'she is gone down' (say, to Calcutta) ; *giṉg kahāṉ chha tala chha*, 'where is Ging ? It is down below'; *jalapahar kati māṉthi chha*, 'how far up is Jalapahar ?'; *jhaṉdai ādhā kos māṉthi chha*, 'it is nearly half a kos up'; *baṛā lāṭ sāheb sabai māṉthiko ho*, 'the Governor-General is over all'; *swarga pṛithiwī dekhi ūṉbho chha*, 'heaven is above the earth'; *pṛithiwī swarga dekhi ūṉdho chha*, 'the earth is below heaven.' The above examples also serve to exemplify the distinction in application of the various synonyms.

On the other hand, the *dekhi* is often unexpressed : *yo bāhik*, 'besides this.'

thāṉi is used only with animate objects : *maṉ thāṉi āwa*, 'come to me'; *maṉ thāṉi dekhi gayo*, 'he went from me' (from my place).

'To' a place is *māṉ* : *tarāīmāṉ gayo*, 'he went to the Terai.'

'To' a thing, in this sense, is *bhayeṭhāṉu* : *rukh bhayeṭhāṉu gayo*, 'he went to the tree' (*lit* : to the tree-been place).

dekhi means 'from,' as source. It is, accordingly, also used for 'by,' in relation to the Passive, when the agent is a volitive being: *man dekhi mānriyo*, 'he was killed by me'; but *dhungole mānriyo*, 'he was killed by a stone.' It is also used in comparison (p. 39).

bāṛo is used only after *bāṭo* and *paṭṭi*: *tyo bāṭo bāṛo koī pani jānnu sakdaina thiyo*, 'no one could go by that road'; *yo prabhuko paṭṭi bāṛo bhayo*, 'this was from the Lord.' *bāṭo baṛo* is sometimes contracted to *bāṭāṛo*.

bittikai is used only after the infin. of verbs: *tyo jānnu bittikai*, 'immediately after his going.'

saña is of elastic use, like the English 'with.' It is sometimes written *sañ*, especially with *ek*: *ek sañ hunnu*, 'to come together.' It may be combined with *samet*: *samet u saña*, 'together with him.'

samet usually attracts the case affix of the word it governs to itself: *dhuirolāi āphnā shiksheharu sametlāi* (not *shiksheharulāi samet*) *bolāyo*, 'he called the multitude, including (or as well as) his disciples'; but *tiniharule aruharuko lāgi samet* (not *aruharu sametko lāgi*) *sewā bigārnan*, 'they will spoil the service for others as well' (where *samet* is really an adverb); *kina tyesle bhūmilāi bikāme samet garāunda chha*, 'why doth it render the ground useless as well?'

samma may be said to come under the *samet* rule: *dosrole pani ani tīsro sātai janā sammale tyesai garye*; 'the second also, and the third, unto the seventh, did likewise.' *yahān samma pugyo*, 'he arrived as far as here,' shews its ordinary use.

sāthamān differs from *saña*, in that it is only used with persons, and these generally superiors, *swāmīko sātha āye*, 'they came with the master.'

sita, like *saña*, is of elastic use: *bachan īshwar sita thiyo*, 'the Word was with God'; *man sita sodhyo*, 'he asked me' (or 'at me'); *man sita bolyo*, 'he spoke to (with) me.' In the last two examples, the dative also would be in order: *manlāi sodhyo, bolyo*. So would *saña*: *man saña sodhyo, bolyo*.

Some of the above prepositions, too, may be used with verbs:—

garyeko dekhi	from, or since, doing
,, ,, *bāhik*	besides ,,
,, *samet*	as well as ,,
garunjyāl samma	as long as ,,
garnu bittikai	immediately on ,,
garne māphikko (ī, ā)	befitting ,,

THE CONJUNCTION.

The mastery of this part of Nepāli speech is half the student's battle of the idioms.

Conjunctions may be classified as co-ordinative and subordinative.

Co-ordinative Conjunctions.

connecting co-ordinate sentences, clauses, or words are used much as in English. The following is a list :—

1.	*ani*	and.
2.	*ra*	,,
3.	*..pani*	also, even.
4.	*..pani ani..pani*	both..and..
5.	*tara*	but.
6.	*tarai* (or *tai*) *pani*	nevertheless.
7.	*ki*	or.
8.	*ki tā* (or *ta*)..*ki tā* (or *ta*)	either..or..
9.	*chāhe..chāhe*	,, ,,
10.	*na..(ani) na*	neither..nor.
11.	*ui pani (ajha)*	and that.

Those with the continuation marks before them follow their word : *ani yo*, 'and this'; but *yo pani*, 'also this.'

1, 2. *ani* differs from *ra*, in that the latter is only a sub-conjunction connecting not distinct words, clauses, or sentences, but those of the same regimen, (it almost corresponds to the Latin—*que*) : *ani usle dhuirāharu ra āphnā shiksheharulāi pani bhanyo shāstrī ra pharīsīharu mūsāko baiṭhakmā̱n basyekā chhan ani tiniharule garhu̱n ani boknu kaṭhin bhayekā bojhā bāndhda chhan bhani*, 'and he said also to the multitudes and his disciples, The Scribes and Pharisees sit in Moses' seat, and they bind on burdens heavy and difficult to bear.' 'And' is often best rendered by the conjunctive participle : *āyera dekhyo*, 'he came and saw'; *hoina bhanye tā aha̱nkārle phulīi shaitānko bichārmā̱n parlā*, 'lest he be puffed up and fall into the judgment of Satan.'

4. *logne pani ani uskī swāsnī pani*, 'both the man and his wife'; *āgomā̱n pani ani pānīmā̱n pani*, 'both into the fire and into the water.' *duwai*, 'the two,' 'both,' also is used : *logne rā uskī swāsnī duwai ; āgo ra pānī duwaimā̱n.*

6. *tarai pani* (or *tai pani*, or *tai*) *pāyenan*, 'nevertheless they found not.'

7. *ki* is used as in English. It is often elliptical at the end of a clause or sentence: *herūn̲ āun̲chha ki*, 'let us see (whether) he will come or (not).' *hoina bhanye tā*, 'or then,' may be substituted for *ki*: *logne ki* (or *hoina bhanye tā*) *uskī swāsnī*, 'the man or his wife'

8. *ki tā* is emphatic: *ki tā dosh lagāun̲dai ki tā uttar din̲dai*, 'either accusing or else excusing.' *ki ta* is argumentative: *ki ta agambhanāī ki ta sikāī*, 'either prophesying or then teaching.'

9. *chāhe* has the special sense of 'choosing'; *chāhe rukhlāi jāti tulyāwa chāhe rukhlāi kharāb tulyāwa*, 'either make the tree good or make the tree bad'

10. *na jāti na* (or *ani na*) *kharāb*, 'neither good nor bad'; *na āyo ani na pachhtāyo*, 'he neither came nor repented.'

11. *Lit.*, 'that also, moreover': *an̲ tara timiharuchain̲le annye ra thagein̲ garda chhau ui pani* (or *ui pani ajha*) *bhāiharu sita po*, 'yea but, as for you, you do wrong and defraud, and that the brethren.'

SUBORDINATIVE CONJUNCTIONS.

1.	*ra..*	in order that.
2.	*...bhani*	
3.	*...bhanyera*	
4.	*...bhannye khātirle*	
5.	*...bhani*	that.
6.	*...bhanyera*	
7.	*...bhanye*	
8.	*...bhanyeko*	
9.	*...bhannye*	
9a	*...bhanye*	as for.
9b	*yeso* (or *uso*) *bhaye tā*	then.
10.	*...bhanye dekhi*	if.
11.	*...bhaye* ,,	
12.	*...yeso bhaye tā*	
13.	*...bhani*	if so be that..may, etc.
14.	*...pani*	though, although.
15.	*...bhanye dekhi pani*	
16.	*..ra pani*	
17.	*kinabhanye*	because, for.
18.	*kasogarībhanye*	
19.	*...bhanyera* or *bhani*	

20.	*na bhaye tā*	lest, otherwise.
21.	*hoina bhanye tā*	
22.	*natra (tā)*	
23.	*na...bhani*	
24.	*ra na*	
25.	*ta...na*	
26.	*...bhani*	
27.	*jaba...ta*	since, seeing that.
28.	*...bhanye jhaiṉ gari*	as if, as though.
29.	*...jhaiṉ gari*	
30.	*cye*	whether.
31.	*kye...kye*	whether,...or...
32.	*...bhaye pani..bhaye pani*	
33.	*... -na bhanye dekhi*	unless, except.
34.	*...na bhaye dekhi tā*	
35.	*yeso ho bhanye dekhi tā*	wherefore.
36.	*yeso bhayekole tā*	so that.
37.	*yahāṉ samma gari*	insomuch that.

'In order that'; 'That.'

1. *ra* (*lit.*, 'and') precedes its clause and generally puts its verb in the Imperat.: *āphu saña ek ki dui janā aru le ra dui ki tīn sākshīharukā mukha dekhi sabai kuro ṭhaharāios*, 'take with thee one or two others, in order that every word may be determined at the mouths of two or three witnesses'; *maṉ ko huṉ ra rājākāṉ jāuṉ*, 'who am I, that I should go to the king?'; *ra yesori usko mahimā garios*, 'that so he may be glorified.' But it puts its verb in the Indic., when it is so in the English, though then its meaning is more the literal 'and': *mānchhe kyā ho ra tyesko samjhanā garnu huṉda chha*, 'what is man, that thou art mindful of him?'; *taiṉle jatan saña oshati khāṉne garis bhanye dekhi āuṉdo sātā sammamāṉ taṉ niko bhayeko holās ra taiṉle pheri kāmmāṉ jāṉnu pāulās*, 'if thou diligently take medicine, thou wilt, by the coming week, have become well, that thou mayest manage to go to work again.'

2. *bhani* (*lit.*, 'saying') follows its clause and puts its verb in the Imperat., generally in the 1st or 2nd pers., changing, that is, indirect to direct speech, as so commonly in Nepālī; *tinale āpastamāṉ sallāh garye uslāi ghāt garāuṉ bhani*, 'they took counsel among themselves that they might (*lit.*, 'saying, let us') put him to death'; *tyesle tinalāi hakāryo chup rahun* (or *raha*)

bhani, 'he rebuked them, that they should hold their peace.' The principal predicate may also go at the end of the sentence, after *bhani*: ..*uslāi ghāt garāūn bhani sallāh garye*; ..*chup rahun* (or *raha*) *bhani hakāryo*.

3. *bhanyera* (*lit.*, 'having said') follows its clause and generally puts its verb in the **Imperat.**, indirect form, in the 3rd pers., that is: *usle tinalāi chetāyo tinale khrisht yei ho bhani* (No. 5) *kasailāi na bhanun bhanyera*, 'he charged them that they should tell no one that (No. 5) this was the Christ.' But it may also put its verb in the **Infinit.**: *usle*..*na bhannu bhanyera*. And the principal predicate may go at the end: *usle*.. *kasailāi na bhanun* (or *bhannu*) *bhanyera chetāyo*.

The **difference** between *bhani* and *bhanyera*, here and elsewhere (Nos. 5, 6, 19, 26), is that between the concurrent and preliminary conjunctive participles (p. 95). The fact expressed by *bhani* is concurrent with that expressed by the principal verb; that by *bhanyera* at least begins before that by the principal verb. The distinction is, however, much disregarded.

4. *bhannye khātirle* (*lit.*, 'for the purpose that') follows its clause and puts its verb in the **Imperat.**: *u āyo jyotiko bishaymān sākshī dewas bhannye khātirle*, 'he came that he might bear witness concerning the light'; *u timiharuko kāranmān kangāli banīyo timiharu dhanī banīyau bhannye khātirle*, 'he became poor on your behalf, that you might become rich.' The *-le* may be dropped, and the principal predicate may go at the end: *u jyotiko bishaymān sākshī dewas bhannye khātir āyo*: *u timiharuko kāranmān timiharu dhanī banīyau bhannye khātirle kangāli banīyo*. The *bhannye* may be separated from the *khātirle*: *tara yo sabai yes khātirle bhayo bachan pūro hawas bhannye*, 'but all this came to pass for this purpose, that the word might be fulfilled.'

Instead of the Imperat. or Indic., with the above conjunctions, the **gerundial infinit.** may be used (p. 91): *sabai kuro thaharāīnnuko lāgi*, 'that every word may be determined'; *uslāi ghāt garāunnulāi*, 'that they might put him to death.'

'That.'

5. *bhani* (*lit.*, 'saying') follows its clause, does not affect the mood of its verb, though it may its tense and person by changing indirect to direct speech, and must, as a rule, be expressed in Nepālī, even when only understood in English: *sodhyen yo ko ho bhani*, 'I asked who it was' (*lit.*, 'that who is this?'); *jānda chhu āyo bhani*, 'I know he is come' (or 'came,' or 'has

come,' or 'had come'); *taba usle uttar dii tyeslāi bhanyo tero ichchhe anśār hawas bhani*, 'then he in reply said to her, Be it according to thy wish.' The principal predicate may go at the end: *mainle yo ko ho bhani sodhyen*.

6. *bhanyera* is used exactly like *bhani*, when the fact it connects with the principal verb is not properly concurrent with it, but more or less anterior to it: *lekhīyeko chha mero ghar prārthanāko ghar bhanīnchha bhanyera*, 'it is written, My house shall be called a house of prayer.' But it is often loosely used without regard to this rule, especially with *bhannu* itself as the principal verb, as in the perpetual Darjeeling colloquialism, ..*bhanyera bhanyo*, 'he said that,' instead of the grammatical *bhanyo.. bhani*; for what he said could not well be said before he said it.

The principal verb may of course go at the end: ..*bhanīnchha bhanyera lekhīyeko chha*.

7, 8. *bhanye* and *bhanyeko* (perf. part. of *bhannu*, 'to say') are really the same word, the former being short for the latter, follow their clause, and are used when their clause is regarded not only as something connected with the principal verb, but as its object. The principal verb generally follows them: *jaba tyesle u yahān bāto jāndai chha bhanye* (or *bhanyeko*) *sunyo taba bhanyo, he prabhu man mānthi dayā garnu hawas*, 'when he heard that he was actually passing that way (*lit.*, 'is passing by here'), then he said, 'Lord have mercy on me.' But the principal verb may also go first: *jaba tyesle sunyo*...It is mainly with such principal verbs as *sunnu* and *dekhnu* that these conjunctions are used.

9. *bhannye*, or *bhanne* (*lit.*, 'named,' 'called,' being probably a corruption of *bhaninne*, the adj. form of the infin. pass. of *bhannu*), is used instead of Nos. 5–8, when the word to be connected with the principal verb is a noun or a noun's equivalent: *karāi bhayo niskī āwa bhannye*, 'there arose the cry, Come out'; *usle prachār garyo khrīsht yei ho bhannye*, 'he preached that this was the Christ'; *usko anugrah jānda chhau u kangāli banīyo bhannye*, 'you know his grace, how that he became poor.' What, in these examples, the *bhannye* connects with the principal clause is the nouns *karāi*, *prachār*, *anugrah*. This becomes all the clearer, when, as is quite legitimate, the principal clause

goes at the end: *niski āwa bhannye karāī bhayo; khrīsht yei ho bhannye prachār garyo; u kangāli baniyo bhannye usko anugrah jānda chhau.* The same thing has already been seen in the conjunction *bhannye khātirle, khātir*, 'purpose,' being a noun.

9*a*. *bhanye* (*lit.*, 'if') is used like a preposition: *aba bhanye*, 'as for now'; *bhitra patti bhanye*, 'as for the inside'; *tara ti āphai bhanye*, 'but as for them themselves.'

9*b*. *Lit.*, 'this (or that) being indeed so': *yeso bhaye tā chhorāharu chain chhutyekā rāchhan*. 'then are the sons let off': *uso bhaye tā uslāi kasogari prabhu bhanda chhan*, 'then how do they call him Lord?'

'If.'

10, 11. *bhanye dekhi* and *bhaye dekhi* [see on the Subj. Mood (pp. 81–86]: *man āphnu bishaymān sākshī dinda chhu bhanye dekhi* (or *ta*) *mero sākshī sachchā chhaina*, 'if I testify concerning myself, my testimony is not true'; *tan īshwarko putra hos bhanye dekhi ta bhani de ra yi dhungā roṭī banīun*, 'if thou be the Son of God, command that these stones become bread' [the *bhani* here is not the conjunction, but, with the *de*, the compound intensive (p. 59]; *tyahān milāpko santān rachha bhanye dekhi* (or *ta*) *timiharu ko milāp tyo mānthi thāmīnchha*, 'if a son of peace be there, your peace will rest upon him'; *tara tyesle sunyena bhanye dekhi tīn janā aru le*, 'but if he hear not, take two persons more'; *man āyera tinihurulāi na bolyeko bhaye dekhi tiniharukān pāp hunne thiyena*, 'if I had not come and told them, they would not have had sin.' In the above examples the principal clause stands last; but the order may be reversed, except when the conjunction is *ta*. Further, the *dekhi* may be dropped: *mero sākshī sachchā chhaina man āphnu bishaymān sākshī dinda chhu bhanye*.

12. *yeso bhaye tā*, besides its common use referred to on p.122, and 9b above, is also used exactly in the sense of 'if': *u āyo yeso bhaye tā kyei āshā dekhnu sakdīnna*, 'if he has come, I cannot see any hope.'

'If so be that..may.'

13. *bhani* is of such elastic usage that another of its uses may be particularized here: *tara kheddai jānda chhu katai jyeko lāgi khrīsht dekhi samāti līnyen tyo samāti liunlā bhani*, 'but I press on, if so be that I may apprehend that for which I was apprehended by Christ.' It puts its verb in the conting. fut. [On *katai*, see p. 114. *samāti linnu* is a compound intensive (p. 60)].

'Though'; 'Although.'

14. *pani* (*lit.*, 'even') follows its clause and puts its verb in whichever of the participles best expresses the connection: *adhikārī sabai thokko dhanī bhai pani dās bhandā beglai chhaina*, 'the heir, though owner of everything, is not different from a slave'; *dhanī bhayera pani kaṅgāli bhanīyo*, 'though he was rich, he became poor'; *sharīrmāṉi hiṉṛdai pani sharīr ansār tā kām gardauṉna*, 'though we walk in the flesh, we do not work according to the flesh'; *timiharukā das hajār janā gurugoṭhāle bhaye pani dherai janā bābu tā chhainan*, 'though ye should have 10,000 tutors, ye have not many fathers'; *katai merai bishwās na garye pani ti kāmaiko bishwās gara*, 'though ye should not believe me, believe those works'; *kinabhanye* (No. 17) *maiṉle tyes patrale timiharulāi shokit pāryeko bhaye pani pachhtāuṉda thiyeṉ bhanye pani* (No. 15) *aba tā puchhtāuṉdīṉna, kasogaribhanye* (No. 18) *dekhda chhu tyes patrale khāli alik ber samma māṉtrai bhaye pani timiharulāi shokit pāryo bhani* (No. 5), 'because though I should have made you sorry by that epistle, I do not now regret it, though I did not regret it; for I see that that epistle did make you sorry, though only for a short time'; *sharīrmāṉ gayel bhaye pani ātmāmāṉ tā timiharu sañai chhu*, 'though absent in the body, I am with you in the spirit'; *bāire mānchhe bigraṉdai jāṉne bhaye pani bhitre chaiṉ tā nayā garāiṉdai jāṉda chha*, 'though the outward man is decaying, the inward one is being renewed'; *maṉchaiṉle tā sharīr māṉthi pani bharosā rākhye pani huṉthyo*, 'though I, indeed, might well have confidence even in the flesh'; *tara byāhā garyei* (emphatic) *pani pāp tā garinas*, but even though thou marry, thou hast not sinned.' The perf. part., then, it appears, is used, in hypothetical connections; the conjunct. or imperf., in actual. In the following: *usle maṉlāi bishwāsyogya ganyo aṉ maṉ pahile nindak ra sdtāuṉne ra upadre bhayekolāi pani*, 'he accounted me faithful, though I was before a blasphemer and a persecutor and injurious,' we see how the 'though' sense may be got from *pani* in its literal meaning, 'even,' and how its conjunctive meaning came about.

15. *bhanye dekhi pani* is just *bhanye dekhi*, 'if,' with *pani*, 'even,' added, and is used exactly like it: *tapāṉi saña maṉrnu paryo bhanye dekhi pani tapāṉilāi aswīkār gardiṉna* 'though I should have to die with Thee, I will not deny Thee.' The *dekhi* is often unexpressed.

'Though' is sometimes translated directly by *tarai pani*, 'nevertheless': *tarai pani u āphaile hoina tara uskā shikshe-*

harule mā̱ntrai baptismā garda thiye, 'though, not he himself, but only his disciples were baptizing.'

16. *ra pani* (*lit.*, 'and even') follows its clause : *kye kye bhanda chhan bhani chāl na pāu̱ndai ra pani*, 'though not knowing what they say'; *ma̱n kyei huinna ra pani ti dekhi ghaṭi chhuinna*, 'though I am nothing, I come not short of them'; *u samundra dekhi bā̱nchyeko thiyo ra pani niyā garnele uslāi jīi rahannu diyena*, 'though he had escaped the sea, the Justice did not allow him to live'; *bhār hunnu sakda thiyū̱n ra pani*, 'though we might have been a burden.'

'Because'; 'For.'

17. *kinabhanye* (*lit.*, 'if you say, Why?') precedes its clause and states the reason why: *kinabhanye manko tiyārī sā̱nmel chha ta tyo sugrahanyogya hu̱nda chha*, 'because if the willingness is present, it is acceptable'; *u bhāgyo kinabhanye ḍarāyo*, 'he fled, because he feared.' This last example may also stand: *u bhāgyo kina bhāgyo bhanye ḍarāyo*, or *u bhāgyo kina bhāgyo ḍarāyo*.

18. *kasogaribhanye* (*lit.*, 'if you say, How?') is used like the above, but states the explanation how: *tinamā̱n pā̱nchwāṭī mūrkha thiin kasogaribhanye tel liinan*, '5 of them (fem.) were foolish, for they did not take oil.' It may be shortened to *kasoribhanye*.

Sometimes No. 18 is used when No. 17 seems called for. It is then to be understood as meaning, 'How is it that you say such a thing?'

19. *bhanyera and bhani*, 'that' (Nos. 6, 5), have sometimes the sense, 'because,' 'because that': *tiniharule uslāi usle bishrāmko dinmā̱n yo garyo bhanyera satāye*, 'they persecuted him, because he had done this on the Sabbath'; *tinalāi bhāi hun bhani tuchchh na ṭhāna*, 'despise them not because they are brethren' (*lit.*, 'saying, They are brothers').

Instead of the above constructions with the conjunctions, the ag. case of the infinit. or the perf. part. may be used: *mai̱nle tyo birsyekole gari̱nna*, 'I did not do it, because I forgot.'

'Lest'; 'Otherwise' (or 'else').

20. *na bhaye tā* (*lit.*, 'if . . have not taken place,' 'failing . . ') precedes its clause and puts its verb in the fut. indef., for 'otherwise,' and in the fut. conting., for 'lest': *tyo ma̱nlāi deu na bhaye*

tā manrchhu, 'give it to me, otherwise I shall die'; *tyo manlāi deu na bhaye tā manrunlā*, 'give it to me, lest I die.'

21. *hoina bhanye tā* (*lit.*, 'if not') precedes its clause and is used exactly like No. 20: ***chārmān hoina hoina bhanye tā khailā-bailā hunchha*** (or ***holā***), 'not during the Feast, otherwise there will be (or lest there be) a tumult.'

22. *natra* (*tā*): *dām pathāunnu parchha natra āunne chhaina*, 'you must send (its) price, otherwise (it) won't come.'

23. *na..bhani* (*lit.*, 'in order that (No. 2) not') goes at the end of its clause, with its verb, in the Imperat., between its two parts, and is best translated 'lest,' not 'otherwise': ***chankha basa kasaile timiharulāi*** (or, in direct speech, ***hānmiharulāi***) ***na bharmāwas bhani***, 'take heed, lest some one mislead you.' [In this particular example, the direct form is ambiguous: it is not clear that the warner is not included with the warned.]

24. *ra...na* (*lit.*, 'in order that (No. 1) not') precedes its clause and puts its verb in the Imperat., with the predicate extension, if there be one, between the *ra* and *na*: *jāgi basa ani prārthanā gara ra parikshāmān na para*, 'watch and pray, lest ye fall into temptation.'

25. *ta..na* (*lit.*, 'then not') is used like No. 24, except that it puts its verb in the fut. conting.: ***man āphuko kyei pani linna ta mainle tyeslāi dhanī garāyen bhani*** (No. 5) ***na bhannu holā*** (honorif. for ***bhanoinas***), 'I won't take aught of thine, lest thou shouldst say thou mad'st me rich' [notice the direct, 'I made him rich'].

26. *bhani* (No. 5) has also the sense of 'lest,' putting its verb in the fut. conting.: ***yeso ho bhanye dekhi tā*** (No. 35) ***man ubhīi rahyeko chhu bhani*** (No. 5) ***thānne larunlā bhani*** (No. 26) ***chankha rahos***, 'wherefore let him that thinketh he standeth' (*lit.*, 'the that I stand thinker') 'take heed lest he (*lit.*, 'I') fall.'

Instead of these conjunctions, the neg. gerundial infin. may be used: ***tara hānmiharule tinalāi thokar na khuwāunnuko lāgi***, 'but lest we cause them to stumble.'

'Since'; 'Seeing that'

27. *jaba..ta* (*lit.*, 'when, or whereas,..therefore') puts its clause between: ***kasogaribhanye*** (No. 18) ***jaba sansārle īshwarlāi chinyena ta īshwar prachārko bātole bachāunnulāi khushi bhayo,***

'seeing that the world did not know God, it pleased God to save through the preaching.' The *ta* is sometimes omitted.

Instead, *ta yeskāraṇ*, 'therefore, for this reason,' may be used: *sansārle īshwarlāi chinyena ta yeskāraṇ īshwar*....

'As if'; 'As though.'

28. *bhanye* (*bhanyeko*) *jhain gari* (*lit.*, 'as if said' follows its clause and does not affect its verb, save that it may of course put it directly, for indirectly: *ta aba āphuharule mahāsabhā sametle sahasrapatilāi āphnu ichchhe janāi dinnu hawas tyesle tyeslāi āphuharuko sānmu utāri lyāi dewas bhannye* (No. 9) *tyesko bishaykā kurā aru ṭhīk gari bichāri thāhā pāunnu khojda chhaun bhanye jhain gari*,' therefore, now, do you, including the Supreme Council, make known to the chief captain your wish that he bring him down before you, as if you sought (*lit.*, 'we seek') to investigate his case more exactly.' The *gari* may be omitted: *usle hānmro bāṭole timiharu sita binti garthyo bhanye jhain*, 'as though he were beseeching you through us.'

29. *jhain gari* (*lit.*, 'doing like as') follows its clause in the imperf. or perf. part. or in the adj. infin.: *mānchheharulāī khush pārdai jhain gari hoina tara īshwarlāi*, 'not as pleasing men, but God'; *ani tiniharu jāndai garyeko tyes gānuko najik āye ani usle aru ṭāṛo jānnu khojyeko jhain garyo*, 'and they came near that village they were going to, and he made as if he wished to go further'; *jye thok chhandai chhainan tinalāi ti bhaye jhain* (*gari* omitted) *bolāunda chha*, 'he calleth the things that are not, as though they were'; *ani na mānchhehāt dekhi sewā linda chha kyei thokko ghaṭī bhaye jhain*, 'nor does he accept service from men's hands as though he had lack of anything'; *sansārkā mūlshikshā dekhi para gari manryau ta kina sansārmān jīi rahanneharu jhain gari bidhi bidhi muni pari rahanda chhau.* 'if you have died to the rudiments of the world, why do you, as though you were living (*lit.*, 'doing as livers') in the world, continue in subjection to ordinances?'

jhain, the conj., is to be distinguished from *jhain* the adv. (p. 116): *lekhīyeko jhain*, 'like what is written.'

'Whether.'

30. *kye* (*lit.*, 'what?') is in this sense merely a sign of indirect interrogation, and is used exactly as in English: *thāhā*

pāuṉchhau kye tyo īshwar dekhi ho rachha bhani, 'you will know whether it be (*lit.*, 'is it ?') from God.'

'Whether..or..'

31. *kye..kye..* (*lit.*, 'whether..whether') is used like the English: *thāhā pāuṉchhau kye tyo īshwar dekhi ho rachha ki kye* (the *ki* is immaterial) *maṉ āphnu paṭṭi bāṭo bolda rāṉchhu bhani*, 'you will know whether it be of God, or whether I be speaking from myself'; *kye jāgūṉ kye sutūṉ*, 'whether we sleep or wake'; *kye logne kye āimāi*, 'whether man or woman' [where it may also be translated 'both..and..'].

Instead,..*ta..ta*, 'if, if,' may be used: *tara kashṭit garāiṉda chhauṉ ta yo timiharuko shānti ra muktiko lāgi ho shānta garāiṉda chhauṉ ta yo timiharuko shāntiko lāgi ho*, 'but whether we be afflicted, it is for your comfort and salvation, or comforted, it is for your comfort'; or, *ki* 'or,' between two imperatives: *timiharu dekhi hawas ki aruharu dekhi hawas*, 'whether it be from you or from others'; *āyera timiharulāi heruṉ ki gayel houṉ*, 'whether I come and see you or be absent.' The *ki* even may be omitted: *sharīr hawas ātmā hawas*, 'whether flesh or spirit'; *bhanos na bhanos*, 'whether he say or not.'

32. ..*bhaye pani..bhaye pani* (*lit.*, 'though..though..') (No. 14) follows the clauses: *maṉ īshwar tira prārthanā garne thiyeṉ thoraile bhaye pani dheraile bhaye pani āphu māṉtrai hoina tara āju mero sunneharu sabai pani maṉ jastai houn bhannye* (No. 9) *khāli yi bandhan chhāṛi*, 'I would to God that, whether with little or with much, not thou only, but also all that hear me this day might become such as I am, excepting only these bonds' [after *mero* understand *kuro*]; *mānchhe bhaye pani pashu bhaye pani*, 'whether man or beast' (or 'both man and beast'). *bhaye* is often shortened to *bhay*.

'Unless'; 'Except.'

33. *-na bhanye dekhi* (*lit.*, 'if not') is used like No. 10: *bhojan kinyūṉna bhanye dekhi*, 'unless (or except) we should buy food.'

34. *na..bhaye dekhi tā* (*lit.*, 'if not') is used like No. 11: *usle yeuṭā baṉsha chhoṛi na diyeko bhaye dekhi tā*, 'unless he had left a seed (posterity).'

Instead, *binā*, 'without,' (p. 117) may be used: *binā hāṉmiharule bhojan kinikana* (or *kinyekole*), 'except we should buy food.'

Comparison of this last example with its form under No. 33, will remind the student of the rule on p. 98, that the subject of participles and infinitives must be expressly stated, unless it can be gathered from the context.

'Wherefore.'

35. *yeso ho bhanye dekhi tā* (*lit.*, 'if it be indeed so') precedes its clause and is used mostly at the beginning of a sentence which sums up a foregoing argument: *yeso ho bhanye dekhi tā yi bachanale ekāle arkālāi shānta garāwa*, 'Wherefore comfort one another with these words.'

Instead, *yeso* (or *uso*) *bhaye tā* (p. 122), or *jaba yeso chha ta* (No. 27), 'since this is so,' may be used.

'So that.'

36. *yeso bhayekole tā* (*lit.*, 'through its being so') precedes its clause: *tyesle pani maṉlāi shāṉta garāyo yeso bhayekole tā jhan jyāsti ramāyeṉ*, 'he also comforted me, so that I rejoiced the more greatly.' 'So that,' in the sense of 'and,' is made by *ra*: *ko karāyo ra nānī uṭhyo*, 'who shouted, so that the baby got up?'

'Insomuch that.'

37. *yahāṉ samma gari* (*lit.*, 'as far as here') precedes its clause and usually follows and repeats the principal verb: *bhāri bhogyūṉ yahāṉ samma bhogyūṉ jīi rahaṉnu pani kasogari ho bhani syāṉṭṭhai anyolmāṉ paryūṉ*, 'we were burdened, insomuch that we were quite at a loss as to how even to survive.' But it is sometimes possible to avoid the repetition: *dherai log yahāṉ samma bhelā bhaye ṭhāṉu aru thiyena*, 'many people assembled, insomuch that there was no more room.'

THE INTERJECTION

is used just as in English and, with one exception, *are*, needs no explanation. The following is a list:—

e	O! (vocative)	*hat teri*	bother!
ei	,, ,, emphatic	*dhanna*	benediction!
he	,, ,, respectful	*dhikkār*	malediction!
hei	,, ,, ,, emphatic	*khabardār*	take care!
āhā	,, admiration	*hāy*	alas!
yei	oh! (surprise)	*jay*	hurrah!

abi	oh! (surprise)	*chhīchhī*	fie!
abuī	,, ,,	*shābāsh*	bravo!
abis	,, ,,	*chup*	silence!
is	,, ,,	*para*	out of the way!
oh	,, (alarm)	*bagal*	to one side!
uh	,, ,,	*lu*	come!
ukh	,, fatigue	*e bābā*	dreadful!
haṛt	,, (disapproval)	*bābainai*	,,
dhat	,, ,,	*uss*	pshaw!
aiyo	,, (pain)	*bes*	well done!
aiyā	,, ,,	*besai bhayo*	,,
aiyai	,, ,,	*swasti*	hail!
āchchhā	,, ,,	*salām*	salutation!
thū	,, (disgust)	*namaskār*	obeisance!
hera	behold! (plu.)	*āge shubhamm*	farewell!
her	,, (sing.)	*are*	———

are, the last, is an exclamation to draw attention, and untranslatable. It is used after a verb setting forth the statement of another person, to give the statement more vivid directness: *tyeslāi bhani dewa āphnu sewāmā̲n̲ tyo pūro garnuko lāgi chan̲kha basnu hawas are bhani*, 'tell him to take heed to his ministry, to fulfil it'; *kye bhanda chhan man̲ ko hun̲ are bhani*, 'who do they say that I am?'; *tinamā̲n̲ phāṭāphāṭ hun̲da chhan are bhani sunda chhu*, 'I hear that there exist divisions among them.' It appears, then, that *are* draws attention to the statement or injunction of a third party.

shubhamm, 'farewell,' in closing epistles is frequently contracted to शुभम *shubhm*. It is often written *subhamm*.

SYNTAX.

In now adding some rules of syntax, it will be sufficient to indicate such as are different from the English. Some have already been indicated and need not now be repeated: those as to the order of words in a sentence (p. 16), and words in apposition (pp. 17, 25, 29), for instance.

Direct for indirect speech.

One of the most important rules, which also has been already referred to (pp. 88, 124, 125, 129), is that in Nepāli the direct form of speech is largely substituted for the indirect in English.

The general effect is to change the 2nd pers. to the 1st, the 3rd to the 1st or 2nd, past tenses to pres., and the subj. mood to the indic.: *jye garda chhau tyo prāṇai dekhi gara sāṭopharkāi pāuṉchhauṉ bhani jānikana,* 'what you do, do from the heart, knowing that you (*lit.*, 'we') will receive recompense'; *usle bhanyo āuṉchhu bhani*, 'he said he would (*lit.*, 'I shall') come'; *tinale tyo sita sān garye usko nāṉu kye rākhchhau bhannye*, 'they made signs to him, as to what name he would (*lit.*, 'you will') give him'; *īshwarle hāṉmiharuko bāṭole manāuṉda chha bhanye jhaiṉ,* 'as though God were (*lit.*, 'is') persuading through us'; *u āyo..katai tyesmāṉ kyei pāuṉlā ki bhani,* 'he came..if haply he might (*lit.*, 'I may') find something on it'; *jye jye tapāṉiko hāt ra manle hawas bhani agāṛi dekhi ṭhaharāyo ti garnuko lāgi,* 'to do those things, which thy hand and counsel fore-ordained to (*lit.*, 'let it') come to pass.'

Relative and antecedent.

Another important general rule is that a relative word or clause precedes its antecedent, as instanced in the last example above, *jye..ti*; *jo āyo tyo* .., 'he who came..'; except when it, not merely defines the antecedent, but introduces a new fact about it: *taba tyo āuṉchha jaslāi prabhule nasāuṉchha,* 'then he will come whom the Lord will destroy,' where 'whom' really = 'and him.'

The antecedent must, as a rule, be expressed, *jaba tyo āyo taba maiṉle tyeslāi dekhyeṉ* 'I saw him (then) when he came'; *jas jaslāi dewaharule pyāro garda chhan ti juwānaimāṉ manri jāṉda chhan,* 'whom the gods love, die young'; *jo māṉthi bharosā rākhyeṉ tyesle mero āshā māṉri diyena,* 'he on whom I relied did not disappoint me.'

The relative and its renderings.

In the above examples the relative is construed, as in English, with a finite verb, but it may also be with an infinitive (gerund), infinitive adjective, or participle: *kām garnumāṉ* (or *gardā*) *khushi chhu,* 'I am happy when I am working: *annye garnele jye annye garyo tyesko phirtā pāuṉchha,* 'he that doeth wrong shall receive again for the wrong that he hath done'; *maiṉle tyeslāi diyeko ghoṛā,* 'the horse which I gave him.'

The advantage of thus making a subordinate relative clause a mere adjectival enlargement is particularly seen when its verb is passive: *dherai dūyeko junsukai dekhi dherai khoji liṉchha ani dherai jimmā rākhīyeko junsukai dekhi logale jhan besi māngchhan,* 'to whomsoever much is given, of him shall much be required; and to whom much is committed, of him will they ask the more'; *ani dhuiroko kāranle u dekhi najik āunnu na sakyekole tiniharule chhānā ujarye ani yo upkāi sakye pachhi tyes arddhāngī pasrii rahyeko khātlāi surkyāi diye,* 'and when they could not come nigh unto him for the crowd, they uncovered the roof, and when they had broken this up, they let down that bed whereon the (man) sick of the palsy lay.' A somewhat similar instance of condensation is: *khāli aile samma bīch dekhi na uthāinjyāl sammako yeutā thuni rākhne chha,* 'only there is one that till now restraineth, until he be removed out of the way' (*lit.*, 'only there is till now an until-he-be-removed-out-of-the-way restrainer').

An adjective, or its equivalent, qualifying the subject of the enlarged clause follows its verb, when that is a participle: *mainle tyeslāi diyeko thulo ghorā,* 'the big horse which I gave him'; *īshwar mānchhele banāundai garyeko tyo sahar hernulāi utri āyo,* 'God came down to behold that city which man was building'; *kinabhanye he bhāiharu ho āshiyāmān bhayeko hanmiharuko kashtako bishaymān thāhā na pāwa bhannye ichchhe gārdaunne,* 'for, brethren, we would not have you ignorant concerning the affliction which befel us in Asia'; *mainle tyesle garyeko tyesko kām jāti jānyen,* 'I considered his work, which he had done, good'; *tyesle āphule garyeko āphnu kām jāti jānyo,* 'he considered his (own) work, which he had done, good.' But while this is the rule with the participle, it is not, with the relative infinitive adjective: *ani tyes āphnu prabhuko ichchhe jānne ani tiyār na banāunne ani na usko ichchhe ansār garne dāsle dherai pitāī khānchha taro na jānne chot pāunne māphikko kām garnechainle thorai pitāī khānchha,* 'and that servant who knew his Lord's will, and made not ready, nor did according to his will, shall be beaten with many stripes; but the one that knew not, and did things worthy of stripes, shall be beaten with few stripes'. Here the *tyes* precedes the inf. adj., far from its subject, *dāsle*.

Proximity of qualifying to qualified word.

It is a general and natural rule that the qualifying word should be as near what it qualifies as possible. The rule already given as to the adjective following the participle, that it may be near its subject, is one example. The position of th. adverb or conjunction, for instance, furnishes other examples: *khāli usle mā̱ntrai maṉlāi 3 diyo*, 'only he gave me 3'; *usle khāli maṉlāi mā̱ntrai 3 diyo*, 'he gave only me 3'; *usle maṉlāi 3 khāli diyo mā̱ntrai*, 'he only gave me 3'; *usle maṉlāi khāli 3 mā̱ntrai diyo*, 'he gave me only 3'; *usle pani maṉlāi diyo*, 'he also gave me'; *usle maṉlāi pani diyo*, 'he gave me also'; *usle maṉlāi diyo pani*, 'he also gave me.' It is plain that the sense depends altogether on the proximity in question.

Emphatic nominative.

An emph. nom., besides taking the emph. termination (p. 14), may also be placed, not at the beginning of the sentence, but at the end, before the verb (p. 17): *bhakti garnu parne īshwarai ho*, 'it is God that is to be worshipped'; *khrīsht yeshūnai ho*. 'Jesus is the Christ'; *rājā maiṉ huṉ*, 'I am the king.'

No nominative absolute.

The English nom. absol. must, in Nepālī, be CONNECTED in some way with the rest of the sentence: *bhānsā sakkīyemāṉ ghar gayūṉ*, 'dinner over, we went home,' where 'dinner over' is absolute in the Eng., but connected (by *māṉ*) in the Nep.

No preparatory nominative.

The Eng. prep. nom., 'it,' is not required in Nep.: *ḍā̱ṉṛā mā̱ṉthi chaṛhnu sāro kaṭhin chha*, '(it) is very difficult to climb the hill.'

No preparatory adverb.

The Eng. prep. adv., 'there,' is not required in Nep.: '*ghar* chha,' '(there) is a house.'

The preparatory conjunction.

The Eng. prep. conj., 'that,' is generally rendered by *yo*, 'this,' standing, not before, but after its clause: *u ghar gayo* yo *sā̱ṉchai chha*, 'that he is gone home is certain.'

Plurality of nominatives.

Two or more singular nouns, that are subjects connected by 'and,' expressed or understood, require their verb in the plu.; or in the sing., in agreement with the last. When the verb is in the plu., it is put in the plu. masc., if the subjects are of different gender: *logne ra uskī swāsnī āye* (or *āī*), 'the man and his wife have come.' The same rules apply, if one or more of the nominative be plu.

The same rules apply in the case of pronouns. If these be of different person, their verb, if in the plu., agrees with the highest person involved: *mānchhe ra maṉ āyūṉ* (or *āyeṉ*), "the person and I came'; *maṉ ra timi āyūṉ*, 'you and I (p. 17) came'; *timi ra u āyau* (or *āyo*), 'you and he came.'

One or more nominatives, joined to another, or others, by *samet*, 'as well as,' 'including,' or by *saña*, 'with,' do not affect the agreement of the verb: *guru āphnā shikshheharu samet* (or *saña*) *āyo*, 'the guru, as well as (or with) his disciples, came.'

Agent Case.

The subject of an act. trans. verb is, with the exceptions as to the 1st pers. sing. noted at p. 98, put in the ag. case: *rājāle garyo*, 'the king did' The other uses of this case are to translate 'by' and its equivalents: *balle*, 'by force'; *hātale* 'with the hands'; *tinale jāti chaiṉ sipāṉigiri garne gar bhannye khātirle*, 'that through them thou mayest war the good warfare.'

'By,' in relation to a verb in the passive, when the agent is capable of volition, is made by *dekhī* (p. 119): *mānchhe dekhi māṉrīyo*, 'he was killed by the person'; but *ḍhuṉgole māṉrīyo*, 'he was killed by the stone.'

Direct object.

When the dir. obj. of a verb is a noun or pronoun, it is put in the accusative: *mānchhelāi bheṭyūṉ*, 'we met the person'; *maṉlāi dekhyo*, 'he saw me.' That of verbs like *sunnu*, 'to hear,' and *mānnu*, 'to obey,' is sometimes apparently in the genitive, *mānchheko sunyo* 'he heard, or listened to, the person'; *mero mānyo*, 'he obeyed me'; but the accus. *kuro*, 'word,' or *ājñā*, 'command,' is understood.

When it is a verbal noun, it is made by the infin., with the perf. part. of *huṉnu*: *laṛnu huṉdai garyeko dekhyeṉ*, 'I saw the fighting.'

When it is an infin., it is made by the infin.: *laṛnu aru jāti jānda chhu*, 'I prefer to fight'; *bhannu thālyo*, 'he began to speak.'

When it is a noun sentence it is made as such: *u gayo bhanyeko* (p. 125) *sunyeṉ*, 'I heard that he had left.'

When it has a cognate meaning to that of the verb it is made by the locative: *jas jiunnimān aba jiunda chhu*, 'the life which I now live.'

Indirect object.

When the ind. obj. is a noun or pron. it is put in the dative · *mānchhelāi ek rupiyā diyen*, I gave the person a rupee'; *manlāi roti diyo*, 'he gave me bread.'

When it is factitive it is made by the uninflected accus.: *uslāi rājā tulyāye*, 'they made him a king'; *uslāi māli jānye*, they took him for the gardener.'

Compound object.

yeslāi (or *yesle*) *bhandai garyeko sunye*, 'they heard him say'; *tyeslāi jāndai garyeko dekhyo*, 'he saw him going'; *hera man swargaharu ughāriyekā ani mānchheko putralāi īshwarko dāhinno hāt patti ubhii rahyeko herda chhu*, 'behold, I behold the heavens opened, and the Son of Man standing at the right hand of God'; *tinale tyeslāi tyesle yeso bhandai garyekomān lohoryāye he prabhu mero ātmālāi grahan garnu hawas bhani*, 'they stoned him, (he) saying, Lord, receive my spirit'; but this last example is of a comp. obj. only in the Eng., not in the Nep., in which it is turned into a subordinate clause connected by *mān* with the principal clause. In *tinalāi āunne dekhyo*, 'he saw them coming,' *āunne* is really the indirect object: 'he saw them comers.'

It will be observed that in the above examples, where the objective verb is put in the part., the time of the two verbs is concurrent; when they are not concurrent the infin. is used, as in Eng.: *tyeslāi merān lekhnu arhāyen*, 'I ordered him to write me.' When the object. vb. is passive, its clause has to be turned into a subordinate conjunctive: *tyo diios bhani arhāyo*, 'he commanded it to be given.'

Subject and object enlargements.

Eng. enlarge. of subj. or obj. may require to be turned into subordinate relative clauses in Nep., and, if more than one, to be connected by an expressed conjunction: *aba kaisariyāmān karniliyus nānu bhayeko ek janā mānchhe thiyo* jo *itāli bhaninne paltanko yeutā kaptān* ani *bhakta* ra *āphnu sabai jahān samet īshwar dekhi darāunne* ra *logalāi dherai dayādān dinne* ra *īshwar sita barābar binti garne thiyo*, 'now there was a certain man in Cæsarea, Cornelius by name, a centurion of the band called the Italian band, a devout man, and one than feared God with all his house, who gave much alms to the people, and prayed to God alway.' [From the context, distinguish the *ḍarāuṉne, diṉne, garne thiyo* from the conditional mood].

Predicate extension.

gari, the concurr. part. of *garnu*, which may be used adverbially with any word or part of a sentence (*chāhā gariko hisāple*, 'in a voluntary manner,' for example) is especially useful in composing extensions of predicate: *uslāi prabhu gari swīkār garyo*, 'he confessed him as Lord'; *yo napanā gari dekhāyo*, 'he shewed this for an example.' See also p. 113.

The genitive.

is, or is not separated from its object by words qualifying its object, as the sense demands or permits: *pāul yeshūko īshwarko ichchheko bāṭole prerit*, 'Paul, an apostle of Jesus by the will of God,' [understand *bhayeko* after *bāṭole*], where *yeshūko* is separated from *prerit*; but *sharīr ansārkā timiharukā ṭhākurharu*, 'your masters according to the flesh,' not *timiharukā sharīr ansārkā ṭhākurharu*, for then it would not be clear whether *timiharukā* governed *sharīr* or *ṭhākurharu* [*ansārkā* is the adjectival gen. (p. 15, 117)]; *hāṉmiharu saña prem garne hāṉmiharuko pita īshwar*, 'God our Father, who loveth us.'

Gerundial infinitive.

The Eng. ger. inf. is made in Nep. by putting the inf in the dat., or in the gen. with *lāgi* (p. 91): *ṭhaṭṭhā garnulāi* (or *garnuko lāgi*) *āyekā mūrkhaharu prārthanā garnulāi* (or *garnuko lāgi*) *rahi gaye*, 'fools that came to scoff remained to pray.'

Construed with a noun, it is usually rendered by the inf. adj. (p. 91); *bikne ghar* 'a house to sell'; or by its cognate noun, used as an adj.: '*bikriko ghar*'; '*khāṉne roṭī*,' 'bread to eat.'

Construed with an adj., it is usually put in the loc.: *hernumāṉ rāmro*; 'beautiful to behold'; but the case affix may be dropped: *boknu kaṭhin* 'difficult to carry'; *sahaṉnu sañlo*, 'easy to bear' (p. 91).

Infinitive adjective.

The infin. adj. (p. 91), as already seen, is very freely used. Let it now be added that it is used regardless of tense, or rather takes its tense from the context, and that it may govern either the gen. or acc., as it is viewed as a noun or verb: *āphnu bhartī garnelāi khush pāros bhannye khātirle*, 'that he may please him that enrolled him'; *usko* (or *uslāi*) *pakarāi diṉne*, 'his betrayer' (or 'he that betrayed him').

Infinitive passive.

The Eng. inf. pass. is sometimes rendered by the active in Nep. : *bhakti* **garnu** *parne īshwarai ho,* 'it is God that is to be worshipped'; *patyāro* **garne** *māphikko,* 'worthy to be believed.' The explanation is that the verb is used in an absolute sense, apart from its connection with its subject.

Perfect participle passive.

The Eng. perf. part. pass. may often be, alternatively, active in Nep. : *man pāūlko* (p. 29) *āphnu hātle lekhīyeko* (or **lekhyeko**) *salām,* 'the salutation of me Paul, written with mine own hand'; *jaso lekhīyeko* (or **lekhyeko**) *chha,* 'as it is written'; *hānmiharuko lāgi dherai janā dekhi—hānmiharulāi dherai janāko bātole dūyeko* (or **diyeko**) *anugrahdānko lāgi—dhannabād garios bhannye khātirle;* 'in order that—for the gift bestowed upon us by means of many—thanks may be given by many persons on our behalf.' Of course, after an agent with **dekhi**, only the pass. could be used : *man dekhi lekhīyeko* (not *lekhyeko*) *patra,* 'the letter written by me' (pp. 119, 137).

On the perf. part., generally, see p. 94.

Imperfect participle absolute.

The imp. part. may be used in an adverbial or absolute way : *pānī hāldā seto hunne oshati,* 'a medicine that becomes white on the application of water,' where *pānī hāldā* is really an absolute construction, not syntactically connected with the rest of the sentence.

On this part., generally, see p. 93.

Conjunctive participles.

The Eng. conj. part. is sometimes best rendered in Nep. by a subordinate clause introduced by the conjunction *kasoribhanye* 'for' or *kinabhanye,* 'because' (p. 128): *usle manlāi bishwās-yogya ganyo kasoribhanye sewāgarāīmān thaharāi rākhyo,* 'he accounted me worthy, appointing me to his service.'

On these part., generally, see p. 95.

VIII. EXERCISE.

This concluding exercise is so framed as to exhibit some typical Nepalī idioms, under English index headings :—

1. **about to ; on the point of—**

garnu ā<u>n</u>tyo	He is on the point of doing
,, *ā<u>n</u>tyeko thiyo*	,, was about to do

2. **ago ; since—**

tīn din bhayo	Three days ago
uile dekhi	Long ago
kaile ,,	How ,, ,, ? Since when ?
,, ,, *ko*	Of ,, ,, ,,
u itāliyā bāṭo āyeko alik din bhayeko thiyo	It was a few days since he had come from Italy
ta usle āyera tyeslāi chihānmā<u>n</u> rākhyeko aba chār din bhayeko bheṭāyo	So when he came, he found that he had been in the tomb four days already

[-*ko ber*, 'a period of,' is understood after *din*.]

3. **as ; as much as—**

ma<u>n</u> pheri tapā<u>n</u>iko chhoṟo bhanī<u>n</u>ne māphikko chhui<u>n</u>na ma<u>n</u>lāi āphnā ba<u>n</u>ni garneharumā<u>n</u>ko yeuṭā jattiko tulyāu<u>n</u>nu hawas	I am no longer worthy to be called thy son ; make me as (much as) one of thy hired servants
timiharulāi rāyoko geṛā jatro bishwās chha bhanye dekhi yes kimbuko rukhlāi bhanne thiyau ukhelīyera samundramā<u>n</u> ropī bhani ani tyesle timiharuko mānne thiyo	If ye had faith as (much as) a grain of mustard seed, ye would say to this sycamine tree, Be rooted up and be planted in the sea, and it would have obeyed you
kasogaribhanye yi sabaile āphnu ubāromā<u>n</u>ko bheṭiharumā<u>n</u> hālye tara yeschai<u>n</u>le tā āphnu apugdomā<u>n</u>ko āphnu sabai jīwikā jati bhayeko hālī	For all these did of their superfluity cast in unto the gifts : but this (woman) of her want did cast (as much as) all the living that she had
aba tyo ṭhā<u>n</u>u saharko najik kos ek jatimā<u>n</u> thiyo	Now the place was nigh unto the city, about (as much as) a kos off

[*jattiko, jatro, jati bhayeko, jatimā<u>n</u>*, are adjectival enlargements *jatro* expresses size ; the others, quantity.]

4. **any longer**—

pānī khānne aru yeso na ho tara āphnu odroko ra lagātār dukhyeko kāraṇ thoṛai dākhrasko chalan gar — Be no longer a water drinker, but on account of thy stomach and often infirmities use a little wine

pānī khānne aru yeso bhayena — He was not a water drinker any longer

5. **according as any**—

ani tiniharule āphnā dhan sampatti bechikana jaslāi jasto khāncho parthyo sabailāi bānṛi dinthye — And they sold their possessions, and parted them to all, according as any had need

jas jaslāi jasto jasto khāncho parda thiyo tyesto janangelāi bānṛi bānṛi dīnda thiyo — Distribution was made to each, according as any had need [*lit.*, such as (was) to whom]

[The 2nd example extends the more compressed construction of the 1st.]

6. **all; every**—

jo junsukai pani mānchheharuko muktidātā ho sabai bhandā besi gari bishwās garneharuchainko — Who is the Saviour of all men, especially of them that believe

tyesle junsukai pani bhalo kām pachchhyāi rahyekī chha — She has continued to follow every good work

ani yeso hunchha prabhuko nānu linne junsukai pani bachāīnchha — And it shall come to pass that every one that calleth upon the name of the Lord shall be saved

īshwarprerṇā bhayeko junsukai pani dharmmashāstra — Every scripture inspired of God

[*junsukai pani* = lit., 'even whosoever.' See pp. 24, 29, 37.]

7. **become of; no small; as soon as**—

aba jasai din bhayo taba tilangāharumān patrus kye bhayo taba bhannye ghabrāī thorai tā bhayena — Now, as soon as it was day, there was no small stir among the soldiers as to what was become of Peter (*patrus kye bhayo taba*)

8. **Before ; by—**

priya swāmī sāhep chhuṭṭī pūro hunnu 10 *din rahandai āunchhu*	Dear Sir, 10 days before the holidays close I shall come
3 *bāji samma hājir hunnu*	Be present by 3 o'clock

9. **Call ; name ; so-called—**

tinamānko yeuṭāle pani kyei thok āphnai bhani bhandaina thiyo	Not one of them called anything his own
uslāi prabhu bhanchhan	They will call him Lord
uṭhyera sojo bhanīnne gallīmān jā	Arise, and go to the street called Straight
guru guru na bhanīyau	Be not called guru
tyesko nānu rāmlāl rākhye	They named him Ramlal
gangā nānu bhayeko ek janā mālī	A gardener named Ganga
jhūṭho nānu bhayeko jñān	Knowledge so-called

10. **Call ; summon ; send for ; fetch ; call to—**

tyeslāi bolāu, or *bolāi deu*	Call him
,, *ḍāka*, or *ḍāki* ,,	,, to him
postak mangāi paṭhāye	They sent for the book
mālī bolāi ,,	,, ,, ,, ,, gardener
tyeslāi ,, *lyāye*	,, ,, and fetched him
bolāīyekā dherai chhan taru chhānīyekā tā thorai chhan	Many are called but few chosen

11. **Compel—**

tinalāi abasse bhitra āunnu lagā	Compel them to come in

12. **Cause ; at random—**

uslāi jatābhābi bolnu lāunnu lāgye	They began to cause him to speak at random

[See pp. 58, 59.]

13. **Cannot but ; but—**

koī thiyena jo usko lāgi manr-nulāi tiyār hunne thiyena	There was no one but would have died for him
yo kyā ho jhūṭh chhāṛi	What is this but a lie ?
yi na boli sakdai sakdaunna	We cannot but speak these things

[*na boli* is not here part of the compound completive (p. 59), but, unconnected with *sakdai*..., means 'not speaking' = 'without speaking'; the primitive of the compound is not expressed].

14. **Every**—

sāṉjh sāṉjh pardā, or *sāṉjh pardā pardā*	Every evening

15. **Henceforth; thenceforth; since; from**—

aba dekhi yeso maṉlāi dekhne chhauna jaile samma bhanne chhauna dhanna prabhuko nāṉumāṉ āuṉne bhani	Henceforth ye shall not see me, till ye shall say, Blessed is he that cometh in the name of the Lord
taba dekhi uso kaile pani āyena	Thenceforth he never came
tīn barsha dekhi yeso phal khojdai āuṉda chhu	(Since) these 3 years I come seeking fruit
dui pahar dekhi yeso tīsro pahar samma	From the sixth hour until the ninth hour

16. **Howsoever; never so; by any means; means**—

tyo kastai ṭhulo bhayo bhanye pani tyo dekhi ḍarāuṉḍīṉna	However big he be, I do not fear him
jattisukai māṉgyau bhanye pani diṉchhu	Ask you never so much, I will give it
jānda chhau jaba anyadesī thiyau taba jaunai parile lihiṉṛālīye pani ti abolā mūrttiharu tira lagīṉthyau bhani	You know that when you were Gentiles, you were led away towards those dumb idols, however you might be led

[These constructions are really those of 'though' (p. 127).]

kunai (or *koī pani*) *parile*	By any means
" " *patyāuṉdauna*	Ye will in no wise believe
jasle īshwarko rājlāi bālakhale jhaiṉ grahaṉ garoina tyo tyesmāṉ kastai garikana pani pasdoina	Whosoever shall not receive the kingdom of God as a little child, shall by no means enter therein
ani hera aṭhārah barsha dekhi nirbaleīṉko ātmā lāgyekī yeuṭī strī thiī ani tyo kuprī ani āphailāi kastai garikana pani sojyāuṉnu na sakne thiī	And behold, a woman which had a spirit of infirmity 18 years; and she was bowed together, and could in no wise lift herself up

kunai parile pani hoina	Not by any means
sabai tira bāṭo	By all means
kastai (or *kaso*) *garikana*	„ what „ ?
ṭhageīn̲ko bāṭole	„ means of fraud
garne upāy	A „ „ doing
hātaparāīko upāy	„ „ „ gain

17. **If; though—**

mānchheko putra tā usko bishay-mān̲ lekhyeko jhain̲ hin̲ṛi jān̲da chha tara hāy tyo mānchhe mān̲thi jasko bāṭole pakarāi dūn̲da chha jāti hun̲thyo tyes mānchheko lāgi tyesko janmai na bhayeko bhaye dekhi	The Son of man goeth, as it is written of him: but woe unto that man through whom he is betrayed! good were it for that man if he had not been born
hun̲nu sakdo ho	If it were possible
tan̲ aulko jarole pakkā bhayeko bhaye dekhi (or *bhayeko hun̲do hos*) *ta tan̲lāi pheri pheri aulko bethā lāgne thiyena*	If thou hadst been seasoned to malarial fever, thou wouldst not have had the malarial sickness coming again and again
tara pakkā bhayeko bhaye pani (or, colloquial, *bhay pani* or *bhāpani*) *pheri man̲lāi jaro āyeko kāraṇ yo ho najāti thok khāi diyen̲*	But, though I have been seasoned, the reason of the fever coming back to me is, that I ate something bad
hoina hoina tain̲le najāti thok khāyekai bhaye pani tan̲ aule jarole pakkā bhayeko thiis bhanye dekhi (quotation—p. 81) *tan̲lāi jaro na āun̲nu parthyo*	No, no; if thou hadst [as thou sayest] been seasoned to malarial fever, the fever ought not to come to thee, even though thou didst eat a bad thing
an̲ tyo belā sammamān̲ man̲ niko bhayeko bhayen̲ bhanye dekhi tā nisse āphnu kāmmān̲ gai sakyeko hun̲chhu	Yea, I shall certainly have already gone to my work by that time, if I shall have been cured
ani tyesai hun̲nulāi dayāluko dayā bhayo bhanye tā aru	And if there be the mercy of the merciful to admit of this,

arule talab thāpdā man̲ pani talab thāpne thiyen̲ ani tyespachhi mainle pani chandā diyeko hun̲chhu holā	when others drew their pay, I also would draw mine, and thereafter I too, it may be, shall have given a collection
tan̲ jati belā man̲ saña bhais bhanye main̲le chandā diyeko dekhlās	If thou shalt be with me so long, thou wilt see me give the collection

18. **Incredible; inconsistent—**

tyeskā kurā patyāī na sakne ra goṭai pichchhe na milne thiye	His words were incredible and inconsistent

[After *patyāī*, which is the noun, 'belief,' understand *hun̲nu*.]

19. **Like; as—**

tai pan̲i tyeslāi satturlāi jasto na gana tara bhāīlāi jasto chetanne dewa	And yet count him not as an enemy, but admonish him as a brother
apavitra garne ra būrhīharukā jastā kahan̲nīharu dekhi māph mān̲g	Decline profane and old wives'-like fables
kasai briddhalāi na hakār tara bābulāi jhain̲ upades de	Rebuke not an elder, but exhort him as a father
ani arko jo tyo jastai chha yei ho tain̲le āphnu kshimeki saña āphai saña jhain̲ prem gar	And a second, like unto it, is this, Thou shalt love thy neighbour as thyself

20. **Lifetime, In one's—**

āphnu jīun̲do jīwanmān̲ tyesai bhanyo	He said so in his lifetime (*lit.*, in his living life)

21. **More than once—**

ek an̲ katti khep āyo	He came more than once (*lit.*, one, yea, several times)

22. **Must; ought; have to; shall; duty; bound; necessary—**

udek na mān main̲le tan̲lāi timiharulāi nayā gari janman̲ne khān̲cho chha bhanyera bhanyen̲ bhani	Marvel not that I said unto thee, Ye must be born anew (*lit.*, there is to you being-born necessity)
timiharu pavitra hun̲nu abasse parda chha	You must be holy

usle abasse yeso garnu parchha	He shall have to do thus
manlāi baptismā hunnu parne yeuṭā baptismā chha ani man kasto sakasmān chhu tyo hoi na sakunjyāl samma	I have a baptism that I must be baptized with, and how am I straitened till it be accomplished
yinalāi garnu ani tinalāi na chhoṛi dīnnu timiharule parthyo	These ought ye to have done, and not to have left the others undone
wahān runnu ra dārā kiṭnu parchha	There shall be the weeping and gnashing of teeth
mainle kye garnu ho jānyen	I am resolved what I shall do
mainle yo garnu chha	I have to do this
tyestai timiharule pani jaba ājñā bhayekā sab kām garyekā hoaulā taba bhana bikāme dās chhaun garnu paryebhariko jattī (p. 116) *māntrdi garyūn bhani*	Even so ye also, when ye will have done all the things which are commanded you, say, We are unprofitable servants : we have but done what it was our duty to do
hānmiharule prārthanā garnu parda chha	We are bound to pray

[N.B.—*parnu* is intrans., and in the above examples its nom. is the whole clause. In the last ex., for instance, *hānmiharule prārthanā garnu* is the nom. to *parda chha ;* and the connection of *hānmiharule* is, not with *parda chha*, but with *garnu*,—hence the ag. case. In *timiharu pavitra hunnu parda chha*, the ag. case would be wrong, because *hunnu* is not an act. trans. verb,—a rule, however, very frequently violated.]

niski gayera tyo hernu manlāi khāncho chha	I must needs go and look at it
kinabhanye jye jye bhannye or (*bhanne*, or *bhannu*) *khāncho chha ti pavitra ātmāle tyesai gharī timiharulāi sikāunchha*	Because the Holy Spirit will teach you in that very hour what things it is necessary to say
yesaigari pashchāttāp garnu khāncho na bhayekā unansai dharmmīharu bhandā jyāsti	Even so there is joy in heaven over one sinner that repenteth, more than over 99

pashchāttāp garne ek janā pāpīko lāgi swargamān ramāhaṭ chha	righteous persons that need not repentance
kye abasse thiyena khrīshṭle yi dukha bhognu	Was it not needful that Christ should suffer these things ?
sabaile mānchheharuko bhandā baru īshwarko ājñā mānnu khāncho chha	All must needs obey God rather than men
timilāi jānne khāncho chhaina	You need not go
khāncho chha man bajārmān jānnu	I must needs go to the bazar
manlāi khāncho pari āyekā thok	My necessities
khānchopariawāī ansār	As need may arise
khānchohuwāīharumān	In necessities
abasse paryekole hoina	Not from necessity
āphuko bhalāī khancho pariko jasto hoina tara chāhā gariko hisāple hawas	Let your beneficence not be as of necessity, but of free will

N.B.—khāncho is used either as a noun, 'necessity,' when it makes its verb an adj and puts its subject in the dat. ; *manlāi jānne khāncho chha*, 'I have going-necessity' ; or as an adj , 'necessary,' when it makes its verb a noun and puts its subject in the nom. or ag. : *man jānnu, mainle garnu, khāncho chha*, 'I-to-go, I-to-do, is necessary.'

abasse is used either as an adj. or adv.

See also p. 87.

On *khānchopariawāī* [see no. 38 below.]

23 **Not that ; imitate—**

hānmiharulāi adhikārai chhaina bhani hoina (or *yeso hoina*) *tara āphulāi timiharulāi—timiharu hānmiharuko jasto chālmān hinrnuko lāgi—napanā tulyāi diūn bhannye khātirle ho* (or *diūn bhani yeso ho*)	(It is) not that we have not authority, but (it is) in order that we may render ourselves an example to you, in order that you may imitate us

23*a*. **Over ; across ; side ; sides ; through ; beyond—**

yetā wāri yes kamānmāṉ hāṉmro gohārmāṉ āija	Come over to this tea-garden and help us
utā pāri jā	Go over
hāṉmilāi kye kām nadī wāri lyāuṉnu bhayo nadī pāri laijāṉnu hawas	To what purpose did you bring us across the river? Take us away across the river
lauro bāhik kyei na lii nadī wār (or *wāri*) *tari āyeṉ tara aba tā dui maṉḍalī bhai rāṉchhu*	I came (*lit.* ferried) across the river with nothing but a stick, but now I am become two bands
nadī pār (or *pāri*) *khwā liṉdauṉna kinabhanye nadī dekhi yeso wārinai paṭṭi tā hāṉmro khwā paṛyo*	We will not take our territory on the other side of the river, because our territory was to be on this side of the river
nadī dekhi pāri jāṉdainas	Thou shalt not go over the river
taṉ nadī wāri tarnu pāuṉdainas tara yi chaiṉ tā wāri tarchhan	Thou shalt not be allowed to come across the river, but these ones shall come across
tyesle mero bāṭolāi āṛ lāyo	He crossed my path (=opposed me)
baru nadī pārinai santok garyera basne thiyūṉ	We would rather have been content to dwell on the other side of the river
ḍāṉṛā kāṭyo	He crossed the hill
chiṉnu na nāṉghnu	Do not cross over the mark
gallībhari aghi gaye ani turantai tyesko sāthī tyo thāṉi dekhi gai gayo	They passed through the street, and suddenly his companion passed away from him
timiharu thāṉi āuṉchhu jaba nepāl des bāṭo nikli jāuṉlā	I shall come to you when I pass through Nepal
kamānko māṉjha bāṭo chhiri gayo	He went through the middle of the tea-garden
des bāṭo chhiri jālā	He will go through the country
maṉ sabai dishā huṉdo chhiri	While I was going through all

jāṉdāmāṉ agghor ramāi rahyeṉ	the districts, I kept rejoicing exceedingly
wārpār kāṭa	Cut it through
maṉlāi waripari gherye	They surrounded me on all sides
kholchāko yeso wāri hoina bhanye tā uso pāri huṉchha	It will do, either on this side of the stream, or on the other
sab tira bāṭo kashṭit pāriyo	He was afflicted from all sides
gharko chheuchhāu	On all sides of the house
ekā paṭṭi jāu	Go to the side (of the road)
tyesko kokhāmāṉ ghāu chha	He has a sore on his side
ani yo sabai dekhi uprānta hāṉmiharu ra timiharuko bīchmāṉ yeuṭā ṭhulo khāṉḍ ṭhaharāiyeko (or ṭhaharāyeko) chha yetā bāṭo uso pāri timiharukāṉ jāṉne ichchhe garneharu na sakun ani na tyetā bāṭo yeso wāri hāṉmiharukāṉ āun bhannye khātirle	And besides all this, between us and you there is a great gulf fixed, that they which would cross over from hence to you may not be able, and that none may cross over from thence to us
ḍāṉṛāko wallo paṭṭi hoina tara pallo paṭṭi chha	It is, not on this side of the hill, but on the other
ūṃbho hoina terchho jāu	Go, not up, but across

[See also p. 115.]

24. **As possible ; as far as—**

huṉnu sakne chha	It is possible
mero sakdobhar	As far as I can
sakdobhari chhiṭo	As quickly as possible
sakyebhari	As far (or much) as possible (with past tense)
huṉnu sakdo ho	Were it possible
tyesko jāndobhar	As far as he knows

25. **Progress : fairly—**

āju melo katiko saryo āju nikai jāti gari melo saryo	What progress has the job made to-day ? To-day the job has progressed fairly well

26. **Right; proper; becoming—**

yestai ritle kām garnu hāṉmiharulāi (or *hāṉmiharule kām garnu*) *uchit chha*	It is right for us to do the work in such a way
tyo yi bandhan dekhi phukāiṉnu uchit thiyo	It was right he should be released from these bonds
kyei pani na garnu mero lāgi suwāuṉda chha	It is proper for me to do nothing
suwāuṉdo pahiran lāi	In becoming apparel

27. **Rather; prefer—**

sunne bhandā baru bolne ichchhe garne chhu	I had rather speak than listen (or I prefer speaking to listening)

28. **Some, one thing; some, another—**

koī kye koī kye bhandai karāuṉda thiye	Some were shouting one thing, some another

29. **Such as; such that**

dhanī huṉne man garneharu chaiṉ yestā kuichchheharu māṉ parda chhan jasle māṉchheharulāi bināsmāṉ burāi diṉda chhan	They that are minded to be rich fall into such lusts as drown men in destruction

30. **Same; same as; that very; one, another—**

ustai (or *tiniharu saña*) *ekai kārigariko huṉnāle u tiniharukāṉ rahyo*	Because he was of the same trade as they, he stayed with them
kye jagātiharule pani tyesai gardainan	Do not even the tax-gatherers the same?
jaslāi chūmā khāuṉ ui ho usailāi samāti rākha	Whomsoever I shall kiss, that same is he: hold him fast
timi ko hau ui huṉ jo thālni dekhi boldai āyeṉ	Who art thou? The same as I have gone on telling you from the beginning
tyesai rātmāṉ	On that very night
sabaiko prabhu ui ho	The same Lord is Lord of all
sabai aṉgako ekai kām chhaina	All the limbs have not the same office

tyesle kye tinai kurā bhandaina	Does he not say the same things ?
anugrahdān waliwalikā chhan tara ātmā tā ui	There are diversities of gifts, but the same Spirit
sabai sharīr ekainā<u>n</u>se sharīr hu<u>n</u>daina tara mānchheharuko sharīr arkai chha ani pashuharuko sharīr arkai	All flesh (corporeity) is not the same flesh : but there is one flesh of men, and another flesh of beasts
jo utri gayo uinai ho jo charhi gayo pani	He that descended is the same also that ascended
ui ekai ho	He is one and the same
ekā thā<u>n</u>umā<u>n</u>	In one and the same place
ti sāṭī<u>n</u>chhan tara tapā<u>n</u>i tā ekainā<u>n</u>se hu<u>n</u>nu hu<u>n</u>da chha	They shall be exchanged, but Thou art the same

[When there is reference to an antecedent the emphatics of the demonstratives are used (p. 22) ; when otherwise, those of *ek, ekainā<u>n</u>se* represents identity in form, as well as in number.]

āpastamā<u>n</u> (or *ekāle arkālāi,* or *ekāle arkāko*) *gohār gara*	Help one another (p. 27).

31. **The same as before ; 'as you were'—**

tyesko hāt jastoko tasto pārīyo	His hand was made the same as before (= was restored) .
jastākā tastā hu<u>n</u>nu	'As you were !'

32. **Set on way—**

tyeslāi yetā alik wara samma puryāwa ra ma<u>n</u> thā<u>n</u>i āwas	Set him forward on his journey, that he may come to me
ma<u>n</u>lāi tyetā alik para samma puryāu<u>n</u>nu hawas ra āphnu gharmā<u>n</u> jāu<u>n</u>	Set me forward on my journey, that I may go to my house

33. **Some or other—**

koī na koī āimāiharu āin	Some women or other have come
kyei na kyei bigri gayo	Something or other has gone wrong
koī na koī parile	Somehow or other

34. **Will ; wish ; would ; like ; willingly ; wilfully—**

kām ma<u>n</u>lāi jāti lāgchha	I like the work

ichchhei gari jāṉnu birsi gayo	He wilfully forgot to go
chāhā gari tā āyo	He came willingly
ichchhehuwāī (or *manko tiyārī*) *chāhiṉchha*	Willingness is desirable
chāhīṉdobhar liṉnu	Take as much as you like
timiharule kye ichchhe garda chhau timiharu thāṉi chharī lii āuṉ ki prem lii āuṉ	What will ye? That I come to you with a rod, or in love?
tyo maṉ na āuṉjyāl samma rahos bhannye mero ichchhe bhayo bhanye dekhi taṉlāi kye	If I will that he should tarry till I come, what is that to thee?
ichchhe garne thiyeṉ aile timiharu thāṉi sāṉmel huṉne	I could wish to be present with you now [or put first three words last]
maiṉle timro lāgi kye garne timro ichchhe chha (or *kye ichchhe garda chhau maiṉle timro lāgi garnu*)	What would you that I should do for you?
yi maiṉle tiniharù māṉthi rāj garuṉ bhannye ichchhe na garne merā satturharulāi yetā lyāwa	Bring hither these mine enemies, that would not that I should reign over them
kahāṉ tiyār pārūṉ bhannye tapāṉiko ichchhe chha	Where wilt Thou that we make ready?
thāhā na pāwa bhannye man gardaina	He is not minded that you should not know
timiharule maṉ alikatā nirbuddhi huṉdāmāṉ maṉlāi sahye tā huṉthyo	Would that ye could bear with me in a little foolishness!
ḍarāuṉda chhu āyera kahīṉ timiharulāi tyestā pāwaiṉna jastā ichchhe garda chhu ani maṉ chaiṉ timiharu dekhi tyesto pāiuṉlā jasto ichchhe gardauna ki bhani kahīṉ timiharumāṉ jhagarā ityādi hunan ki bhani	I fear, lest by any means, when I come, I should find you not such as I would, and should myself be found of you such as you would not; lest there should be quarrels, et cetera, among you [See also p. 82.]

35. **While yet—**

tyo jiun̲do chhan̲dākheri	While he was yet alive
man̲ timiharu saña hun̲daikheri	While I was yet with you
din chhaun̲jyāl samma	While it is yet day
jiun̲dai pani man̲rī	She is dead while she liveth
tyo boldainai thiyo hera tyesko pakarāi din̲ne tyo thān̲i pugyo	While he was yet speaking, behold, his betrayer arrived where he was
tyo nirbal bhai rahyekaimān̲ pani	While he was yet weak (lit., on his yet remaining weak)
bālakha janmyekai thiyenan ani na ki ta bhalo ki ta buro (p. 122) *kyei garyekā thiye tabai yeso kahīyo jeṭho kān-chhoko dās hun̲chha bhani*	While yet the children were unborn, and had done nothing either good or bad, it was said as follows, The elder shall serve the younger

36. **Whosoever; whatsoever—**

tan̲ koī hos jasle bichār garda chhas niruttar chhas	Thou art without excuse, whosoever thou art that judgest
jastā thiye tyestai thiye man̲lāi kyei bhed māphikko chhaina	Whatsoever they were, it makes no matter to me
jyesukai houn̲	Whatever I am

37. **Word Discrimination: to fall, descend, behold, know—**

larnu	To fall (from an erect position)
khasnu	To fall (from a higher position)
orhlan̲nu	To descend (down a thing)
utran̲nu	To descend (through space)
dekhnu	To behold (see)
hernu	To behold (look at)
jānnu	To know (from comprehension)
thāhā pāun̲nu	To know (from information)
chāl ,, ...	To know (from observation)
chinnu	To know (from identification)
kye yes mānchhelāi chinchhau	Do you know this person?

[The above examples are given to show how rich the Nepāli

vocabulary of simple words is, and how carefully discriminating in its use the student must be.]

38. Word Compounding.—While rich in concrete, Ṇepālī is poor in abstract words. It makes up for this, however, by admitting, as easily as German or Greek, of the formation of verbal and compound words, as the following typical examples are intended to show :—

mānchhehāt	(two nouns)	Human hands
bhāīprem	(two nouns)	Brotherly love
dharmmānsārbichār	(two nouns + one prep.)	Righteous judgment
pavitrājñā	(adj. + noun)	Solemn commandment
garāī	(from *garnu*)	Doing
awāī	(from *āuṉnu*)	Coming
jawāī	(from *jāṉnu*)	Going
liwāī	(from *liṉnu*)	Taking
diwāī	(from *diṉnu*)	Giving
huwāī	(from *huṉnu*)	Being
ṭhaharāī	(from *ṭhaharnu*)	Decision
khānchopariawāī	(noun + two verbs)	Necessities
khāṉchochuwāī	(noun + verb)	Needfulness
atithisewāgarāī	(two nouns + verb)	Practice of hospitality
gharjawāī	(noun + verb)	Home-going
dharmmīhuwāī	(adj. + verb)	State of righteousness
dharmmīṭhaharāī	,,	Justification
dharmmīṭhaharāīgarāī	(adj. + two verbs)	Act of Justification
pavitrahuwāī	(adj. + verb)	State of holiness
pavitragarā	,,	Sanctification
mānmāphikkohuwāī	(noun + prep. + verb	Worshipfulness, gravity
pharkiawāī	(two verbs)	Return

APPENDIX.

Pending the publication of a Dictionary, it may be useful to furnish here, however meagrely, (I) a general vocabulary; and (II) an Army phrase-list. The usefulness will be multiplied if the lessons as to **Causal and Compound Verbs and Abstract and Compound Nouns** (pp. 58, 59, 155) be applied.

I. General Vocabulary.

[Numbers refer to foregoing pages. (A.) = Accusative.

(a.) = adjective	(adv.) = adverb	(D.) = Dative
(*d.*) = *dinnu*	(f.) = feminine	(G.) = Genitive
(*g.*) = *garnu*	(g.) = governs	(*h.*) = *hunnu*
(i.) = intransitive	(n.) = noun	(ob.) = object
(sub.) = subject	(t.) = transitive	(v.) = verb]

A, An—13, 26
Able (v.)—*saknu* (59)
About—56, 59, 117, 141
Above—*mānthi*, *ūmbho* (119)
Absent—*bihājir*, *gayel*
Abundance—*dherai*, *parasasta* (59)
Abuse (n.)—*gālī*, (misuse) *kubhog*
Accident—*sanyog*
According—117, 142
Account—*hisāp*, 117
Accusation—*dosh*
Acknowledge—*mānnu*
Acquaintance, An,—*chinājānā*
Acquit—*chhoṛi dinnu*
Acre—*ropni*, *bīghā*
Across—149
Act of, In the,—75, 93
Add—*joṛnu*
Address (direction)—*patā*, *thegānā*
Admonition—*chetanne*
Adult—*siyānā*
Advance (money)—*pesgī*, (to take an a.) *kharcha linnu*
Advice—*sallāh*
Adze—*bachhila*
Afford—*butā h.* (g. D. of sub. and G. of ob.)
Afraid of (v.)—*dekhi ḍarāunnu*
After—*pachhi* (117, 115, 70)
Again—*pheri*
Against—*biruddha* (117)
Age—*umer*
Aggressor—*agāṛi hāt chhāṛne*
Ago—*bhayo* (141, 56)

Agree—*lau bhannu*
Agreement—*bandabasta*
Ague—*aulko jaro*
Ails ?, What,—*kye bhayo*
Aim (v.)—*tāknu*
Air—*hāwā*
Alike—*barābar*
Aliment—*khurāk*
Alive—*jiundo*
All—*sab* (29, 37, 142)
Allow—*dinnu*
Allowance—*bāṭā*
Almost—*jhandai*
Alone—*eklai*
Along—*lanmai tira, bāṭo* (g. G.)
Already—*aile ;* 60, 116
Also—*pani* (121, 136)
Alter—*phernu*
Alternately—*pālo pālo*
Although—93
Altogether, *syānṭṭhai, chhuṭṭi*
Always—*sadhain, barābar*
Ambush—*ghā*
Amends—*sāṭo*
Ammunition—*bāruk golī*
Among—13, 15, 28
Amount—*jamā*
And—*ani, ra, ta* (121, 115)
And that—121
Anger—*ris ;* (v.) *risāunnu*
Angle—*kunnā*
Animal—*pashu*
Annoy—*khijyāunnu*
Another—*aru, arko* (26, 151)
Answer—*juwāp*
Anvil—*līhī*

Any—*koī, kyei, kunai* (25)
Anyhow—*kastai gari pani*
Anything—*kyei*
Anywhere—*kahīn pani* (114)
Any longer—142
Apologize—*māph māngnu*
Apparatus—*tānābānā*
Apparently—*dekh gari*
Appeal—*dohaī ;* (v.) *d. d.*
Appetite—*bhok*
Application—*arjī*
Apply—(ask) *māngnu ;* (put) *lagāunnu*
Appoint—*khaṭāunnu ; bhartī g.* (g. A.)
Appointment—(post) *khānki*
Apprehend—*samātnu*
Approval—*manjūrī*
Approximation—*aṛkal*
Arable—*kheti māphikko*
Arbitrate—*dui tira milāunnu*
Arch (n.)—*dhanurūpī sirān*
Area—*nāpo*
Argue—*bibād g.*
Arithmetic—*hisāp*
Arm—*bānhān, hāt ;* (v.) *bhirnu*
Armful—*añālobhariko*
Arms—*hatiyār*
Army—*laskar*
Arrange—*ṭhīk pārnu*
Arrears—*bānkī*
Arrest—*pakrannu*
Arrive (at)—(*samma*) *pugnu*
Artisan—*kārigar*
As—*jaso, jasto, gari, jhain* (115, 116, 141, 146, 152) ; as far as—150 ; as for—*chain,*

bhanye (13, 38, 121); as if—123; as long as—89; as much as—139, 141; as much as there is—*bhayebhari*; as soon as—*jasai* (142); as though—123; as well as—*samet* (119, 120)

Ascend—*charhnu*

Ascent (acclivity) *ukālo*

Ashamed (of), To be,—(*dekhi*) *sharminnu*

Ashes—*kharāni*

Aside—*ekā paṭṭi*

Ask—*sodhnu* (g. A.)

Ass—*gadāhā*; (f.) *gadahī*

Assault (v.)—*mānthi āi lāgnu, mānrpīṭ g., hānāmānr g.*

Assent—(v.)—*rājī h.*

Assessment—*sirtu*

Assets—*jaujāt*

Assist—*gohār g.* (g. G. or D.)

Assort—*rakam* 2. *g.*

Astride—*goṛā pasāri*

At—*thāni,-mān,-kān, hoi* (13, 15, 57, 95, 113, 116, 119, 120)

Attend—(listen) *sundai rahannu*; (watch) *herdai rahannu*

Auction—*līlām*

Auger—*pechī*

Authority—*aktiyār*

Average—*ausat*

Awake—(i.) *jāgnu*; (t.) *jagāunnu*

Awl—*sutārī*

Axe—*bancharo*

Axle—*dhurī*

Baby—*nānī*

Back—(n.) *pīṭh*; (adv.) *pharki*

Bad—*najāti, buro, kharāb* (122)

Bag—*thailo*; (sack) *borā*

Baggage—*jhiṭimiṭi, sārdām*

Bag and baggage—*kumlosumlo*

Bail—*jamāni*

Bait—*chāro*

Bake—(dry) *seknu*; (cook) *polnu*

Balance—(weighing) *kānṭā, tarājū*; (remainder) *bānkī*; to b. accounts—*hisāp milāunnu*

Bale—*kumlo*

Ball—*golī*

Bamboo—*bāns*

Band—(tie) *bandhan*

Bandage—*paṭṭī*

Bangle—*churā*

Bank—(earth) *ḍhiskā*; (river) *tīr*

Bankrupt—*phakīrī*

Bar—(rod) *ghārā*; (bolt) *āglo*; (gate) *tagāro*

Barbed—*kānṛe*

Barefoot—*nāngā goṛāko*

Bark—(tree) *bōkra*; (dog) *bhuknu*

Barley—*jau*

Barrel—*pīpā*; (gun) *nāl*

Barren—*bānjhī*; (land) *rūkho*

Barricade—*āṛ*

Barrow—*hātgāṛī*

Basement—*bhūinṭalā*

Basin—*chilimchī*

Basket—*ḍoko, thunse*; (small) *ḍālo, ṭokarī*

Bat—(animal) *chamero*

Batch—*gaṭṭhā*

Bathing—*nuhāī, snān* (9)

Batten—*ghochā, baṭam*
Be—*hunnu* (66)
Beads, string of,—*mālā*
Beam (timber)—*dalān*; (small) *balo*
Bean—*simi*
Bear (animal) *bhālū*
Bear (v.)—(endure) *sahannu*; (fruit) *phalnu*
Beast—*pashu*
Beat—*piṭnu*; (game) *ṭhaṭāk-ṭhuṭuk g.*
Beautiful—*rāmro*
Because—*kinabhanye* (123); b. of—*kāraṇle* (g. G) (117, 14)
Become—*hunnu, hoi jānnu* 58, (95, 142)
Becoming (a.)—*suwāundo*(151)
Bed—*ochhyān, khāṭ*; (plants) *byāṛ*
Befitting—*māphikko* (119)
Before—*agāṛi, aghi, sānmu, mukhenji* (117, 143)
Begin—*thālnu, lāgnu* (59)
Behaviour—*chalan*
Behind—*pachhāṛi* (117)
Behold—*hernu* (154, 133)
Believe—*patyāunnu* (g. A.)
Bell—*ghanṭi*
Bellows—*bhānṭi, āgo phukne*
Belly—*peṭ, bhunṛi*
Belly-band—*peṭi*
Belong—*hunnu* (g. D. or G.) (68)
Below—*muni, tala, ūndho*(119)
Belt—*paṭukā*: (machinery) *doāl*
Bent—*bāngo*
Beseech—*binti g.* (130)
Beside—*nira, paṭṭi, chheu* (117, 119)
Besides—*uprānta, bāhik* (117, 119)
Besiege—*gheri basnu*
Besom—*jhāṛū*; (soft) *kucho*; (hard) *kharyāṭo*
Best—*jāti, assal* (37, 39)
Between—*bich, mānjha* (117)
Beyond—*dekhi uso, dekhi punṛo* (118, 149)
Bid—*hukum d.*; (offer) *ḍāk bolnu*
Bill (acct.) *hisāh*; (exchange) *hunḍi*
Bird—*panshi*; (small) *charā*
Birth—*janma*
Bit—(bridle) *kareli*
Bite—*ṭoknu, khānnu*
Bitter—*tito*
Black—*kālo*
Blacksmith—*lohār*
Blade—(grass) *biruwā*; (knife) *dhār*
Blame—*dosh*
Blanket—*rāṛi, kambal*
Blast (v.)—(powder) *suruñ hānnu*
Blemish—*khoṭ*
Blight—*rātopahenlo*
Blind—*andhā* (37)
Blister—*phokā*
Blockhead—*laṭheprā*
Blood—*ragat*
Blossom—*pos*

Blow (v.)—(as wind) *bahannu* ; (the fire) *phuknu*

Blow (n.)—*hirkāi*; (fist) *ghussā*, *murki*

Blow out—*nibhāunnu*

Blue—*nīlo*

Blunt—*na lāgne*, *bodho*

Boat—*dungā*

Body—*jīu* (16)

Bog—*hilebhūin*

Boil—*umālnu*, *usinnu*

Boil (n.)—*pīlo*

Bolt—*āglo*, *chhitkanī*

Bond—(deed) *hātchitthā*

Bone—*hār*

Bonus—*bakshiprāpti*

Book—*kitāp*

Book-keeping—*lekhājokhā*

Boot—*juttā*

Bore—*chhenrnu*

Boring-tool—*barmā*

Born, to be,—*janmannu*

Borrow—*rin linnu*

Both—*duwai* (44) ; (conj.) 121, 131

Bottom—*tala*, *puchhār*, *thāh*

Bound—(obliged) 146

Boundary—*simānā*, *sānd*

Bow—(arrow) *dhanu* ; pellet) *guleli* ; stoop (v.)—*niurannu*

Box—*sampat*, "*bākas*"

Boy—*ketā*

Branch—*hāngā*

Brand—(fire) *agultho* ; (mark) *dām*

Brass—*pītal*

Bravery—*ānt* ; (a.) *āntilo*

Bread—*roti*

Breadth—*gaj*

Break—*bhānchnu* ; (shatter) *phornu* ; (open) *upkāunnu*

Bribe—*ghūs* ; (v.) *gh. d.*

Brick—*intā*; (-layer) *gārokarmī*

Bride—*byāulī* ; (-groom) *byāulā*

Bridge—*pul*

Bridle—*lagam*

Brim—(vessel) *nimtho*

Bring—*lyāunnu*

Brittle—*phutnu sahaj* (91)

Broad—*gajilo*, *pharāk*

Bronze—*kānsā*

Brook—*kholchā*

Brother—*dājyu* ; (younger) *bhāi*

Bruise—(grain) *pinnu*

Brush—*kuchī*

Buckle—*chaprās*

Buckwheat—*phāpar*

Bud—*kopilā*

Buffalo—*bhainsi*

Bug—*urus*

Bugle—*bikul*

Build—*banāunnu*

Bull—*sānr goru*

Bullock—*goru*

Bullet—*golī*

Bunch—*jhuppā*

Bundle—*bitā*; *gatthā*

Burden—*bhāri* ; (a.) *bhārī*

Burglar—*ghar phorne*

Burn—*jalnu*, *balnu*, *darnu* (58)

Bury—*gārnu*, *purnu*

Bush—*pothrā* ; *jangal*, *jhor*

Business—*kām*
Busy—*lāgyeko*
But—*tara* (121), 143
Butt—(gun) *kunjā*
Butter—*ghiu, makkhan*
Buy—*kinnu*
By—12, 14, 44, 117, 119, 137, 143
By-way—*chorbāṭo*
Calf—*bāchchho*
Calk—*ṭālnu*
Call—*bolāuṉnu, ḍāknu* (143)
Called—*nāṉu bhayeko* (143)
Can (n.)—*ghaṛā* ; (v.) *saknu* (59, 88)
Candle—*mom battī*
Cane—*bet*
Cannon—*top*
Carcase (animal)—*siṉnu*
Cardamoms—*alaiṉchi*
Care—*phikri* ; (keeping) *jimmā*
Careful—*khabardār*
Carpenter—*kāṭhkarmi, baṛhaī*
Carpet—*darī*
Carriage—*baggī* ; (porterage) *bokāī*
Carry—*boknu* (59)
Cart—*gāṛi*
Cash—*nakhati*
Cast—*hālnu*
Caste—*jāt*
Castrated—*khasi*
Catch—*pakraṉnu*
Cattle—*gāī goru*
Cause—*kāraṇ* ; (v.) 58, 59, 117, 143
Cavalry—*risāla, truksawār*
Ceiling—*chhāṉnā*
Cement—*bilāitī maṭṭī*
Census—*nāṉulekhāī*
Certain—*sāṉchai* ; *koī, phalānā* (93)
Certainly—*nisse*
Chaff—*bhūs*
Chain—*jhinjiri, sikri*
Chair—*chaukī*
Chalk—*khalimāṭi*
Challenge—*laṛāīṉ māṉgnu* ; (sentry) *paharshabda māṉgnu*
Chance—*sanyog* ; (opportunity) *belā*
Change—*phernu* ; (money) *reji*
Charcoal—*koilā*
Charge (cost)—*dām* ; (accusation) *phirāt* ; (keeping) *jimmā* ; (enemy) *hamlā g.*
Cheap—*sasto*
Cheat—*ṭhagnu*
Cheerful—*khushi* ; (n.) *khushī*
Cheese—*panīr*
Chew—*chabāuṉnu*
Chicken—*challā*
Chief—*mūl* ; (n.) *mukhiyā*
Child—*bālakha* : (plu.) *lālābālā, keṭākeṭi*
Chin—*chiuṉṛā*
Chips—*jhūs, choiṭāchoiṭ*
Chisel—*chhinu*
Cholera—*haizā*
Choleraic diarrhœa—*upartali*
Choose—*chhānnu*
Cinnamon—*sinkaulī*
Circumference—*gherā*
Cistern—*kūp*

City—*sahar*
Claim—*dāwā*
Clay—*mā<u>n</u>ṭo*
Clean—*chokho*
Climate—*hāwāpānī*
Climb—(*mā<u>n</u>thi*) *charhnu*
Cloth—*kaparā*
Clothes—*lugā*
Coal—*patthar koilā*
Coarse—*bāklo*
Coin—*reji*
Coir—*nariwalko nasā*
Cold—*chiso ;* (n.) *jāṛo ;* (sickness) *sardī*
Collect—*jamāu<u>n</u>nu*
Colour—*ra<u>n</u>g*
Come—*āu<u>n</u>nu* (108); (out) *nikla<u>n</u>nu* (58)
Common—*majhaule, sādhāraṇ*
Companion—*sāthi*.
Company—*sātha* (117); (soldiers) "*kampū*"
Compare—*milāi hernu*
Compel—*abasse lagāu<u>n</u>nu* (143)
Concerning—*bi<u>sh</u>ay* (117)
Condition—*paṇ ;* (state) *gat*
Conduct—*chāl ;* (v.) *chalāu<u>n</u>nu*
Confess—*kāel h.* (g. G.)
Conquer—*jitnu*
Consider—*bichārnu*
Constantly—*barābar*
Continue—*raha<u>n</u>nu* (59, 61)
Continuous—*nirantar*
Contrary—*ulṭāulo* (117)
Convict—*ḍo<u>sh</u>i ṭhaharāu<u>n</u>nu*
Cook—*pakāu<u>n</u>nu;* (n.) *bāwarchī*
Copper—*tāmbā ; paisā* (46)

Coppersmith—*bā<u>n</u>ṛā*
Corner—*ku<u>n</u>nā*
Corpse—*murdā, loth*
Cost—*dām*
Cough—*khoki*
Could—87
Counsel—*sallāh*
Count—*gannu*
Country—*des*
Couple—*joṛā* (45)
Cover—*ḍhāknu, chhopnu*
Cow—*gāi*
Coward—*kāṭar*
Cradle—*kokro*
Creditor—*sāhū*
Crime—*aparādh*
Crooked—*bā<u>n</u>go*
Cross—*pāri jā<u>n</u>nu* (g. G.)
Cross-examine—*sawāl kāṭnu*
Crowbar—*jhampal*
Crush—*michnu*
Cry—*karāu<u>n</u>nu* (61)
Cultivation—*khetipāti*
Cunning—*chhaṭṭu*
Cup—*baṭuko*
Custom—*rīt, behorā*
Customer—*gāhaki*
Cut—*kāṭnu*
Cutting (of plant)—*kalam*
Dagger—*chupi*
Daily—*dinahū<u>n</u>*
Damage—*noksān*
Danger—*jagjagi, jokhim*
Dark—*a<u>n</u>dhyāro* (50)
Date (day)—*tithi* (10, 51); (fruit) *khajur*
Dawn—*bihāna prātai*

Day—*din*
Day-time—*diunso*
Dead—*manryeko*
Deaf—*bahiro*
Dear—*priya;* (costly) *mahango*
Death—*kāl, mrityu*
Debt—*rin*
Debtor—*āsāmi*
Deceive—*thagnu*
Decide—*thaharāunnu*
Decrease—*ghati ;* (v) *ghatnu*
Declivity—*orhālo*
Deduct—*ghatāunnu*
Deep—*gahiro*
Defeat—*jitnu ;* (n.) *hār*
Defence—*bachāi ; uttar*
Deficiency—*apugdo* .
Delay—*biyānlo*
Demolish—*bhatkāunnu*
Deny—*aswikār g.* (127)
Descend—*utrannu, orhlānnu* (154)
Deserter—*bhagaurā*
Desirable—*chāhindo*
Despise—*tuchchh thānnu* (128)
Destitute—*harikangāl*
Detachment (party)—"*kamān*"
Dew—*sit*
Diarrhœa—*chherauti*
Die—*manrnu* (58)
Difference—*bhed*
Different—*farak, beglai*
Difficult—*kathin, sāro*
Dig—*khannu*
Diligence—*dāsti; jatan*
Diligent—*dāste, jatane*
Dip—*chobhnu*

Direction—*tira ;* 115, 119
Dirty—*mailo*
Disappoint—*āshāmānrnu*(g.G.)
Discharge—*chhutti ; nānu katāunnu*
Disciple—*shikshe*
Discipline—*shikshā, ainmanāi*
Disease—*bethā, rog*
Dishonest—*beimān*
Disloyal—*nimakharām*
Dismissal—*chhutti*
Disobedience—*namanāi*
Distance—*tāro*
Disturbance—*gulmul*
Ditch—*khāral*
Divide—*bhāg bhāg g.*
Diviner—*jhānkri* (14)
Do—*garnu* (58, 97)
Do, It will,—*hunchha*
Doctor—*baidya*
Dog—*kukur*
Door—*dailo*
Double—*doharo* (46)
Doubt—*shankā*
Down—*tala, ūndho, muntira* (119)
Drain—*kulo ;* (stone) *mohori*
Draw—*tānnu*
Drink—*piunnu, khānnu* (58)
Drive—*hānknu*
Drop—*thopo ;* (v. i.) *chuhunnu*
Drought—*obāno*
Drown—*dubi manrnu, burnu*
Drum—*dhol*
Drunk—*mātyeko*
Drunkard—*matwāl*
Dry—*sukye ;* (v. t.) *sukāunnu*

Dumb—*gongā*
Dung—*mal*
Dust—*dhūlo*
Duty—*parne kām* (146)
Dysentery—*ragatmānsi*
Each—*ek ek, janange, gotā* (37)
Ear—*kānn*
Early—*saberai ;* (morning) *bihānai*
Earn—*kamāunnu*
Earnings—*kamāī*
Earnest (pledge)—*bainnā*
Earth—*prithiwī ;* (soil) *mānto*
East—*pūrba*
Easy—*sajilo*
Eat—*khānnu* (58)
Edge—*chheu ;* (knife) *dhār*
Effort—*jatan*
Egg—*phul*
Either (a.) 38 ; (conj.) 121
Elbow—*kuino*
Elder—*jetho, baro*
Elephant—*hāthī*
Else—(conj.) 128 ; (a.) *aru*
Embers—*bhubro*
Empty—*khālī*
End—*anta*
Enemy—*sattur*
Engine—*kal*
Enlist—*bhartī h.* (i.), *g.* (t.)
Enmity—*dushmanī*
Enough—*dherai ; bhayo* (!)
Enquiry—*tāluk*
Enrol—*bhartī g. ; nānu lekhāunnu*
Enter—*pasnu* (g Loc.)
Entire—*gairha ;* (horse) *bokā*
Entrust to—*jimmāmān rākhnu* (g. G.)
Equal—*barābar*
Erect—*thāro*
Escape—*bānchnu*
Escort—" *eskāut* "
Especially—*assal gari*
Estimate—*arkal kātnu*
Et cetera—*ityādi, ādi* (153)
Even—*samma ;* (adv.) *pani* (114, 121)
Evening—*sānjh, belukā*
Ever—*kaile pani* (113);–ever—*sukai* (24, 26, 154)
Every—*sabai* (24, 37, 142, 144)
Evidence—*gawā*
Evil—*dushta*
Exact—*thīk*
Examine—*jānchnu*
Example—*naparā*
Excavate—*khopnu*
Except—*bāto hernu* (g. G.)
Exchange—*sātnu*
Excuse—*niun. uttar* (122, 154)
Exhausted—*sakye ;* (fatigued) *galye*
Exhortation—*upades*
Expect—. . *chhāri ;* (conj.) 123
Expel—*nikālnu* (58)
Expense—*kharcha*
Extend—*barhāunnu*
Extra—*fālto*
Eye—*ānkhā*
Face—*mukh*
Factory—*godām*
Fairly—*nikai* (150)
Faith—*palyāro;* (v.)*palyāunnu*

Faithful—*imāndār*
Fall—*laṛnu, khasnu* (154); *parnu* (60, 147, 155)
False—*jhūṭho*
Family—*jahān*
Fan—*nāñlo*
Far—*ṭāṛo*
Fare—*tiro*
Farewell—*shubhamm* (133); *bidā*
Fat—*moṭo*
Fatal—*prāṇ māṉrne*
Father—*bābu*
Fatigue—*thakāi*
Fault—*kasūr*
Favour—*anugrah*; (partiality) *panpasāi*
Fear—*ḍar*; (v.) *ḍarāuṉnu* (138)
Feel—*khuwāuṉnu* (58)
Feel—*thāhā pāuṉnu*
Fell—*ḍhālnu*
Fence—*bār bārnu*
Fetch—*lyāuṉnu*, 143
Fetter—*nel*
Fever—*jaro*
Few—*thorai* (37)
Field—*khet*
Fight—*laṛāiṉ g.*
Fill—*bharnu* (g. Loc.)
Find—*pāuṉnu bheṭāuṉnu*
Fine—*masiṉno*; (n.) *jaribāṉā*
Finger—*auṉlo*
Finish—*pūro g.*; *saknu* (59)
Fire—*āgo*; (gun) *paṛkāuṉnu*
Fireplace—*chulhā*
Firewood—*dāuro*
First—*pahilo, pratham*
First-rate—*assal*
Fish—*māchchhā*
Fist—*muṛki*
Fit—*māphikko* (119, 120)
Flag—*dhajā, jhaṉḍī*
Flame—*juwālo*
Flank—*chheu*
Flat (a.)—*chepṭo*
Flax—*sunpāṭ*
Flea—*upiṉyā*
Flee—*bhāgnu*
Float—*pauraṉnu*
Flock—*baṭgāl*
Floor—*majheri, bhūiṉ*
Flow—*bahaṉnu* (58)
Flower—*phūl*
Fly—*uṛnu*; (n.) *jhiñgā*
Fold—*behernu*; (enclosure) *khor*; (-fold) *guṇā* (45)
Follow—*pachchhyāuṉnu*
Food—*khāṉne thok*
Fool—*mūrkha*
Foot—*goṛā*; (on f.) *paidalai*
Footstep—*ḍoro*
For—*lāgi* (g. G.) (conj.) *kasogaribhanye* (123); *gari* (139); 138
Forbid—*manāhi g.*
Force—*bal*
Ford—*jañār, ghāṭ*; (v.) *tarnu*
Foreign—*anyadesi*
Forfeit—*gumāuṉnu* (59)
Forget—*birsaṉnu* (60)
Fork—*kāṉṭā*
Former—*agāṛiko* (117)
Forth from—*paṭṭi bāṭo* (117)
Fortified position—*balliyo āṛ*

Fortune—*sanyog* ; (good) *su-sanyog*
Forward—*aghi*
Fowl—*kukhrā*
Frequently—*bārambār*
Fresh—*tājā*, *ālo*
Friend—*mitra*, *mit* (14)
From—*dekhi*, *bāto* (14, 116, 117, 119, 144)
Front—*agāri*, *aghi* (117)
Frost—*tusāro*
Fruit—*phal* ; (v.) *phalnu*
Full—*pūro*, *bharye*, *bhari* (116)
Funeral—*malāmī*
Furlough—*razāy*
Furniture—*ālmāl*
Further—*ajha*, *aru* (114)
Gallop—*phardāwāl dugurnu*
Gamble—*juwā khelnu*
Garden—*bārī* ; *kamān*
Gardener—*mālī*
Garrison—*chhāunnī*
Gate—*dhokā*
Gather—*batulnu* ; (i.) *jamnu*
Gelding—*khasi*
Gently—*bistārai*
Ghee—*ghiu*
Gift—*dān*
Girl—*keti*
Girth—*peti*
Give—*dinnu* (97)
Glass—*ainā*
Go—*jānnu* (97)
Goat—*bākhrā*
Gold—*sun*
Gong—*ghantā*
Good—*jāti* (36); (normal) *bhalo*
Gorkha (a.)—*gorkhālī*, *gorkhe* (1)
Grain—*anna* ; (corn) *dānā* ; (weight) *ratti* (48)
Gram—*chānā*
Grass—*ghāns*
Gratis—*sitteinmān*
Graze—(i.) *charnu* ; (t.) *charāunnu*
Great—*baro*, *thulo* (36)
Green—*harīyo*; (unripe) *kāncho*
Greeting—*sewā salām*
Grind—(crush) *pinnu*
Groom—*sais*
Ground—*bhūin*
Grow—*umrannu* ; (increase) *barhnu*
Guard—*chaukī paharā* ; (v.) *ch. p. basnu*
Guess—*bichār kātnu*, *arkalnu*
Guide—*bāto dekhāunnu*
Guilt—*dosh* ; (a.) *doshī*
Gun—*banduk*
Gunner—*golandāz*
Gutter—*kulo* ; (roof) *dunī*
Habit—*bānni* ; (v.) *b. basnu* (g. G.)
Habitually—59, 60, *barābar*
Hail—*asinnā*
Half—*ādhā* (45)
Halt—*ubhinnu*, *arinnu*
Hammer—*mārtaul* ; (large) *ghan* ; (gun) *ghorā*
Hand—*hāt*
Handcuff—*hatkari*
Handful—*muthi*, *hātbhari* (42, 115)

Handle—*benr*

Hang—(i.) *jhundinnu* ; (t.) *jhundyāunnu*

Hard—*sāro*

Hardly—*kathin saña*

Haste—*hatār* ; (v. i.) *hatārinnu*

Have—*hunnu* (68, 73, 72, 87, 91, 127, 146)

Haversack—*jholī*

He—*u*, *tyo* (20, 21)

Head—*sir*, *kapāl* ; (animal's) *ṭāuko*

Healthy—*niko*, *bhalāchangā* (36)

Heap—*thupro*

Hear—*sunnu*

Heart—*mutu*

Heat—*tāp* ; (v.) *tattāunnu* ; (sun) *ghām*

Heavy—*garhun*

Heel—*kurkucho*

Help—*gohār* (152), *upakār* (36)

Henceforth—144

Herd—*bathān*

Herdsman—*goṭhālā*

Here—*yahān*, 92

Hereupon—*yetimān*

Hew—*kundnu*

Hide—*luknu* ; (t.) *lukāunnu*

High—*algo*

Hill—*ḍānṛā*, *parbat*, *pahāṛ* ; (a.) *parbate*, *pahāṛe*

Hillside—*kachhār*

Hinder—*thunnu*

Hinge—*kabjā*

Hire—(person) *banni* ; (v.) *b. lagāunnu* (g. A.) ; (thing) *jyālā*, *kirāī*

Hither—*yetā* (115)

Hoe—*kodālo*, *faruwā*

Hole—*chhenṛ*, *ḍop*, *dulo*

Hollow—*khāṛal* ; (a.) *khālī*

Holy—*pawitra*

Home—*ghar* ; (v.) *ghar jānnu*

Honest—*īmāndār*

Honour—*mān*, *ijjat*

Hoof—*khur*

Hope—*āshā* ; (v.) *ā. dekhnu* (g. G.)

Horse—*ghoṛā*

Hot—*tāto*

Hour—*ghar* ; (50)

House—*ghar*

How—*kaso*, *kasto*

How much—*kati*, *katti* (27, 37)

However—*tā* (115) ; (conj.) *jaunai parile pani* (144)

Human—155

Hunger—*bhok* ; (a.) *bhoko* ; (v.) *bhokāunnu*

Hunt—*sikār khelnu*

Hunter—*sikārī*

Hurt—*choṭ*

Husband—*logne*, *khasam*

Husbandman—*kisāni*

I—*man*

Identify—*chinnu*

Idle—*alchhe*

Idol—*mūrtti*

If—81, 123, 145

If I am, be—85

If so be that—123

Ignorant of—*dekhi ajñānī h.*

Ill—*dukhye* ; (adv.) *najāti narāmro*

Immediately—*turantai*, 120
Impertinent—*ḍhīṭo*
Impossible—*huṉdaina* (78)
In—13, 15, 92, 116, 117
In order that—122
In order to—118
Inasmuch as—114
Inch—*aiṉchi*
Incline—(ascent) *ukālo*
Including—*samet* (119, 120)
Inconsistent—146
Increase—*baṛhtī*; (v. i.) *baṛhnu*
Incredible—146
Indeed—*tā*, *po* (14, 38, 115)
Indian corn—*makai*
Infectious—*desānko*
Inform—*janāuṉnu*
Injustice—*annye*
Innocent—*nirdoṣh*
Inside—*bhitra* (117)
Insomuch that—123
Instalment—*kisti* ; *bhāg*
Instead of—*sāṭo* (117)
Insubordination—*namanāī*
Intention—*man*
Intentionally—*jāni būjhikana*
Interest—(money) *byāj*
Interpreter—*domāse*
Intervene—60
Into—13, 15
Intrenchment—*āṛ*
Investigate—*ḍhūṉṛalnu*
Invitation—*nimto* ; (v.) *nimtaṉnu*
Iron—*phalam*
It—*tyo* (21, 136)
Jackal—*syāl*
Jewel—*gahanā*
Job—*melo*, *kām*
Join—*joṛnu*
Joint—*joṛni*, *gāṉṭho*
Journey—*yātrā*, *pardes*
Judge—*bichārnu* ; (n.) *bichārī*
Juice—*ras*
Jump—*phāl hānnu*, *uphraṉnu*
Jungle—*jaṉgal* ; (cutting) *phaṉṛāī*
Just—*niyālu*
Justice—*niyā*
Keep—*rākhnu* (60)
Key—*chābī*
Kick—*lāttale hirkauṉnu*
Kill—*māṉrnu* (58), *kāṭnu*
Kiln—*bhaṭṭi*
Kin—*kuṭumba* (f.—*benī*)
Kind—*rakam* ; (a.) *hitkārī*
Kindle—(t.) *salkāuṉnu*
Knee—*ghuṉṛā*
Kneel—*ghuṉṛā ṭeknu*
Knife—*chhuri*, *karda*
Knock—*ṭhok* ; (v.) *ṭhoknu* ; (down) *bhatkāuṉnu*
Knot—*gāṉṭho*
Know—*jānnu* (97), etc. (154)
Knowledge—*jñān*, *bidye*
Knuckle—*auṉlāko gāṉṭho*
'Kookree'—*khukuri*
Labourer—*kūli* ; (field) *khetālā*
Ladder—*lisnu*
Lame—*khoraṉḍe* ; (v.) *khochyāuṉnu*
Lamp—*battī*
Land—*jimīn*
Landslip—*pairo*

Language—*bolī*
Large—*ṭhulo*
Last—*pachhillo*
Late—(tardy) *aberko, ḍhilo*
Laugh—*hāṉsnu*
Law—*ain*
Lay—*rākhnu ;* (eggs) *phul pārnu ;* (table) *ochhyāuṉnu*
Lazy—*alchhe*
Lead—(metal) *sīsā ;* (v.) *li-hiṉṛālnu*
Leaf—*patti*
Lean—*dublo ;* (v.) *aṛes lāgnu* (g. L.)
Learn—*siknu*
Least—*sāṉnu* (39) ; (at l.) *kamko kam*
Leather—*chhālā*
Leave—*chhoṛnu ;* (n.) *chhuṭṭī ;* (farewell) *bidā*
Leech—*jugā*
Leg—*khuṭṭā*
Leisure—*belā*
Lend—*ṛiṇ d.*
Length—*laṉmai*
Leopard—*chituwā*
Less—*sāṉnu* (39), *kam, ghaṭī*
Lest—81, 123, 129
Let—(allow) *diṉnu* (88); (land) *kutmāṉ d. ;* (house, &c.) *jyālāmāṉ d. ;* (down, by a rope, *e.g.*) *surkyāi d.*
Letter—*chiṭṭhī*
Level—(a.) *samma, samthar ;* (tool) *sādni ;* (v.) *sam-myāuṉnu*
Lid—*ḍhakani*

Licence—*parwānā*
Lie—(n.) *ḍhāṉṭ, jhūṭh ;* (v.) *ḍhāṉṭnu*
Lie—(down) *ḍhalkaṉnu*
Life—*jiuṉni*
Lifetime—*jīuṉdo jīwan* (146)
Lift—*uṭhāuṉnu uchālnu*
Light—(not heavy) *haluñ ;* (not dark) *ujiyālo* (50)
Like—*jasto ; jhaiṉ, sari* (146, 119) ; (v.) 152
Lime—*chun*
Line—*lahar*
Lintel—*sañār*
List—*bahī*
Little—*sāṉnu, chhoṭo ;* (not much) *alik*
Live—*jīuṉnu* (58) ; (dwell) *basnu*
Load—*bhāri, bojhā*
Lock—*tālchā ;* (gun) *chāṃp*
Loft—*machān*
Log—*choiṭā, phablyāṉṭo*
Long—*lāṉmo*
Look—*hernu*
Loose—*khukulo ;* (v.) *phukāuṉ-nu* (151)
Lose—*harāuṉnu*
Loss—*noksān ;* (at a l., *i.e.*, puzzled) *anyolmāṉ* (132)
Loud—*sāro, charko*
Low—*hoṉcho*
Machine—*kal*
Mad—*pāgal, baulāhā* (36)
Maid—*kannye*
Main—(a.) *mūl*
Make—*banāuṉnu, tulyāuṉnu, garnu*

Mallet—*mungro*
Man—*lognemānchhe*
Manage—*chalāunnu*
Mange—*luto*
Mango—*āmp*
Manner—*rīt*
Manners—(breeding) *dhanga*
Manure—*mal*
Many—*dherai* (37)
Mark—*chinnu*
Marriage—*byāhā, bihā*
Marsh—*aul*
Mason—*gārokarmī, rāj*
Master—*mālik, swāmī*
Matter—*kuro, bishay* (9); (suppurating) *pip*
Maund—*man* (48)
May—(v.) 80, 88 ; (month) 51
Meaning—*ariha*
Means—*upāy* ; 144 ; 117
Measles—*pānīsaro, dādurā*
Measure—*nāp* ; (v.) *nāpnu*
Measuring-rod—*ṭāngo*
Medicine—*oshati* (9), *dawāi*
Meet—*bheṭnu*
Melt—*galnu* (i.); *gālnu* (t.)
Mend—*sudhārnu, ṭālnu, tunnu*
Merciful—*dayālu* (37)
Mercy—*dayā*
Message—*samāchār, khabar*
Metal—*darba*
Midday—50
Middle—*bīch, mānjha* (117)
Midnight—50, *ādhā rāt*
Might—*sāmartha* ; (v.) 87, 88
Mile—*mail, ādhā kos*
Milk—*dut, dud* ; (v.) *duhunnu* (97)
Mind—man; (v.) *dhandā mānnu* (g. G.)
Mine—*mero* ; (pit) *khāni*; (sapping) *suruñ*
Minus—*kam* (57)
Minute—50
Miscarry—*tuhunnu* (97)
Miss—*na pāunnu, na lāgnu, birāunnu*
Mist—*kuiro*
Mistake—*bhūl*
Mix—*misāunnu*
Moment—*chhin, palā* (50)
Money—*rupiyā paisā*
Month—*mahīnā, mās* (51)
Moon—*jūn*
More—*besi, jyāsti, aru* (27, 146) ; (the m.) 114 ; (m. than once) 146.
Moreover—*aru pani, ajhai*
Morning—*bihān* ; (next m.) *bholi palṭo* ; (in the m.) *bihāna*
Mortar—(vessel) *okhlī* ; (cement) *gāro chunpāni, muchhyeko mānṭo*
Moss—*jhyāu*
Most—*dherai*, 39
Mother—*āmmā*
Mould (matrix)—*sāncho*
Mount—*mānthi charhnu*
Mouth—*mukh*
Move—(i.) *chalnu, chalahala g.*; (t.) *sārnu*
Much—*dher* ; (as m.) *jati* ; (so

m.) *yeti, tyeti, tati* ; (how m.) *kati*
Mud—*mānṭo, hilo*
Mule—*khachchar*
Multiply—(t.) *guṇā g.*
Muslin—*malmal*
Must—78, 146
Mutiny—*baluwā*
Muzzle—*mahalā* ; (gun) *moṉhoṛā*
My—*mero*
Nail—(finger) *nañ* ; (metal) *khīl, kānṭi*
Naked—*nāṉgo*
Name—*nāṉu* (16, 73, 143)
Namely—*arthāt*
Narrow—*sāṉguro*
Native—*desī* ; (n. place) *janmades*
Nay—*nāhīṉ*
Near—*najik* (117)
Necessarily—*abasse*
Necessary—*khāṉcho* (146)
Neck—*galā*
Needle—*suiro*
Neighbour—*kshimeki* (14)
Neither—38, 121
Net—*jāl*
Never—*kaile pani hoina* (113) ; (n. so) 144
Nevertheless—121
New—*nayā*
News—*khabar*
Next—*dosro* ; (n. year) *āghuñ*
Night—*rāt* ; (at n.) *rāti*
Nip—*chimaṭnu*
Nip off—*chuṉṛnu*
No—*hoina, ahaṉ* (67, 78, 113, 115) ; (no small) 142
Noise—*khailābailā*
None—27
Nor—*ani na*
North—*uttar*
Nose—*nākh*
Not—*na* (113, 62) ; (n. that) 148
Nothing—*kyei pani hoina*
Now—*aile, aba* (113, 116)
Number—*ganti*
Nut—*bādām* ; (bolt) *ḍhibri*
O—132
Oath—*kasam, pashṭan*
Obey—*mānnu*
Objection—*rokṭok, chhekthun*
Obstinate—*aṭṭeri* (36)
O'clock—*baji* (50)
Odd—*fālṭo, fuṛkaro*
Of—12
Off—*māṉthi bāṭo* (119) ; (gone) *gai gayo*
Often—*bārambār*
Oh—132 ; (oh that) 81
Oil—*tel*
Old—(person) *būrho* ; (thing) *purāṉnu*
On—13, 15, 119
Once—*ek khep*
One—*ek* (38, 44, 151) ; (o. another) 151, 27
Only—*khāli* (114, 136)
Open—*ughārnu, kholnu*
Opinion—*mato, bichār*
Opportunity—*belā*

Opposite—*sānmu*, *sānmunne*, *ulṭāulo*, *biblyānto* (117)
Opposition—*birodh*
Or—*ki* (121)
Orange—*suntalā*
Order—*hukum*; (v.) *arhāunnu*; (mandate) *chalān*; (arrangement) *melo*, *ṭhakān*
Other—*aru* (26, 27, 36)
Otherwise—123
Ought—87, 146, *chāhinchha*, *chāhinthyo*
Our—*hānmro*
Out—*bāira*; (117, 133); (v.) *niklannu* (58)
Outstrip—*uchhinnu*
Oven—*aghennā*
Over—*mānthi* (119, 136, 148)
Overseer—*dafādār*
Overtake—*phelā pārnu*
Overturn—*ulṭāunnu*
Owe—*riṇ kārnu*, *riṇī h.*
Own—*āphnu* (37)
Owner—*dhani*
Ox—*goru*
Pack—*pokā pārnu*
Pail—*ḍol*
Pain—*dukha*
Paint—*rang*
Pair—*joṛā* (45)
Palm—(hand) *hatkelā*
Paper—*kāgat*
Pardon—*māf*
Part—*bhāg*, *ansha*, *hissā*
Particle—*rati*
Partly—*ek chheu*, *ali ali*

Pass—(away) *bitnu*; (time) *kāṭnu*; (outstrip) *uchhinnu*; (by) *bāṭo jānnu* (125); (mt.) *ghāṭī*; (clearance) *chalān*; (permit) *parwānā*
Pasture—*kharka*
Pay—*tirnu*, *dām dinnu*
Peace—*mel*, *milāp*
Peg—*phesā*
Pen—*kalam*
Pencil—*pilsiñ*
Pension—*pinshan*
People—*log* (16)
Per cent.—*saikaṛā* (45)
Perhaps—*holā*, *koni* (114)
Perjury—*jhūṭhkasam*
Permanent—*pakkā*, *sadhainko*
Permission—*ājñā* (78)
Permit—*dinnu* (59); (n.) *parwānā*
Person—*janā*, *mānchhe*, (44, 19)
Personally—*khud*, *āphai*
Persuade—*manāunnu* (60)
Pick—*ṭipnu*; (axe) *gainti*
Piece—*ṭukro*; (p. work) *ṭhīkā*
Pig—*sungur*
Pillar—*khāmbo*
Pioneer—(soldier) *beldār*
Pious—*bhakta*
Pit—*khāṛal*
Pitch—*rokan*; (tent) *ṭāngnu*
Pitcher—*ghailā*
Place—*ṭhānu*, 117
Plague—*ruṛhi*
Plain—*maidān*; (a.) *samma*, *sāf*
Plains—*mades*
Plaint—*dāwā*

Plaintiff—*phirāte, sāhū*
Plait—*bunnu*
Plan—*rīt, ḍhāṉchā*
Plane—(tool) *raṉḍhā*
Plank—*phalyāk*
Plant—*ropnu, lagāuṉnu* ; (n.) *biruwā*
Plantain – *kerā*
Plate—*thāl*
Play—*khelnu*
Please—*khush pārnu* (g. A.)
Pleased—*khushi*
Pleasure—*khushī*
Pledge—*bandhak*
Plenty—*saha, dherai*
Plough—*halo* ; (v.) *h jotnu*
Pluck—*ṭipnu*
Plummet—*sāhul*
Plunder—*lūṭ* ; (v.) *lūṭnu*
Point—*ṭuppā* ; 141
Poison—*bikh*
Police Office—*thānā*
Polish—*chamkāuṉnu*
Pommel—*kāṭhī, pāṉgro*
Pond—*pokhari*
Poor—*kaṉgāli*
Possible—*huṉnu sakne*, 150
Post—(door) *sañār* ; (letter) *hulāk, ḍāk*; (military) *chaukī*
Postpone—*ṭārnu*
Potato—*ālū*
Pouch—(cartridge) *tosdān*
Pour—*jhārnu, khanyāuṉnu*
Powder—*bāruk* ; (dust) *dhūlo*
Practise—*sādhnu*
Prefer—137, 151
Prepare—*tiyār pārnu*
Presence—*sāṉmel*, 117
Present—(place) *hājir* ; (time) *huṉdo barttamān* ; (gift) *bakshish* ; (give) *bakshi diṉnu*
Preserve—*bachāi rākhnu*
Press—(down) *khāṉdnu*; (urge) *ḍhipi lāuṉnu* (g. A.); (squeeze) *niṉcharnu*; (crowd) *ghachcha diṉnu* (g. D.); (printing) *chhāpākhānā*
Pretence—*niuṉ*
Prevent—*roknu*
Price—*dām*
Print—*chhāpnu*
Private—*ekāntako, nij*
Probably—*holā* (80)
Profit—*nāfā*
Progress—(v.) *sarnu* (150), *baṛhnu*
Promise—*karahār*
Promotion—*baṛhtī*
Proof—*sābuṭi*
Proper (v.)—*suwāuṉnu* (151)
Protection—*rakshe*
Provisions—*rasad*
Provoke—*jiskyāuṉnu*
Prune—*kalam kāṭnu*
Pull—*tānnu*; (down) *bhatkāuṉnu*
Punishment—*daṉda*
Purpose—*artha, man*, 117
Pursue—*khednu*
Push—*ṭhelnu, ghacheṭnu*
Put—*rākhnu* ; (off) *jhiknu* ; (on) *lagāuṉnu*
Quarrel—*jhagarā*
Quarrelsome—*jhagarelu*
Quench—*nibhāuṉnu*
Question—*sodhni* ; (v.) *sodhnu*

Quick—*chhiṭo*
Quiet—*chāmchum*
Quite—*syāṇṭṭhai*, *sarāsar*, 60
Race—*hoṛābāji*
Race-course—*akhāṛā*
Rafter—*ḍāṇṛā*
Rag—*jhumro*
Rain—*parne pānī*
Raise—*uṭhāuṇnu*
Ramrod—*gaj*
Random—*jatābhābi* (143)
Rank—*darjā*
Rate—*hisāp*, *bhāu*
Rather—*baru*, *jhan* (114, 115, 151)
Ravine—*kholṭhā*
Raw—*kāṇcho*, *kachchā*
Reach—*summa pugnu*
Read—*parnu*
Ready—*tiyār*
Rebellion—*balwā*
Rebuke—*dhamkī*; (v.) *hakārnu*
Receive—*pāuṇnu*; *grahaṇ g.*
Recently—*asti*, *alik din bhayo*
Recognize—*chinnu*
Recommend—*sarkāuṇnu*
Reconnoitre—*khoji hernu*
Recruit—*bhartī g.*
Red—*rāto*, *lāl*
Refuse—*kasingar*; (v.) *nāhīṇ bhannu*
Regiment—*palṭan*
Regularly—*barābar*
Rein—*lagam*
Relay—*ḍāk*; (v.) *ḍāk basāuṇnu*
Relief—(military) *badalī*
Remain—*rahaṇnu* (61, 139)
Remainder—*bāṇki*
Remember—*samjhaṇnu*; (n.) *samjhanā*
Remind—*samjhāuṇnu*
Rent—*tiro*, *kirāī*, *bāhāli*
Repair—*sājnu*, *sudhārnu*
Repent—(*dekhi*) *pachhtāuṇnu* (61)
Reply—*juwāp*
Reprimand—*ghurki*
Reproof—*dhamkī*
Request—*binti*
Require—*māṇgnu*
Reserve—*rakhi chhoṛnu*
Resolve—*ṭhaharāuṇnu*
Respect—*mān*
Respectable—*sajjan*
Responsible—*juwāp diṇnu parne*
Rest—*bishrām*; (v.) *bisāuṇnu*; (platform) *phalaiṇchā*
Result—*nikās*, *phal*
Retire—*pharki jāṇnu*
Retreat—*haṭi jāṇnu*
Return—*pharkaṇnu*; (t.) *pharkāuṇnu*; (in r. for) *sāṭomāṇ*
Reverse—(opposite) *ulṭāulo* (117)
Revetment—*parkāl*
Reward—*inām*
Rice—*chāṇwal*; (cooked) *bhāt*; (growing) *dhān*
Riches—*dhan*
Ride—*sawārī h.*
Ridge—*lekh*, *ḍeṅ*; (piece) *balo*
Right—*ṭhīk*, 151; (n.) *aktiyār*; (hand) *dāhiṇno*

Ring—*mundro*
Ripe—*pākye, pakkā*
Rise—*uṭhnu* (58)
River—*nadī* ; (small) *kholā*
Road—*bāṭo* ; (paved) *saṭak*
Road-metal—*roṛā*
Roast—*sekaunnu*
Rob—*ṭhagnu*
Rock—*shilāpatthar* ; (out-standing) *ḍhānṛ*
Rod—*lauro*
Roll—*palṭaunnu*; (tea) *mānṛnu*
Roof—*chhānā*
Room—*koṭhā* ; (space) *ṭhānu*
Root—*jarā* ; (up) *ukhelnu*
Rope—*ḍorī* ; (porter's) *nāmlo*
Rot—*kuhunnu* (58)
Rough—*khasro* ; (ground) *kharbar*
Round—*ḍallo* ; (spherical) *gol* ; (prep.) *chheuchhāu* ; (all r.) *chārai tira*
Row—*lahar*
Rub—*malnu*
Rubbish—*kasingar*
Rule—*bidhi*
Run—*dugurnu*
Rush upon—*mānthi jāi lāgnu*
Rust—*khīyā*
Sack—*borā*
Saddle—*jīn* ; (v.) *j. kasnu*
Sake—*lāgi* (117)
Sale—*bikri*
Salt—*nun* ; (a.) *nunīlo*
Saltpetre—*sorā*
Same—*tyei, jastai* (23, 151, 152)
Sand—*bāluwā*
Satisfied—*santushṭa*
Save—*bachāunnu*
Saw—*ārā*
Say—*bhannu, kahannu*
Scabbard—*khol, dāp*
Scarce—*thorai*
Scatter—(t.) *phinjāunnu*
Scissors—*kainchi*
Scoff—*ṭhaṭṭhā g.*
Scrape—*khurkannu*
Screw—*pech*
Screwdriver—*pechkas*
Seal—*chhāp*
Seat—*pīrhā*
Season—*ṛitu, samay*
Seasonable—*belā māphikko*
Seasoned—(matured) *pakkā*
Second—*dosro*
Secret—(a.) *gupta*
Secretly—*luki luki*
See—*dekhnu*
Seed—*biu* ; (tea) *geṛā* ; (-ling) *biruwā*
Seeing that—123
Seek—*khojnu*
Seem—*jasto h.*
Seer—(weight) *ser* (48, 49)
Seize—*samātnu*
Seldom—*kaile 2 māntrai*
Select—*chhānnu*
Self—*āphai* (27, 28)
Sell—*bechnu* (58)
Send—*paṭhāunnu* (143)
Sentry—*senṭri, paharū* ; (v.) *paharā* (or *chaukī*) *basnu*
Sentry-box—*tauwā*

S. parate—*alag* ; (v.) *a. g.*
Serpent—*sāp*
Servant—*nokar*, *chākare*
Set—*rākhnu* ; (fire to) *āgo lagāunnu* ; (out) *sidhārnu* ; (on way) 152
Several—*dherjaso* (36)
Sew—*silāī g.*
Shake—*hallāunnu*
Shall—78, 146
Shallow—*jañāre*
Shape—*ḍawal*, *rūp*
Share—*bhāg*
Sharp—*lāgne*
Sharpening-stone—*sān*
Shavings—*jhūs*
She—*u*, *tyo* (20)
Sheath—*dāp*
Shed—*kaṭerā*
Sheep—*bhenṛā*
Sheet—*chaddar*
Shelter—*āṛ*
Shepherd—*gothālā*
Shew—*dekhāunnu*
Shoe—*juttā* ; (horse) *nāl*
Shoot—*banduk paṛkāunnu*, *golile hānnu* ; (plant) *ṭusā*
Short—*chhoṭo* ; (to be s. of) 130
Shortly—(soon) *alik dinmān*
Should—87
Shoulder—*kum*, *kāndh*
Shout—*karāunnu*
Shower—*jharī*
Shut—*thunnu*
Shutter—*jhilmile*
Sick—*bimār*, *madhauro*
Sickle—*hansiyā*
Sickly—*rogī* ; (plant) *sikro*
Side—*chheu*, *paṭṭi*, *tira* ; (on this s.) *yeso* (or *wallo*) *paṭṭi* ; (on that s.) *uso* (or *pallo*) *paṭṭi* ; (on all s.) *chheuchāu*, *waripari* (117, 119, 148, 133)
Sieve—*chālni*
Sift—*chālnu*
Sight—(gun) *makkhī*, *ḍig*
Sign—*chinnu*
Signal—*sān*
Signature—*sahī*
Silence—*chup*
Silver—*chāndī*
Sin—*pāp* ; (v.) *p. g.*
Sinner—*pāpī* (14)
Since—119, 123, 129, 141, 144
Singe—*alik ḍaṛāunnu*
Single—*eklo*, *ekā* (44)
Singly—*ek ek garī*
Sister—*didī*, (younger) *bainnī*
Sit—*basnu*
Size—*ḍāl*, *kad*
Skill—*sip*
Skilful—*sipālu*
Skin—*chhālā*
Slack—*ḍhilo*
Slave—*kamānrā*, *dās*
Sleep—*sutnu* ; (n.) *nind*
Slip—*chiplinnu*
Slippery—*chiplo*
Slow—*susto*, *ḍhilo*
Small—*sānnu*, *chhoto* (36)
Small-pox—*māī*
Smear—*lipnu*
Smell—*gandha* ; (v. t.) *sūnghnu*
Smoke—*dhuwān*

Smooth—*chillo*
Snake—*sāp*
Snow—*hiṉu*
So—*yeso, tyeso, yesto, tyesto; ta* (114–116)
Soever—26
So much—*yeti, tyeti*
So that—123
So then—*ta taba tā* (115)
So-called—143
Soft—*naram*
Solder—*rāṉg*
Soldier—*tilaṉgā, sipāṉi*
Some—*koī, kyei, kati* (26,27,37, 151; (s. or other) 25, 27, 152
Somehow—*katai, kunai parile* (144)
Sometimes—*kaile kaile* (113)
Somewhere—*kahīṉ, katai*
Son—*chhoro* (12)
Soon—*chāṉṛai*; (as s. as) *jasai*
Sore—*ghāu*
Sorrow—*shok*
Sort—*rakam*; (v.) *chhānnu*
Sound—*sor*; (a.) *niko*; (v.) *bajāuṉnu*
Sour—*amīlo*
South—*dakkhin*
Sow—*chharnu*
Spade—*belchā*
Spare—(a.) *fālṭo*; (v.) *ṭiṭhāuṉnu*
Speak—*bolnu* (61, 120)
Spear—*bhālā*
Special—*nij*
Speed—*dhāwā*
Spend—*kharchaṉnu*; (time) *kāṭnu*

Spider—*mākuro*
Spill—*pokhnu*
Spin—*kāṭnu*
Spit—*thūknu*
Splinter—*chirā*
Split—*chirnu*
Split bamboo—*kapṭerā*
Spoil—*bigārnu*
Spoke—*pakheṭo*
Spoon—*chamach, ḍāṛu*
Spread—(t.) *phailāuṉnu*
Spring—(gun) *kamāni*; 52
Spring-water—*jaruwā pānī*
Sprout—*ṭusā*
Spy—*bhediyā*
Square—(s.) *chārpāṭe, chārkuṉne*
Squeeze—*niṉcharnu, chepnu*
Stab—*ghochnu*
Stair—(stone) *bharyāñ*; (wood) *siṉṛhi*
Stale—*bāsi*
Stalk—*ḍāṉṭh*
Stall—*kaṭerā*
Stand—*ubhiṉnu*
Standing-order—*chalyeko ain*
State—(condition) *gat*
Stay—*basi rahaṉnu*
Steal—*chornu*
Steam—*bāf*
Steel—*ispāt*
Steep—(up) *ukālo*; (down) *orhālo*
Step—*phaṛkā*; (stair) *khuṛkilo*; foots.) *ḍoro*
Stick—*lauro*; (be caught) *al jhaṉnu*

Still—(adv.) *aile samma, ajha* (114); (v.i.) *na chali basnu*
Stirrup—*rikāb*
Stone—*ḍhungā*
Stool—*chaukī*
Stop—(t.) *thāmnu*; (i.) 58
Store—*bhanṛār*; (room) *godām*
Storey—*talā*
Storm—*āndhī*
Straight—*sojo*
Strange—*parāyko, udekko*
Straw—*parāl*
Strength—*sāmartha, shakti, bal*
Stretch—(t.) *pasārnu*
Strike—*hirkāunnu*; (o'clock) *bajnu* (50)
Strip—*nikhārnu*; (clothes) *kāṛnu*
Strong—*balliyo*
Stubble—*buchkā*
Stumble—*ṭhes khānnu*
Subjection—*tābi*
Substantial—*pakkā*
Substitute—*badalī*
Such—*yesto, tyesto* (151)
Suddenly—*ekkāsi*
Suffering—*dukha* (16)
Sufficient—*dherai*; " *bho* " (77)
Suitable—*māphikko* (119, 120)
Sulphur—*gandhak*
Summon—143
Sun—*ghām*; (-rise) *uday*
Supply—*lyāi d., pāri d.*
Support—*sambhālnu*; *pālnu*; (n.) *ṭekan*
Surely—*sānchai*
Surrender—*pakarā parnu*; (t.) *sumpi d.*
Surround—*ghernu*
Survive—*jīi rahannu*
Suspicion—*shankā*
Swear—*kasam khānnu*
Sweat—*pasīnā*
Sweep—*baṛhāṛnu*; (up) *sohar* [*nu*
Sweet—*miṭho*
Swim—*paurannu*
Sword—*tarawār, kharga*
Table—*mej*
Tail—*puchhar*
Take—*linnu, lyāunnu*; (away) *laijānnu, lānnu*; (out) *nikāl-nu, jhiknu*
Tame—*taha lāyeko, paluwā*
Tank—*pokhari*
Target—*tārā*
Task—*kām*
Taste—*chākhnu*
Tea—*chiyā*
Teach—*sikāunnu*
Teak—*ṭuni*
Tear—*phāṭnu*
Telegraph—*tār*
Telescope—*durbin*
Tell—*bhani d.*
Temporary—*kachchā*
Tent—*pāl, chhāhārī*
Than—*bhandā* (39)
Thank—*guṇ mānnu* (g. G.); (" thank you ") *āphukā guṇ*
That—*tyo, u* (22, 136); *bhani* (88, 122)
Thatch—*khar*
The—13

Their—*tinako* (23, 20)
Then—*taba, ta* (113, 115, 121)
Thence—*tyahān bāṭo*
Thenceforth—144
There—*tyahān* 114, 115, 136)
Thereabouts—92
Therefore—*ta, yeskāraṇ* (115)
Thereupon—*tyetimān* (94)
These—*yi* (23)
They—*ti* (23, 20)
Thick—*moṭo ;* (dense) *bāklo*
Thief—*chor ;* (v.) *chornu*
Thin—*pātulo ;* (lean) *dublo*
Thing—*thok*
Think—*ṭhānnu ;* (care) *sochnu*
Thirst—*tirkhā;* (v.) *tirkhāunnu*
This—*yo* (22)
Thistle—*bihīn*
Thither—*utā* (115)
Thorn—*kānṛā*
Thorough—*pakkā*
Though—123, 128, 145
Thread—*dhāgo*
Threat—*dhamkī*
Through—*mānjha bāṭo* (14, 115, 117, 92, 148)
Throughout—*bhari* (115)
Throw—*āphālnu* (60)
Thumb—*buṛhiaunlo*
Thus—*yeso* (115)
Tidy—*ṭhikṭhāk*
Tie—*kasnu*
Tile—*jhiñgaṭi*
Till—*samma* (88, 119, 120)
Time—*belā ;* (season) *samay ;* (turn) *phero, khep, bār, pālo*
Tip—*ṭuppo*
To—12, 13, 14, 15, 116, 119
To-day—*āju*
Toe—*aunlo*
Together—*ek saña*
To-morrow—*bholi ;* (day after t.) *parsi*
Tongue—*jibro*
Too—(adv.) *sārai, hunnu na sakne gari ;* (conj.) *pani*
Tool—*hatiyār*
Tooth—*dānt*
Top—*ṭuppo, thāpli, phurkā*
Torch—*rānko*
Torrent—*chhāngo*
Total—*jamā*
Touch—*chhunnu*
Towards—*tira* (119)
Town—*sahar*
Trace—*goho*
Track—*pāilo*
Trade—*bepār*
Trample—*dalnu*
Trap—*pāso*
Tray—*ārhi* (50)
Treachery—*kapaṭ*
Tread on—*kulchi d. ;* (grain) *dānīn g.*
Treason—*rājdroh*
Treasury—*dhansār*
Tree—*rukh*
Trench—*khāwā*
Trespass—*nānghi pasnu*
Tribute—*kar*
Trigger—*liblibi, ṭrigar, aunlā-* [*kal*
Trigger-guard—*ṭrigargāraṭ*
Trip—*ṭhes khānnu*
Triple—*teharo* (46)

Trot—*kadam dugurnu*
Trouble—*dukha*
Trough—*ḍoṉṟ*
Trowel—*khurpi*
True—*sāncho, sachchā*
Trust—*bharosā*
Try—*khojnu ;* (judge) *bichār g.*
Turn—(i.) *ghumnu ;* (back) *pharkannu*
Turns, By,—*pālo pālo*
Twist—*bāṭnu*
Umbrella—*chhātā*
Unawares—*bithāhā*
Under—*muni ; tala* (119)
Understand—*būjhnu* (58)
Ungrateful—*auguni*
Uniform—(n.) *bānā, urdi*
Uniformly—*ekaināṉse*
Unite—*saña joṟnu*
Unjust—*anyāi*
Unless—123
Unload—*bhāri orhālnu*
Unripe—*kāṉcho*
Unite—*phukālnu*
Unwilling—*aman*
Up—*māṉthi, ūmbho* (119)
Up and down—115
Upper—*māṉthillo*
Uproot—*ukhelnu*
Upside down—*ulṭā*
Upwards—*māstira*
Use—*kām;* (v.) *lāuṉnu; chalan g.* (g. G.)
Useful—*kāmako*
Useless—*berthai*
Vaccinate—*khopāuṉnu*
Valid—*pakkā*
Valley—*tari*
Value—*mol*
Various—*waliwalikā* (152)
Vegetable—*sāgpāt*
Velocity—*beg*
Verdict—*bichārājñā*
Very—*baṟo, agghor* (151)
Vessel—*bhāṉṟā*
Via—*bāṟo* (117, 119)
Victory—*jīt*
View to, With a,—*nimti* (117)
Village—*gāṉu*
Violence—*bal*
Visit—*bheṭ ;* (v.) *darsanmāṉ jāṉnu* (g. G.)
Voluntarily—*āphaile, āphnu khushīle, chāhā gari*
Wages—*talab, dormāhā*
Waist—*kammar*
Wait—*parkhi basnu*
Wake—(i.) *jāgnu ;* (t.) *jagāuṉnu*
Walk—*hiṉṟnu ;* (about) *ḍulnu* (115)
Wall—*gāro, bhittā, dewāl ;* (large) *parkhāl*
Wander—*abāṭo lāgnu*
Want—*ghaṭī ;* (v.) *māṉgnu*
Wanted—*chāhīṉdo*
Wanting in—*rahit* (119)
Warm—*tāto*
Warn—*chetāuṉnu*
Warrant—*parwānā*
Wash—*dhuṉnu* (97)
Waste—*noksān*
Watch—*gharī, pahar* (50) ; (v.) *heri rahaṉnu*
Water—*pānī ;* (v.) *p. lagāuṉnu*

Way—*pari* ; (road) *bāṭo*
Weak—*nirbal*
Wear—(clothes)*lāuṉnu*;(away. i.) *khīīṉnu*, (t.) *khīyāuṉnu*
Weary—*thākye*
Weed—*jhār*
Week—*sātā* (50)
Weep—*ruṉnu* (97)
Weigh—*jokhnu*, *taulaṉnu* (48)
Weighing-machine—*kāṉṭā* ; (large) *tulo*, *tarāju*
Weight—*bhār*: (measure) *ḍhak*, *ser*
Well—(a.) *rāmro* ; (healthy) *niko* ; (adv.) *jati* ; (n.) *kuwā*
West—*pachchhiuṉ*
Wet—*bhijāuṉnu*
What—*kye*, *kyā* (25)
Whatever, Whatsoever—24, 25, 26, 154
Wheat—*gahūṉ*
Wheel—*paiyā*
When—*kaile* ?, *jaba* (94, 113, 134)
Whence—*kahāṉ bāto* ?, *jahāṉ bāṭo*
Where—*kahāṉ* ?, *jahāṉ* (114)
Whereas—*jaba*. . *ta* (129)
Wherefore—123
Whether—123
Which—*kun* ?, *jo*, *jun* (23, 25)
Whichever—24
While—75, 93, 94 ; (wh. yet) 154
Whistle—*swisalā*
White—*seto*
Whitewash—*chun lāuṉnu*
Whither—*katā* ?, *jatā*
Who—*ko*, *kun* ? ; *jo*, *jun* (23, 24)
Whoever, Whosoever—(24, 81, 154)
Whole—*sabai*, *siṉgai*
Why—*kina*
Wick—*saleto*
Wide—*gajilo*, *pharāk*
Widow—*bidhuwī*
Wife—*swāsnī*, *mukheṉnī*, *ghar-bār*
Wilfully—152
Will—*ichchhe*, 78, 152
Willing—*rāji*
Willingly—152
Wind—*batās*
Window—*jhyāl*, *khirkī*
Winnow—*niphannu*,*battāuṉnu*
Winter—*hiṉudo*, *jāṛo*, 52
Wipe—*puchhnu*
Wisdom—*buddhi*
Wish—*ichchhe*, *man* (59, 78, 152)
With—*saña*, *sita* (12, 14, 116, 119, 120)
Wither—(i.) *oilhīṉnu*
Within—*bhitra* (117)
Without—*binā* (116, 117)
Witness—*gawāī* ; (testimony) *gawāh*
Woman—*āimāi*, *strī*
Won't—78
Wood—*kāṭh*
Wool—*ūn*
Word—*kuro* ; *shabda*
Work—*kām*
World—*lok*, *jagat*, *saṉsār*

Worm—*aunsā, kirā*
Worship—*pūjā*
Worth—*mol*
Worthy—*yogya, māphikko* (36, 117)
Would—87, 152
Wound—*choṭ ; ghāu*
Wrap—*behernu*
Wring—*nimaṭhnu*
Wrist—*ḍunṛulo*
Write—*lekhnu*
Wrong—*anuchit* ; (n.) *annye* ; (error) *bhūl*
Yard—*gaj* ; (court) *āghan*
Yea—*aṉ*
Year—*barsha, sāl* (51)
Yearly—*bārshik, sālenni*
Yellow—*pahenlo*
Yes—*jyu, ho, aṉ* (67, 78)
Yesterday—*hijo* ; (day before y.) *asti*
Yet—*aile samma* ; (conj.) *tai*
Yield—*dihālnu* ; (fruit) *upjāunnu* ; (assent) *swīkār g.*
You—*timiharu* (20, 21)
Young—*juwān*; (progeny) *bāchchho* ; (of birds, serpents, &c.), *bacharā*
Younger—*kānchho, chhoṭā*
Youth—(time) *jobhān, jawāni* ; (lad) *taruṇ* (f. *taruṇī*)
Zeal—*dhuni, ish* (9)

II. Army Formulary.

[The following sample set of conventional words and sentences is founded, by kind permission, on the "Manual of Khas Gurkhali or Parbatiya, by Major A. G. F. Browne, D.S.O.: 2nd Edition: Lucknow: 1892;" collated with Lieutenant M. E. Dopping-Hepenstal's "Khas Gurkhali Grammar and Vocabulary: 1899."]

Who is it ?	*ko ho.*
Who are you ?	*timi ko hau.*
What is your name ?	*nāṉu kyā ho.*
What is your caste ?	*kun jātkā hau.*
What branch [of the caste] ?	*thar kyā.*
How old are you ?	*umer kati barshako bho.*
I am 21.	*maṉlāi ekkāis barsha bho.*
Can you read and write ?	*parnu lekhnu jānda chhau ki.*
Where do you come from ?	*kahāṉ bāṭo āyau.*
Where are you going ?	*katā jāṉchhau.*
Where do you live ?	*kahāṉ baschhau*
How long have you lived there ?	*tyahāṉ basyeko kati din bho.*
How long will you remain ?	*kaile samma rahanchhau holā*
Stop, I wish to speak to you.	*parkha timilāi kyei bhannu chhau*

What service have you ?	*nokarī garyeko katiko bho.*
What regiment are you ?	*kun palṭanmān̲ chhau.*
Have you any acquaintances ?	*kye timrā koi chinhāru chhan.*
Are you married ?	*bihā* [or *byāhā*] *bhayo.*
Where is your wife ?	*swāsnī* [or *gharbār*] *kahān̲ chha.*
How many children have you ?	*timrā kati chhorā chhorī chhan.*
Were you at drill and on parade to-day ?	*āju ḍalel ra pareḍmān̲ thiyau.*
No ; I was on guard.	*hoina paharāmān̲ thiyen̲.*
Which is the way to the Orderly-room ?	*ārdali rum jān̲ne bāṭo kun chain̲ ho.*
How far is the Mess from here ?	*messkoṭ yahān̲ dekhi kati tāṛo chha.*
How many men are in your company ?	*timro kampanimān̲ kati janā chhan.*
Are you a marksman or first-class shot ?	*kye mārksman ki fastkilas hau.*
Can one see the range from here, or not ?	*yahān̲ bāṭo chān̲dmārī dekhnu sakchha ki sakdaina.*
No, Sir, it is on the other side of the hill, not on this.	*sakdaina sāhep ḍān̲ṛāko pallo paṭṭi chha wallo paṭṭi hoina.*
I have never been on active service.	*laṛāīn̲mān̲ po kaile pani gain̲na.*
Go and report yourself sick at the hospital.	*aspaṭālmān̲ gayera bimār chhu bhani raporṭ gara.*
Give over your orders.	*āphule pāyekā hukum bhani deu.*
Several days' march.	*katti dinko bāṭo.*
Do you understand what I say ?	*main̲le bhanyeko kye būjhchhau.*
Give my salaams to the subadar-major and tell him I wish to see him	*subidār-mejar sāhepkana mero salām diyera bhana uniko bheṭ mān̲gchhu bhani.*
Call the havildar-major.	*hawaldār-mejarkana bolāu.*
Call to him.	*uslāi ḍāka.*
When is your furlough due ?	*timro razāy kaile parlā.*
When your elder brother was wounded was your younger brother with him ?	*jaba timro dājyu ghāyal pāriyo taba timro bhāī kye usko sāthman̲ thiyo.*

Tell your family they may go to the "lines."	*āphnu jahānlāi bhana lainmān jānnu hunchha bhani.*
What is your height, and chest measurement?	*kati algo ani chhātiko nāp kati.*
Please, be seated.	*basāi hawas.*
How many medals have you?	*timrā kati tagmā bhaye.*
Are you a good shot?	*goli hānnumān assal chhau ki.*
I heard him saying there would be drill to-day.	*mainle tyesle yeso bhandai garyeko sunyen āju ḍale hunchha bhani.*
Call them by name.	*nānu kāṛi kāṛi bolāu.*
Come what may, you must stay.	*jo hos so hos* [or *jye jye holā holā*] *timi rahi jānnu parchha.*
Before he had done speaking I came.	*tyesle bhani sakyeko thiyena* [or *bhani sakdā na sakdā*] *man āyen.*
Here is the wood, but where is the fire?	*i dāurā tā chha tara āgo khoi.*
Tell the bugler to sound the "fall in"	*bigul arlāi fālin bajāunnu bhana*
Hold yourself up.	*sojo hou.*
Look to the right, not straight to your front.	*dāhinno hera sojo hoina.*
Heads up!	*manto uchāla.*
Do not crowd up on the left.	*debre tira na ḍhalka* [or *micha*].
Don't lose your dressing.	*ḍresiñ na bigāra.*
Don't move.	*chalahala na gara.*
Close to the left.	*debre tira mila.*
Keep step.	*kadam milāi hinṛa.*
Work smartly.	*phurti saña gara.*
At the gate of the fort [firing exercise].	*killāko ḍhokā mānthi.* [*lagāu.*]
Aim lower.	*aru tala tāka* [or *sirristā ali tala*
Take a fine sight.	*masinno tāka.*
Adjust your sights.	*makkhi ṭhīk ṭhīk pāra.*
Keep in your proper section of fours.	*āphnu āphnu sekshanafforz ṭhīk rākha.*

You are not working together.	*mili mili gardauna.*
Tell the band to march away for practice.	*benḍlāi prākṭis garnulāi mārach garnu bhana.*
All your accoutrements are upside down.	*timro sabai asbāb ulṭā chha.*
No talking !	*bāt na mānra* [or *chup raha*].
The bayonets and rifle-barrels of this whole file are all very dirty; they must after this be kept thoroughly clean.	*yes singai failkā sangin ra pāfalkā berral sārai mailā chhan aba dekhi khūb safā rākhnu parchha.*
Shew me your kookree scabbards.	*manlāi āphnu āphnu khukuriko dāp dekhāwa.*
The rear rank is not properly dressed.	*riar renk rāmro ḍres bhayena.*
Eight days' imprisonment with hard labour.	*sāro mihinnat sañako āṭh din kaidkhānā.*
Dismiss the parade	*pareḍ ḍismis garnu hawas.*